Budgeting

The Comprehensive Guide

Third Edition

Steven M. Bragg

Published by AccountingTools, Inc., Centennial, Colorado.

For more information about AccountingTools® products, visit our Web site at www.accountingtools.com.

ISBN-13: 978-1-938910-40-1

Printed in the United States of America

Table of Contents

Table of Contents

Table of Contents

Table of Contents

Table of Contents

Preface

It can be extremely difficult to assemble all of the information needed for a creditable corporate budget in a timely manner, and then continue to refer back to it throughout the budget period. Many companies have become so frustrated with the process that they have either given up budgeting or done the reverse and implemented an oppressive, top-down system of adherence to the budget.

This new edition of *Budgeting: The Comprehensive Guide* addresses all aspects of the budgeting conundrum – how to create a budget, whether there are variations on the concept that may work better, and how to operate without any budget at all. In Chapters 1-17, we inspect all parts of a traditional corporate budget, including such areas as the production budget, inventory budget, and master budget, as well as the unique aspects of nonprofit budgeting. In Chapters 18-20, we discuss flexible budgeting and zero-base budgeting, which are variations on the traditional budgeting model. In Chapters 21-22, we cover the concept of operating without a budget. And finally, we address a variety of budget-related systems, such as procedures, reporting, and controls. An appendix contains a sample budget, showing subsidiary budget schedules rolling up into a master budget. A great many topics are covered in the book, including:

- What are the advantages and disadvantages of budgeting?
- What is the system of budgets?
- What are the sources of information for the revenue budget?
- When should I use the crewing method to compile the direct labor budget?
- When should I use the roll-up method to calculate the direct materials budget?
- How do I derive the correct amount of research and development funding?
- How does bottleneck analysis impact capital budgeting?
- What are the inputs to a budgeted balance sheet?
- How do I create a flexible budget?
- What are the steps involved in creating a zero-base budget?
- What alternative systems are needed to operate without a budget?
- What efficiencies can I impose on the budgeting process?

Budgeting: The Comprehensive Guide is designed for both professional accountants and students, since both can benefit from its detailed descriptions of budgeting systems, reports, and controls. As such, it may earn a place on your book shelf as a reference tool for years to come.

Centennial, Colorado
August 2014

About the Author

Steven Bragg, CPA, has been the chief financial officer or controller of four companies, as well as a consulting manager at Ernst & Young. He received a master's degree in finance from Bentley College, an MBA from Babson College, and a Bachelor's degree in Economics from the University of Maine. He has been a two-time president of the Colorado Mountain Club, and is an avid alpine skier, mountain biker, and certified master diver. Mr. Bragg resides in Centennial, Colorado. He has written the following books and courses:

Accountants' Guidebook
Accounting Controls Guidebook
Accounting for Inventory
Accounting for Investments
Accounting for Managers
Accounting Procedures Guidebook
Budgeting
Business Ratios
CFO Guidebook
Closing the Books
Constraint Management
Corporate Cash Management
Cost Accounting Fundamentals
Cost Management Guidebook
Credit & Collection Guidebook

Financial Analysis
Fixed Asset Accounting
GAAP Guidebook
Human Resources Guidebook
IFRS Guidebook
Inventory Management
Investor Relations Guidebook
Lean Accounting Guidebook
Mergers & Acquisitions
New Controller Guidebook
Nonprofit Accounting
Payroll Management
Public Company Accounting and Finance
Revenue Recognition

On-Line Resources by Steven Bragg

Steven maintains the accountingtools.com web site, which contains continuing professional education courses, the Accounting Best Practices podcast, and hundreds of articles on accounting subjects.

Budgeting is also available as a continuing professional education (CPE) course. You can purchase the course (and many other courses) and take an on-line exam at:

www.accountingtools.com/cpe

Chapter 1
Introduction to Budgeting

Introduction

A budget is a document that forecasts the financial results and financial position of a business for one or more future periods. At a minimum, a budget contains an estimated income statement that describes anticipated financial results. A more complex budget also contains an estimated balance sheet, which includes the entity's anticipated assets, liabilities, and equity positions at various points in time in the future.

A prime use of the budget is to serve as a performance baseline for the measurement of actual results. Budgets may also be linked to bonus plans in order to direct the activities of various company employees. A budget may also be used for both tax planning and treasury planning. Despite these valid uses, there are also a number of problems with budgeting that have given rise to a movement dedicated to the elimination of budgets.

In the following sections, we will address both the advantages and disadvantages of budgeting, and then cover how budgeting has become thoroughly integrated into the command and control system of management. After this discussion, you may still be willing to install a thoroughly traditional system of budgeting, or a modified version, or even prefer to adopt a system that does not use a budget at all – the choice is up to you.

> **Related Podcast Episode:** Episode 130 of the Accounting Best Practices Podcast discusses the problems with budgeting. You can listen to it at: **accounting-tools.com/podcasts** or **iTunes**

The Advantages of Budgeting

Budgeting has been with us a long time, and is used by nearly every large company. They would not do so if there were not some perceived advantages to budgeting. These advantages include:

- *Planning orientation*. The process of creating a budget takes management away from its short-term, day-to-day management of a business and forces it to think longer-term. This is the chief goal of budgeting, even if management does not succeed in meeting its goals as outlined in the budget - at least it is thinking about the company's competitive and financial position and how to improve it.
- *Model scenarios*. If a company is faced with a number of possible paths down which it can travel, it is possible to create a set of budgets, each based

on different scenarios, to estimate the financial results of each strategic direction.

- *Profitability review.* It is easy to lose sight of where a company is making most of its money, during the scramble of day-to-day management. A properly structured budget points out which aspects of a business generate cash and which ones use it, which forces management to consider whether it should drop some parts of the business or expand in others. However, this advantage only applies to a budget sufficiently detailed to describe profits at the product, product line, or business unit level.

- *Assumptions review.* The budgeting process forces management to think about why the company is in business, as well as its key assumptions about its business environment. A periodic re-evaluation of these issues may result in altered assumptions, which may in turn alter the way in which management decides to operate the business.

- *Performance evaluations.* Senior management can tie bonuses or other incentives to how employees perform in comparison to the budget. The accounting department then creates budget versus actual reports to give employees feedback regarding how they are progressing toward their goals. This approach is most common with financial goals, though operational goals (such as reducing the scrap rate) can also be added. We will address a countervailing argument in the Command and Control System section later in this chapter.

- *Predict cash flows.* Companies that are growing rapidly, have seasonal sales, or which have irregular sales patterns have a difficult time estimating how much cash they are likely to require in the near term, which results in periodic cash-related crises. A budget is useful for predicting cash flows in the short term, but yields increasingly unreliable results further into the future.

- *Cash allocation.* There is only a limited amount of cash available to invest in fixed assets and working capital, and the budgeting process forces management to decide which assets are most worth investing in.

- *Cost reduction analysis.* A company that has a strong system in place for continual cost reduction can use a budget to designate cost reduction targets that it wishes to pursue.

- *Shareholder communications.* Large investors may want a benchmark against which they can measure the company's progress. Even if a company chooses not to lend much credence to its own budget, it may still be valuable to construct a conservative budget to share with investors. The same argument holds true for lenders, who may want to see a budget versus actual results comparison from time to time.

These advantages may appear to be persuasive ones, and indeed have been sufficient for most companies to implement budgeting processes. However, there are also serious problems with budgets that we will outline in the following sections.

The Disadvantages of Budgeting

There are a number of serious disadvantages associated with budgeting. This section gives an overview of the general issues, while the following sections address the particular problems associated with capital budgeting, as well as the use of budgets within a command and control management system. The disadvantages of budgeting include:

- *Inaccuracy.* A budget is based on a set of assumptions that are generally not too far distant from the operating conditions under which it was formulated. If the business environment changes to any significant degree, then the company's revenues or cost structure may change so radically that actual results will rapidly depart from the expectations delineated in the budget. This condition is a particular problem when there is a sudden economic downturn, since the budget authorizes a certain level of spending that is no longer supportable under a suddenly reduced revenue level. Unless management acts quickly to override the budget, managers will continue to spend under their original budgetary authorizations, thereby rupturing any possibility of earning a profit. Other conditions that can also cause results to vary suddenly from budgeted expectations include changes in interest rates, currency exchange rates, and commodity prices.

- *Rigid decision making.* The budgeting process only focuses the attention of the management team on strategy during the budget formulation period near the end of the fiscal year. For the rest of the year, there is no procedural commitment to revisit strategy. Thus, if there is a fundamental shift in the market just after a budget has been completed, there is no system in place to formally review the situation and make changes, thereby placing a company at a considerable disadvantage to its more nimble competitors.

- *Time required.* It can be very time-consuming to create a budget, especially in a poorly-organized environment where many iterations of the budget may be required. The time involved is lower if there is a well-designed budgeting procedure in place, employees are accustomed to the process, and the company uses budgeting software. The work required can be more extensive if business conditions are constantly changing, which calls for repeated iterations of the budget model.

- *Gaming the system.* An experienced manager may attempt to introduce budgetary slack, which involves deliberately reducing revenue estimates and increasing expense estimates, so that he can easily achieve favorable variances against the budget. This can be a serious problem, and requires considerable oversight to spot and eliminate.

- *Blame for outcomes.* If a department does not achieve its budgeted results, the department manager may blame any other departments that provide services to it for not having adequately supported his department.

- *Expense allocations.* The budget may prescribe that certain amounts of overhead costs be allocated to various departments, and the managers of those departments may take issue with the allocation methods used. This is a particular problem when departments are not allowed to substitute services provided from within the company for lower-cost services that are available elsewhere.

- *Use it or lose it.* If a department is allowed a certain amount of expenditures and it does not appear that the department will spend all of the funds during the budget period, the department manager may authorize excessive expenditures at the last minute, on the grounds that his budget will be reduced in the next period unless he spends all of the authorized amounts. Thus, a budget tends to make managers believe that they are entitled to a certain amount of funding each year, irrespective of their actual need for the funds.
- *Only considers financial outcomes.* The nature of the budget is numeric, so it tends to focus management attention on the quantitative aspects of a business; this usually means an intent focus on improving or maintaining profitability. In reality, customers do not care about the profits of a business – they will only buy from the company as long as they are receiving good service and well-constructed products at a fair price. Unfortunately, it is quite difficult to build these concepts into a budget, since they are qualitative in nature. Thus, the budgeting concept does not necessarily support the needs of customers.

The disadvantages noted here are widely prevalent and difficult to overcome. Unfortunately, we have not yet presented all of the problems with budgeting. There are additional issues with capital budgeting, as well as the use of budgeting within the command and control style of management. We describe these problems in the next two sections.

Capital Budgeting Problems

The traditional budgeting system has an especially pernicious impact on capital budgeting. Under capital budgeting, managers apply for funding for whichever fixed assets they feel are needed in their areas of responsibility. A considerable amount of detailed analysis is needed for these requests, since the amount of funding requested can be quite large. The problem is that the budgeting timeline forces most capital budgeting requests to be submitted within a short time period each year, after which additional funds are only grudgingly issued. In effect, this means that the corporate "bank" is only open for business for a month or two every year! Thus, someone may spot an excellent business opportunity for the company, but not be able to take advantage of it for many months, when the "bank" is again open for business. This can be a massive impediment to the continuing growth of a business.

Given the "bank" issue just noted, managers fight hard for the maximum amount of funding as soon as the "bank" opens – and they spend *all* of it. But when was the last time that you saw a manager return allocated funds, because he did not feel that the expenditure was needed any longer? That is indeed a rare event! Instead, many managers receive their annual allocation of capital expenditure funds and then push for *more* funds throughout the budget year for additional projects. In short, the

4

capital budgeting process really creates a *minimum* funding level, above which a company is very likely to go as the year progresses. It is a rare company that only spends what it initially budgets for fixed assets.

In summary, the budgeting process creates two capital budgeting problems. First, it is unusually difficult to obtain funds outside of the budget period, even for deserving projects. And second, managers tend to game the system, so that the capital budgeting process nearly always ends up absorbing more funds than senior management originally intended.

The Command and Control System

The single most fundamental problem underlying the entire concept of a budget is that it is designed to control a company from the center. The basic underpinning of the system is that senior management forces managers throughout the company to agree to a specific outcome (that portion of the budget for which they are responsible), which senior management then monitors to control the activities of the managers. This agreement is usually a formal agreement under which each manager commits to achieve a fixed target in exchange for receiving a bonus. Examples of target commitments are:

- A revenue target, which may be defined for a specific product, product line, or geographic region.
- An expense target, which may be a single block expense for an entire department or expenditures for individual line items.
- A profit target, which a manager may achieve by any combination of revenue increases or expense reductions.
- A cash flow target, such as producing a specific amount of net positive cash flow.
- A metrics target, such as return on assets or return on equity.

These targets may be combined to further control the actions of managers. For example, there may be a combination geographic revenue target and profit target, so that a manager is forced to commit resources to sales in a new sales region while still maintaining overall profitability. When there are many targets to achieve, managers find that their actions are entirely constrained by the budget – there is no time or spare funding for any other activities. Thus, the combination of the budget and a bonus system create an extremely tight command and control system.

Formal performance agreements are the source of an enormous amount of inefficiency within a company, and can also reduce employee loyalty to the company. They require a great deal of time to initially negotiate, and may be altered over time as changing conditions give managers various excuses to complain about their agreements. Further, if the recipient of a bonus agreement misses out on a substantial bonus, how does he feel about the company? He may complain bitterly that the bonus system was rigged against him, and leave to work for a competitor.

In short, when budgeting is used within a command and control management system it imposes a rigid straightjacket on the actions of any managers who want to earn their designated bonuses. This level of rigidity makes it particularly difficult for a company to react quickly to changes in its competitive environment, since managers are constrained by their performance plans from proceeding in new directions.

Behavioral Impacts

The command and control nature of the budget results in an immediate behavioral change in the management team before the budget has even been completed, because managers understand that they can influence their bonus plans in advance by negotiating the amount of improvement that they will be required to achieve. This calls for fierce protection of their existing funding levels, as well as committing to the lowest possible improvement levels in their areas of responsibility. They will have an excellent chance to earn maximum bonuses, because their performance commitments under the budget are so minimal. In short, the concept of the budget forces managers to fight for *minimal* improvements.

The marketplace may change with alacrity, so that a manager struggling to meet his budgeted targets must also somehow meet competitive pressures by altering products and services, changing price points, opening and closing locations, cutting costs, and so forth. This means that a manager is faced with the choice of either earning a bonus (or a promotion) by meeting his budget, or of improving the company's competitive position. A manager's willingness to work in the best interests of a company's competitive position is further hampered by the sheer bureaucratic oppressiveness of the budgeting system, where a manager has to obtain multiple approvals to achieve a reorientation of funding. It is simply easier to not deviate from the budget. Therefore, the budget priority wins out and a company finds that its competitive position has declined specifically because of a tight focus on achieving its budget.

The pressure to meet a budgeted target can cause managers to engage in unethical accounting and business practices in order to control their reported results. Examples of such practices are:

- Recording revenue that was shipped after the month-end deadline
- Using a discount offer to stuff sales into a sales channel during a bonus period
- Overbilling customers
- Not entering supplier invoices in the accounting system during a bonus period
- Taking unwarranted discounts from supplier invoices
- Firing employees and using contractors to avoid headcount targets

Unethical behavior is a poison that can spread through an organization rapidly; unsullied managers may leave, while the remainder engages in increasingly egregious behavior to meet their performance commitments.

There are other actions caused by the budget that are not precisely unethical, but which result in behavior by managers that does not properly support the company. Here are several examples:

- *Expenditure deferral.* When the amount of budgeted funds is running low, managers delay spending any more money until the next budget year. But what if they need funds right now to meet a golden business opportunity, or to avoid a much larger expense later? They still defer the expenditure in order to remain within their budgeted expense goals and earn their bonuses, even though the expenditure should be made right now from the perspective of the entire business.
- *Bloated budget requests.* Managers request more funding than they actually need, so that any future expense cuts will still allow them to run their departments, as well as more easily meet their performance targets.

Bureaucratic Support

Once the budget and bonus plan system takes root within a company, a bureaucracy develops around it that has a natural tendency to support the status quo. Here are several such areas:

- *Human resources.* Bonus agreements may include specific budget-based goals, due dates, and resources to be allocated; this can be one of the largest tasks of the human resources department.
- *Accounting.* The accounting staff routinely loads the budget into its accounting software, so that all income statements it issues contain a comparison of budgeted to actual results. Thus, the accounting staff incorporates the budget into its system of reports.
- *Analysts.* The budget may be used as a baseline for cost controls, where financial analysts investigate why costs are higher or lower than the budgeted amounts. These analysts report to the controller or CFO, who will therefore want to retain the budget in order to keep tight control over costs.
- *Investment community.* If a company is publicly held, the investor relations officer may routinely issue press releases, stating how the company performed in comparison to its budget. The investment community may rely on this information to estimate a share price for the company's stock, and will want the same information to be reported to it in the future.

Consequently, there are many constituencies, both inside and outside of a company, that have a vested interest in retaining the budget and bonus plan system.

Information Sharing

A related issue in a command and control environment is that senior management has a propensity to only release financial information pertinent to the operations of each manager. This means that there is a great deal of information available at the top of the organization, but very little at the bottom. In addition, managers have a tendency to massage information as they pass it down to their subordinates. The result is a paltry amount of actionable information in the hands of front line employees.

We can only presume that managers engage in this information filtering because they assume that employees below them in the corporate hierarchy are not capable of making their own decisions. Instead, the system is designed to hoard information with those people authorized to make decisions. Therefore, by default, those people receiving a *minimum* amount of information are *not* authorized to make decisions.

This type of restricted information sharing has a profound impact on the budget, because most employees never know what their budgets are, or how they are performing in relation to the budget. Since there is no knowledge of the budget, there can be no acceptance of it by employees, and therefore little chance that it will be achieved.

Summary

The discussion of budgeting in this chapter has cast serious doubts on the need for a detailed and rigorously-enforced budgeting system, especially one that integrates the budget model with bonus plans. Nonetheless, the decision to install a budget is up to the reader. In the following chapters, we will begin with complete coverage of the construction of a typical budget model, and then progress to several variations on the budgeting concept that may be a better fit for the budgeting needs of the reader. Finally, we will address the concept of operating with no budget at all, and how a company can remain competitive (if not improve) in such a situation. The choice is up to you. But first, we will address in the next chapter the concept of cost-volume-profit analysis, which is an essential prerequisite to budget modeling.

Chapter 2
Cost-Volume-Profit Analysis

Introduction

When constructing a budget, it is essential to understand the relationships between costs, unit volumes, and profitability. In this chapter, we examine the concept of contribution margin, as well as how it can be employed in a different income statement format. We then use contribution margin to derive the breakeven point of a business, and discuss the uses to which breakeven analysis can be put. The breakeven concept is then extended to calculate the margin of safety. These issues are all components of cost-volume-profit analysis, for which we provide a number of examples. Finally, we address sales mix, which impacts the results of a cost-volume-profit analysis. In total, this chapter is intended to provide the reader with a view of how sales volumes interact with the cost structure of a business to achieve profitability.

Contribution Margin

The contribution margin is a product's price minus its variable costs, resulting in the incremental profit earned for each unit sold. The total contribution margin generated by an entity represents the total earnings available to pay for fixed expenses and generate a profit. The contribution margin concept can be applied throughout a business, for individual products, product lines, profit centers, subsidiaries, and for an entire organization.

The measure is useful for determining whether to allow a lower price in special pricing situations. If the contribution margin is excessively low or negative, it would be unwise to continue selling a product at that price point. It is also useful for determining the profits that will arise from various sales levels (see the next example). Further, the concept can be used to decide which of several products to sell if they use a common bottleneck resource, so that the product with the highest contribution margin is sold.

To determine the amount of contribution margin for a product, subtract all variable costs of a product from its revenues, and divide by its revenue. The calculation is:

$$\frac{\text{Product revenue} - \text{Product variable costs}}{\text{Product revenue}}$$

EXAMPLE

The Iverson Drum Company sells drum sets to high schools. In the most recent period, it sold $1,000,000 of drum sets that had related variable costs of $400,000. Iverson had $660,000 of fixed costs during the period, resulting in a loss of $60,000.

Revenue	$1,000,000
Variable expenses	400,000
Contribution margin	600,000
Fixed expenses	$660,000
Net loss	-$60,000

Iverson's contribution margin is 60%, so if it wants to break even, the company needs to either reduce its fixed expenses by $60,000 or increase its sales by $100,000 (calculated as the $60,000 loss divided by the 60% contribution margin).

EXAMPLE

The president of Giro Cabinetry is examining the gross margins on the five products that his company sells. A summary of this information is:

Product	Sales Price	Variable Cost	Fixed Cost	Gross Margin	Contribution Margin
A	$100	60	30	10%	40%
B	200	100	60	20%	50%
C	75	25	23	36%	67%
D	400	300	120	-5%	25%
E	325	230	98	-1%	29%

Fixed costs are comprised of factory overhead, which are assigned to products based on their prices. Thus, a high-priced product will be assigned more fixed cost than a lower-priced product. However, there is no linkage between price and fixed cost, so the fixed cost allocations are artificial.

Based on the information in the table, the president might be tempted to cancel products D and E, since both have negative gross margins. However, if he were to do so, the factory overhead would still remain, and would not be allocated among the smaller number of remaining products, which would reduce their gross margins. Only by examining the contribution margin is it obvious that *all* of the products are profitable, and should be retained in order to generate sufficient profits to offset the total amount of fixed costs incurred by the company.

Contribution Margin Income Statement

A contribution margin income statement is an income statement in which all variable expenses are deducted from sales to arrive at a contribution margin, from which all fixed expenses are then subtracted to arrive at the net profit or loss for the period. Thus, the arrangement of expenses in the income statement corresponds to the nature of the expenses. This income statement format is a superior form of presentation, because the contribution margin clearly shows the amount available to cover fixed costs and generate a profit or loss. The format is particularly useful for determining the contribution margin for an entire product line or business unit, rather than for an individual product, as was described in the last section.

In essence, if there are no sales, a contribution margin income statement will have a zero contribution margin, with fixed costs clustered beneath the contribution margin line item. As sales increase, the contribution margin will increase in conjunction with sales, while fixed costs should remain approximately the same.

This form of income statement varies from a normal income statement in the following three ways:

- Fixed production costs are aggregated lower in the income statement, after the contribution margin;
- Variable selling and administrative expenses are grouped with variable production costs, so that they are a part of the calculation of the contribution margin; and
- The gross margin is replaced in the statement by the contribution margin.

Thus, the format of a contribution margin income statement is:

+	Sales
-	Variable production expenses (such as materials, supplies, and variable overhead)
-	Variable selling and administrative expenses (such as commissions)
=	Contribution margin
-	Fixed production expenses (including most overhead)
-	Fixed selling and administrative expenses (such as corporate expenses)
=	Net profit or loss

The key difference between the gross margin found in a normal income statement and the contribution margin in this format is that fixed production costs are included in the cost of goods sold to calculate the gross margin, whereas they are not included in the same calculation for contribution margin. This means that the contribution margin income statement is sorted based on the variability of the underlying cost information, rather than by the functional areas or expense categories found in a normal income statement.

It is useful to create an income statement in the contribution margin format when you want to determine that proportion of expenses that truly varies directly with revenues. In many businesses, the contribution margin will be substantially higher than the gross margin, because such a large proportion of its production costs are fixed, and few of its selling and administrative expenses are variable.

Breakeven Point

The breakeven point is the sales volume at which a business earns exactly no money, where all contribution margin earned is needed to pay for the company's fixed costs. The concept is most easily illustrated in the following chart, where fixed costs occupy a block of expense at the bottom of the table, irrespective of any sales being generated. Variable costs are incurred in concert with the sales level. Once the contribution margin on each sale cumulatively matches the total amount of fixed costs, the breakeven point has been reached. All sales above that level directly contribute to profits.

Breakeven Table

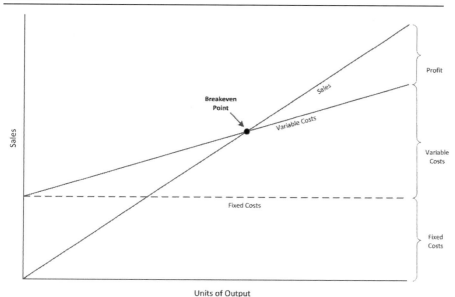

Knowledge of the breakeven point is useful for the following reasons:
- Determining the amount of remaining capacity after the breakeven point is reached, which reveals the maximum amount of profit that can be generated.
- Determining the impact on profit if automation (a fixed cost) replaces labor (a variable cost).
- Determining the change in profits if product prices are altered.
- Determining the amount of losses that could be sustained if the business suffers a sales downturn.

In addition, the breakeven concept is useful for establishing the overall ability of a company to generate a profit. When the breakeven point is near the maximum sales level of a business, this means it is nearly impossible for the company to earn a profit even under the best of circumstances.

Management should constantly monitor the breakeven point, particularly in regard to the last item noted, in order to reduce the breakeven point whenever possible. Ways to do this include:

- *Cost analysis.* Continually review all fixed costs, to see if any can be eliminated. Also review variable costs to see if they can be eliminated, since doing so increases margins and reduces the breakeven point.
- *Margin analysis.* Pay close attention to product margins, and push sales of the highest-margin items, thereby reducing the breakeven point.
- *Outsourcing.* If an activity involves a fixed cost, consider outsourcing it in order to turn it into a per-unit variable cost, which reduces the breakeven point.
- *Pricing.* Reduce or eliminate the use of coupons or other price reductions, since they increase the breakeven point.
- *Technologies.* Implement any technologies that can improve the efficiency of the business, thereby increasing capacity with no increase in cost.

To calculate the breakeven point, divide total fixed expenses by the contribution margin (which was described in an earlier section). The formula is:

$$\frac{\text{Total fixed expenses}}{\text{Contribution margin percentage}}$$

A more refined approach is to eliminate all non-cash expenses (such as depreciation) from the numerator, so that the calculation focuses on the breakeven cash flow level. The formula is:

$$\frac{\text{Total fixed expenses} - \text{Depreciation} - \text{Amortization}}{\text{Contribution margin percentage}}$$

Another variation on the formula is to focus instead on the number of units that must be sold in order to break even, rather than the sales level in dollars. This formula is:

$$\frac{\text{Total fixed expenses}}{\text{Average contribution margin per unit}}$$

EXAMPLE

The management of Ninja Cutlery is interested in buying a competitor that makes ceramic knives. The company's due diligence team wants to know if the competitor's breakeven point is too high to allow for a reasonable profit, and if there are any overhead cost opportunities that may reduce the breakeven point.

Cost-Volume-Profit Analysis

The following information is available:

Maximum sales capacity	$5,000,000
Current average sales	$4,750,000
Contribution margin percentage	35%
Total operating expenses	$1,750,000
Breakeven point	$5,000,000
Operating expense reductions	$375,000
Revised breakeven level	$3,929,000
Maximum profits with revised breakeven point	$375,000

The analysis shows that the competitor has an inordinately high breakeven point that allows for little profit, if any. However, there are several operating expense reductions that can trigger a steep decline in the breakeven point. The management of Ninja Cutlery makes an offer to the owners of the competitor, based on the cash flows that can be gained from the reduced breakeven level.

A potential problem with the breakeven concept is that it assumes the contribution margin in the future will remain the same as the current level, which may not be the case. You can model the breakeven analysis using a range of contribution margins to gain a better understanding of possible future profits and losses at different unit sales levels. See the Sales Mix section for a discussion of variations in contribution margin.

EXAMPLE

Milford Sound sells a broad range of audio products. The CFO is concerned that the average contribution margin of these products has been slipping over the past few years, as customers have been switching to personal audio devices. The current average contribution margin is 38%, but the declining trend indicates that the margin could be 30% within two years. The CFO uses this information to construct the following breakeven analysis for the company:

	Current Case	Projected Case
Total fixed costs	$20,000,000	$20,000,000
÷ Contribution margin	38%	30%
= Breakeven sales	$52,632,000	$66,667,000

The calculation shows that the breakeven point will increase by $14 million over the next two years. Since Milford's current sales level is $58,000,000, this means that the company faces the alternatives of driving a massive sales increase, fixed cost reductions, or margin improvements in order to remain profitable.

Margin of Safety

The margin of safety is the reduction in sales that can occur before the breakeven point of a business is reached. The amount of this buffer is expressed as a percentage.

The margin of safety concept is especially useful when a significant proportion of sales are at risk of decline or elimination, as may be the case when a sales contract is coming to an end. By knowing the amount of the margin of safety, management can gain a better understanding of the risk of loss to which a business is subjected by changes in sales. The opposite situation may also arise, where the margin of safety is so large that a business is well-protected from sales variations.

To calculate the margin of safety, subtract the current breakeven point from sales, and divide the result by sales. The breakeven point is calculated by dividing the contribution margin into total fixed expenses. The formula is:

$$\frac{\text{Total current sales} - \text{Breakeven point}}{\text{Total current sales}}$$

To translate the margin of safety into the number of units sold, use the following formula instead:

$$\frac{\text{Total current sales} - \text{Breakeven point}}{\text{Selling price per unit}}$$

If the margin of safety is expressed as the number of units sold, the result works best if a company only sells one type of product. Otherwise, it can be difficult to translate the result into a range of products that have different price points and contribution margins.

EXAMPLE

Lowry Locomotion is considering the purchase of new equipment to expand the production capacity of its toy tractor product line. The addition will increase Lowry's operating costs by $100,000 per year, though sales will also be increased. Relevant information is noted in the following table:

	Before Machinery Purchase	After Machinery Purchase
Sales	$4,000,000	$4,200,000
Contribution margin percentage	48%	48%
Fixed expenses	$1,800,000	$1,900,000
Breakeven point	$3,750,000	$3,958,000
Profits	$120,000	$116,000
Margin of safety	6.3%	5.8%

The table reveals that both the margin of safety and profits worsen slightly as a result of the equipment purchase, so expanding production capacity is probably not a good idea.

Cost-Volume-Profit Analysis

Cost-volume-profit (CVP) analysis is designed to show how changes in product margins, prices, and unit volumes impact the profitability of a business. It is one of the fundamental financial analysis tools for ascertaining the underlying profitability of a business. The components of cost-volume-profit analysis are:

- *Activity level.* This is the total number of units sold in the measurement period.
- *Price per unit.* This is the average price per unit sold, including any sales discounts and allowances. The price per unit can vary substantially from period to period, based on changes in the mix of products and services, which may be caused by old product terminations, new product introductions, and the seasonality of sales.
- *Variable cost per unit.* This is the totally variable cost per unit sold, which is usually just the amount of direct materials and the sales commission associated with a unit sale. Nearly all other expenses do not vary with sales volume, and so are considered fixed costs.
- *Total fixed cost.* This is the total fixed cost of the business within the measurement period. This figure tends to be relatively steady from period to period, unless there is a step cost transition where the company has elected to incur an entirely new cost in response to a change in activity level (such as adding a production line).

These components can be mixed and matched in a variety of ways to arrive at different types of analyses. For example:

- What is the breakeven unit volume of a business? We divide the total fixed cost of the company by its contribution margin per unit. Thus, if a business has $50,000 of fixed costs per month, and the average contribution margin of a product is $50, then the necessary unit volume to reach a breakeven sales level is 1,000 units.
- What unit quantity is needed to achieve $__ in profits? We add the target profit level to the total fixed cost of the company, and divide by its contribution margin per unit. Thus, if the CEO of the business in the last example wants to earn $20,000 per month, we add that amount to the $50,000 of fixed costs, and divide by the average contribution margin of $50 to arrive at a required unit sales level of 1,400 units.
- If I add a fixed cost, what sales are needed to maintain profits of $__? We add the new fixed cost to the target profit level and original fixed cost of the business, and divide by the unit contribution margin. To continue with the last example, the company is planning to add $10,000 of fixed costs per month. We add that to the $70,000 baseline fixed costs and profit and divide by the $50 average contribution margin to arrive at a new required sales level of 1,600 units per month.
- If I cut unit prices by $__, how many additional units must be sold to maintain profit levels? To continue with the last example, the baseline fixed

costs are $60,000, profits are $20,000, and the contribution margin is $50 per unit. The plan is to reduce the unit price by $10 in an attempt to increase sales. Doing so will decrease the contribution margin to $40. To calculate the total number of unit sales required, we divide the $40 contribution margin per unit into the combined fixed costs and profits to arrive at total unit sales of 2,000. Thus, if prices are cut by $10, unit sales must increase by 400 units from the last example in order to maintain profit levels.

In short, the various components of CVP analysis can be used to uncover the financial results arising from many possible scenarios.

EXAMPLE

The president of Micron Metallic is working through the annual budgeting process, and wants to know how many stamping machines the company must produce in the upcoming year in order to earn a target before-tax profit of $3,000,000. The business has $24,000,000 of fixed costs, and its contribution margin per unit is $20,000. The calculation of units to sell is:

$$\frac{\$24,000,000 \text{ Fixed costs} + \$3,000,000 \text{ Target profit}}{\$20,000 \text{ Contribution margin per unit}}$$

$$= 1,350 \text{ Units}$$

The analysis can be refined to include the impact of income taxes, so that the formula for establishing a target after-tax profit for a certain number of units sold becomes:

$$\frac{\text{Fixed costs} + (\text{Target profit} \div (1 - \text{Tax \%}))}{\text{Contribution margin per unit}}$$

EXAMPLE

To continue with the last example, the president of Micron Metallic wants to determine the number of stamping machines that must be sold in order to achieve an *after-tax* profit of $3,000,000, using the same information. The tax rate is 35%. The calculation is:

$$\frac{\$24,000,000 \text{ Fixed costs} + (\$3,000,000 \text{ Target profit} \div (1 - 35\%))}{\$20,000 \text{ Contribution margin per unit}}$$

$$= 1,431 \text{ Units}$$

We do not present a single cost-volume-profit formula, for there is no single formula that applies to all situations. Instead, the basic concept must be revised to meet the requirements of each financial analysis topic as it arises.

Sales Mix

Sales mix refers to the proportions of different products and services that comprise the total sales of a company. In most cases, each product or service that a company provides has a different contribution margin, so changes in sales mix (even if the total sales level remains the same) usually result in differing amounts of profit.

EXAMPLE

The CFO of Creekside Industrial is examining the sales and profit figures for the past two months, and is having difficulty understanding why sales were identical, but profits were radically different in the two months. He creates the following analysis of sales of the company's two types of batteries:

	January			February		
	Product A	Product B	Total	Product A	Product B	Total
Sales	$2,000,000	$3,500,000	$5,500,000	$4,000,000	$1,500,000	$5,500,000
Variable costs	1,600,000	1,400,000	3,000,000	3,200,000	600,000	3,800,000
Variable cost %	80%	40%	55%	80%	40%	69%
Contribution	400,000	2,100,000	2,500,000	800,000	900,000	1,700,000
Fixed costs			2,000,000			2,000,000
Profit (loss)			$500,000			-$300,000

Because sales have shifted between the two products, which have radically different contribution margins, the profit level is heavily impacted by the sales mix.

If a company introduces a new product that has a low profit, and which it sells aggressively, it is quite possible that profits will decline even as sales increase. Conversely, if a company elects to drop a low-profit product line and instead push sales of a higher-profit product line, total profits can increase even as total sales decline.

A cost accounting variance called the *sales mix variance* is used to measure the difference in unit volumes in the actual sales mix from the planned sales mix. Follow these steps to calculate it at the individual product level:
1. Subtract budgeted unit volume from actual unit volume and multiply by the standard contribution margin.
2. Do the same for each of the products sold.
3. Aggregate this information to arrive at the sales mix variance for the company.

The formula is:

(Actual unit sales – Budgeted unit sales) × Budgeted contribution margin

---

EXAMPLE

Oberlin Acoustics expects to sell 100 platinum harmonicas, which have a contribution margin of $12 per unit, but actually sells only 80 units. Also, Oberlin expects to sell 400 stainless steel harmonicas, which have a contribution margin of $6, but actually sells 500 units. The sales mix variance is:

Platinum harmonica: (80 actual units – 100 budgeted units) × $12 contribution margin = -$240
Stainless steel harmonica: (500 actual units – 400 budgeted units) × $6 contribution margin = $600

Thus, the aggregated sales mix variance is $360, which reflects a large increase in the sales volume of a product having a lower contribution margin, combined with a decline in sales for a product that has a higher contribution margin.

Summary

The interaction of unit costs, fixed costs, sales volumes, and contribution margins is critical to an understanding of cost management, since these concepts can be used to model financial results. By altering the inputs to a cost-volume-profit model, you can estimate how the results of a business will change, which affects management's decisions to invest in fixed assets, withdraw products, cut back business units, hire staff, and so forth.

A note of caution must be inserted into this discussion. Cost-volume-profit analysis assumptions are not entirely under the control of an organization. It may be possible to adhere to planned changes in costs, but unit sales and product price points may not be accepted by customers, rendering a financial model invalid. Consequently, it may be necessary to revise these models frequently in response to pilot tests in the market; alternatively, incorporate worst-case scenarios for unit sales and price points, in case customer acceptance of a new company initiative is indifferent.

Chapter 3
The System of Budgets

Introduction

Only in the smallest company can a budget be contained within a single page or spreadsheet. In most cases, the level of complexity of the business demands a much more segmented approach, so that key elements of the budget are modularized and then aggregated into a master budget. In this chapter, we show the complete system of budgets, summarize the function of each element of the budget, and show how they are linked together to form a complete budget. We also address how to review the system of budgets to see if its various components work together to create an achievable budget.

The System of Budgets

The key driver of any budget is the amount of revenue that is expected during the budget period. Revenue is usually compiled in a separate revenue budget. The information in this budget is derived from estimates of which products or services will sell, and the prices at which they can be sold. Forecasted revenue for this budget cannot be derived just from the sales staff, since this would limit the information to the extrapolation of historical sales figures into the future. The chief executive officer provides additional strategic information, while the marketing manager addresses new-product introductions and the purchasing staff provides input on the availability of raw materials that may restrict sales. Thus, a group effort from many parts of a company is needed to create the revenue budget.

Once the revenue budget is in place, a number of additional budgets are derived from it that relate to the production capabilities of the company. The following components are included in this cluster of budgets:

- *Ending inventory budget.* As its name implies, this budget sets the inventory level as of the end of each accounting period listed in the budget. Management uses this budget to force changes in the inventory level, which is usually driven by a policy to have more or less finished goods inventory on hand. Having more inventory presumably improves the speed with which a company can ship goods to customers, at the cost of an increased investment in working capital. A forced reduction in inventory may delay some shipments to customers due to stockout conditions, but requires less working capital to maintain. The ending inventory budget is used as an input to the production budget.
- *Production budget.* This budget shows expected production at an aggregated level. The production budget is based primarily on the sales estimates in the revenue budget, but it must also take into consideration existing inventory

levels and the desired amount of ending inventory, as stated in the ending inventory budget. If management wants to increase inventory levels in order to provide more rapid shipments to customers, the required increase in production may trigger a need for more production equipment and direct labor staff. The production budget is needed in order to derive the direct labor budget, manufacturing overhead budget, and direct materials budget.

- *Direct labor budget.* This budget calculates the amount of direct labor staffing expected during the budget period, based on the production levels itemized in the production budget. This information can only be generally estimated, given the vagaries of short-term changes in actual production scheduling. However, direct labor usually involves specific staffing levels to crew production lines, so the estimated amount of direct labor should not vary excessively over time, within certain production volume parameters. This budget should incorporate any planned changes in the cost of labor, which may be easy to do if there is a union contract that specifies pay increases as of specific dates. This budget provides rough estimates of the number of employees needed, and is of particular interest to the human resources staff in developing hiring plans. It is a key source document for the cost of goods sold budget.

- *Manufacturing overhead budget.* This budget includes all of the overhead costs expected to be incurred in the manufacturing area during the budget period. It is usually based on historical cost information, but can be adjusted for step cost situations, where a change in the structure or capacity level of a production facility strips away or adds large amounts of expenses at one time. Even if there are no changes in structure or capacity, the manufacturing overhead budget may change somewhat in the maintenance cost area if management plans to alter these expenditures as machines age or are replaced. It is particularly important to adjust this budget if management contemplates running a production facility at close to 100% utilization, since doing so requires a considerable incremental increase in many types of expenditures. This budget is a source document for the cost of goods sold budget.

- *Direct materials budget.* This budget is derived from a combination of the manufacturing unit totals in the production budget and the bills of material for those units, and is used in the cost of goods sold budget. The bills of material must be accurate if this budget is to be remotely accurate. If a company produces a large variety of products, this can become an excessively detailed and burdensome budget to create and maintain. Consequently, it is customary to estimate material costs in aggregate, such as at the product line level. It may also be necessary to state expected scrap and spoilage levels in this budget, especially if management plans to improve its production practices to reduce scrap and spoilage below their historical levels.

- *Cost of goods sold budget.* This budget contains a summarization of the expenses detailed in the direct material budget, manufacturing overhead budget, and direct materials budget. This budget usually contains such additional information as line items for revenue, the gross margin, and key production statistics. It is heavily used during budget iterations, since management can consult it to view the impact of various assumptions on gross margins and other aspects of the production process.

Once the revenue and production-related budgets have been completed, there are still several other budgets to assemble that relate to other functions of the company. They are:

- *Sales and marketing budget.* This budget is comprised of the compensation of the sales and marketing staff, sales travel costs, and expenditures related to various marketing programs. It is closely linked to the revenue budget, since the number of sales staff (in some industries) is the prime determinant of additional sales. Further, marketing campaigns can impact the timing of the sales shown in the revenue budget.
- *Administration budget.* This budget includes the expenses of the executive, accounting, treasury, human resources, and other administrative staff. These expenses are primarily comprised of compensation, followed by office expenses. A large proportion of these expenses are fixed, with some headcount changes driven by total revenues or other types of activity elsewhere in the company.

A budget that is not directly impacted by the revenue budget is the research and development budget. This budget is authorized by senior management, and is set at an amount that is deemed appropriate, given the projected level of new product introductions that management wants to achieve, and the company's competitive posture within the industry. The size of this budget is also influenced by the amount of available funding and an estimate of how many potentially profitable projects can be pursued.

Once these budgets have been completed, it is possible to determine the capital budgeting requirements of the company, as well as its financing needs. These two topics are addressed in the capital budget and the financing budget:

- *Capital budget.* This budget shows the cash flows associated with the acquisition of fixed assets during the budget period. Larger fixed assets are noted individually, while smaller purchases are noted in aggregate. The information in this budget is used to develop the budgeted balance sheet, depreciation expense, and the cash requirements needed for the financing budget.
- *Financing budget.* This budget is the last of the component budgets developed, because it needs the cash inflow and outflow information from the other budgets. With this information in hand, the financing budget addresses how funds will be invested (if there are excess cash inflows) or obtained through debt or equity financing (if there is a need for additional cash). This budget also incorporates any additional cash usage information that is typically addressed by the board of directors, including dividends, stock repurchases, and repositioning of the company's debt to equity ratio.

The interest expense or interest income resulting from this budget is incorporated into the budgeted income statement.

Once the capital budget and financing budget have been created, the information in all of the budgets is summarized into a master budget. This master budget is essentially an income statement. A more complex budget also includes a balance sheet that itemizes the major categories of assets, liabilities, and equity. There may also be a statement of cash flows that itemizes the sources and uses of funds.

The complete system of budgets is shown in the following exhibit.

The System of Budgets

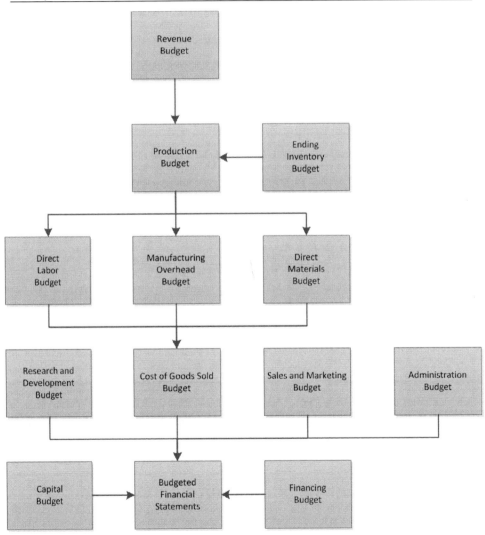

Employee staffing levels are usually included in each of the various budgets, so that employee compensation is fully integrated into the expenses in each budget.

However, since compensation comprises a major proportion of all company expenses, it may be useful to also create a staffing budget that summarizes headcount and compensation for all areas of the business. This information is useful for determining whether there will be a sufficient number of employees to support planned revenue levels, as well as to provide guidance for the recruiting and layoff plans of the human resources department.

Though not included in this book, some companies like to separate facilities costs into a separate budget. It is useful to segregate this information into a separate budget when there is a facilities manager, since this person will want to see the expenses for which he is responsible. Otherwise, facilities expenses are usually entered into either the production budget or the administration budget, or both. The facilities budget is usually one of the last budgets to be constructed, since it depends upon the number of employees to be housed and the requirements for production and warehousing facilities, all of which are established in other parts of the budget.

It may be useful to append a ratios page to the budget. These ratios are most useful when compared to historical trends, to see if the results generated by the budget model appear reasonable. Typical ratios to consider for this page are revenue per person, inventory turnover, accounts receivable turnover, and working capital as a percentage of sales.

The system of budgets frequently includes another activity that is not officially a part of the budget – compensation plans. These plans are prepared by the human resources department for selected individuals within the company, and define exactly which budgeted targets a person must attain in exchange for a bonus payment. There is a separate compensation plan for each person, so they are not mentioned in the system of budgets, other than as a budgeted amount of additional compensation.

In summary, the system of budgets ultimately depends upon the revenue budget and the amount of planned ending inventory. These two budgets directly or indirectly influence the amounts budgeted in many other parts of the corporate budget.

The System of Budgets for a Multi-Division Company

The same system of budgets just noted also applies to a company that has multiple operating divisions, with the following differences:

- *Corporate budget.* There will be a separate budget for the corporate headquarters group, which may include such additional items as directors and officers insurance, and the treasury and internal audit departments, which may not be found at the subsidiary level. This budget can usually be constructed independently of the subsidiary budgets.
- *Corporate allocation.* Each subsidiary may be asked to shoulder a portion of the cost of the corporate overhead group, in the form of an overhead allocation. This allocation is not recommended, since the subsidiaries have no control over the amounts allocated.

- *Financing feedback.* Financing needs are generally handled at the corporate level, so there may be capital rationing by the corporate headquarters group that reduces the expenditures for fixed assets that are itemized in the budgets of the subsidiaries. Thus, the corporate financing budget is used as input for the various capital budgets.
- *Cash repatriation.* If some subsidiaries are located in countries that restrict the outflow of cash back to the parent company (known as "cash repatriation"), then this issue must be integrated into the budget, so that the company does not mistakenly allocate cash from such locations to other parts of the company. This can have a significant impact on local financing needs.

Thus, there are additional levels of budgeting complexity in larger businesses. This complexity usually extends the budget preparation process into a multi-month endeavor that can be so complicated that there is a dedicated budgeting staff whose job continues throughout the year.

Operating Decisions Impacting the System of Budgets

As senior management oversees the construction of the system of budgets each year, it must be mindful of how certain operating decisions can impact the results of the budget. If management does not incorporate the trickle-down effects of these decisions into the budget, it will likely see variances from the budget in the near future. Some of the operating decisions that may have multiple impacts on the budget include:

- *Increase prices.* If management decides to increase the price of the company's goods or services, this may trigger a decline in demand. This decline may result in a reduced need for overtime in the direct labor budget. Also, a demand reduction may reduce machine utilization levels, so there will be less need for additional investments in fixed assets.
- *Lower prices.* If management lowers prices, it can expect increased utilization of production equipment, which in turn may call for increased maintenance expenditures, as well as the purchase of more fixed assets in the production area. Also, lower prices may result in significantly lower cash flow per customer if sales volume does not increase to offset the price reduction, so verify that there is sufficient cash or debt available to offset any negative cash flow issues.
- *Add new sales territory.* If the company is moving into a new sales territory, this may require a significant increase in distribution costs into that area (especially if warehousing facilities are needed). Also, the travel and entertainment expenditures by the sales staff assigned to this area may be disproportionately high, as they travel to meet with prospective customers. Further, be prepared for higher-than-normal marketing expenditures to build brand awareness in the region. Finally, it is possible that you may have to reduce prices in the region, due to price wars initiated by competitors in that area.

- *Relax credit terms.* When management approves the use of relaxed credit terms to customers, the obvious intention is to increase sales. However, doing so will very likely increase the amount of bad debts, so there should be a corresponding increase in the allowance for doubtful accounts in the budget. This may also call for the hiring of additional collections staff, as well as budgeting for additional fees payable to outside collection agencies. Relaxing credit terms also creates the issues already noted when management lowers prices.
- *Increase inventory levels.* Management may want to keep more inventory in stock in order to increase the speed with which it can fill customer orders. This change is made to the ending inventory budget. This change can cause a ripple effect throughout the budget, since doing so may require expenditures for additional production equipment, more direct labor staff, overtime, and inventory storage space. It will also increase the amount of budgeted working capital, and may increase the reserve for obsolete inventory.
- *Reduce inventory levels.* Management may want to reduce the company's investment in working capital by shrinking the amount of inventory on hand. There are a number of implications to this. First, there may be an increase in freight expenses, since some items may go out of stock and require overnight delivery. Second, the obsolete inventory expense may increase, since drawing down stocks will be more likely to reveal any items that are not in usable condition. Third, fewer inventories may equate to longer intervals before customer orders are shipped, which may result in some cancelled customer orders and therefore reduced revenues.

The operating decisions noted here are only a few of the multitude that can impact a budget. Management should examine any prospective change in its current operating policies to determine how alterations to them can impact the budget, and then incorporate those changes in the budget as appropriate.

The Reasons for Budget Iterations

There are several very good reasons why the first version of a corporate budget is sent back for additional work. We do not refer to the requirement by an egotistical senior manager to create "better" numbers, irrespective of the ability of the company to achieve such numbers. Instead, there are other serious issues that must be considered in depth to ensure that a budget is realistic. These issues are:
- *Constraints.* If there are bottlenecks within the company that interfere with its ability to generate additional sales, does the budget provide sufficient funding to impact these bottlenecks? If not, the company can budget whatever results it wants, but it has virtually no chance of achieving them. For example, a machine in the production area may be a bottleneck that keeps a company from producing any more products – if the bottleneck is not dealt with, sales will not increase, irrespective of improvements anywhere else in the company.

- *Pacing*. If a company intends to expand operations in new geographical areas, or to open new distribution channels, or to offer entirely new products, it should build into the budget an adequate amount of time to ramp up each operation. This issue of pacing should include consideration of the sales cycle of customers, which may be extremely long. For example, expanding the customer base to include municipal governments may be an excellent idea, but may require a sales cycle of greater than a year, given the advance notice needed by governments to budget for purchases.
- *Financing*. If a company has a hard cap on the amount of funding that it will have available during the budget period, then the requirements of the budget must not exceed that funding limitation. This is one of the more common reasons for budget iterations, especially in small companies, where it may be difficult to obtain new funding.
- *Historical metrics*. If a company has been unable to achieve certain performance benchmarks in the past, what has changed to allow it to do so now? The chances are good that the company will still have trouble improving beyond its historical ability to do so, which means that the budget should be adjusted to meet its historical metrics. For example, if a business has historically been unable to generate more than $1 million of sales per salesperson, the preliminary budget should continue to support a similar proportion of sales to salespeople. Similarly, a historical tendency for accounts receivable to be an average of 45 days old prior to payment should probably be reflected in the preliminary budget, rather than a more aggressive collection assumption.

This section has highlighted the need to conduct a close examination of preliminary versions of a budget to see if it meets a number of reasonableness criteria. This usually calls for a number of adjustments to the budget, which typically begins with excessively optimistic assumptions, followed by a certain amount of retrenching.

The Number of Budget Scenarios

Most companies prepare just a single budget scenario, which is their best guess regarding how the next year will turn out. This scenario is based upon a range of supporting assumptions, any one of which can lead to diverging results - and usually does. So, though you may spend a considerable amount of time on that "mainstream" budget scenario, just that one version will not be enough to prepare for what may - and probably will - happen.

It may make sense to add two more scenarios, one for the absolute worst case, where bankruptcy is looming, and one for the most phenomenal sales success. Sounds unlikely that either one will ever happen? If you don't plan for success, it never *will* happen, and bankruptcy scenarios are far more frequent than you might think. Consequently, it is useful to know what resources will be needed for a phenomenally successful year, and how deep expenses will have to be cut to avoid bankruptcy. Of these two outlier scenarios, it is more important to spend additional time on the worst case scenario, perhaps matching the worst business conditions that the company has ever experienced in its history. The result should be a contingency plan for how the company can deal effectively with a catastrophic situation, coupled with a commitment to fast execution of the plan.

Is that a sufficient number of scenarios? No.

There are key variables that could significantly skew the company's results if specific events arise, and you should have a rough, high-level budget in place that is based on changes in those variables. The types of variables will differ by business. Here are examples of key variables:

- *Commodity costs*. For example, the price of aviation fuel is of extraordinary importance in the airline industry, since it comprises such a large proportion of an airline's expenses.
- *Credit availability*. For example, the fortunes of the home building industry rise and fall based on the availability of credit for home owners.
- *Government action*. For example, increases in the government-mandated capital reserve requirement for banks restricts the ability of banks to lend, and therefore reduces their ability to earn a profit.
- *Supplier availability*. For example, the combined earthquake and tsunami in Japan in 2011 interrupted the flow of automobiles and related parts to other markets.

Thus, it is useful to have one thoroughly-constructed budget scenario, and two other budgets dealing with best-case and worst-case scenarios that require a lesser amount of detail, as well as other high-level budget models to deal with key variables.

All of this talk of multiple models does not mean that it is necessary to spend an equal amount of time on each one. The mainstream scenario requires the most work, because it is (presumably) the most likely, with less work needed for the less likely alternatives. Nonetheless, at least spend some time determining financial results at a high level for each scenario, and conceptualize what those situations will do to the company's operations.

The discussion of budget scenarios so far has been about constructing budget versions that are essentially based on probability of occurrence. Another possibility is to construct a top-down model and a bottom-up model, and reconcile the two. Under this approach, ask the senior management team to construct a budget based on their view of the business (the top-down model), while front-line managers and staff independently create a budget that is based on their street-level view of the company's business (the bottom-up model). The top-down model is largely derived from senior management's presumably better strategic view of the industry and general trends, while the bottom-up model is derived from the more immediate, short-term view of those people dealing directly with customers and products. Since these two budgets are derived from fundamentally different sources of information, there will inevitably be significant differences. Examining these differences can yield valuable insights into the business, and can lead to the creation of an integrated model that better represents the capabilities of the company and the industry within which it operates.

Summary

The discussion in this chapter has described in general terms the multitude of component parts that must be completed, compared with each other, and revised before they are assembled into a comprehensive budget. This requires a close examination of a variety of operational decisions and how they impact all facets of the budget. It is also necessary to review the budget in light of the company's historical results, ability to obtain financing, effects of operational bottlenecks, and other issues. Thus, considerable contemplation of each budget version is needed to discern which aspects of company operations may require budget adjustments.

In the following chapters, we will delve into each of the various components of the budget in greater detail. The intent of the following chapters is to present the budget in sufficient detail to allow you to create your own budget.

Chapter 4
The Revenue Budget

Introduction

Revenue is the key driver of a business, and so we begin the discussion of how to create a traditional budget model with the revenue budget. It can also be called a sales budget, but to avoid any confusion with the budget of the sales department (which is comprised of expenses), we will call it the revenue budget. This chapter describes several possible formats for the revenue budget, as well as who is responsible for it, additional sources of information for the budget, and the impact of pacing and revenue variability on the budget.

Overview of the Revenue Budget

The basic revenue budget contains an itemization of a company's sales expectations for the budget period, which may be in both units and dollars. If a company has a large number of products, it usually aggregates its expected sales into a smaller number of product categories; otherwise, the revenue budget becomes too unwieldy. The sales budget is usually presented in either a monthly or quarterly format.

The basic calculation in the sales budget is to itemize the number of unit sales expected in one row, and then list the average expected unit price in the next row, with the total revenues appearing in the third row. If any sales discounts or returns are anticipated, these items are also listed in the revenue budget.

It is extremely important to do the best possible job of forecasting revenue, since the information in the revenue budget is used as an input by most of the other budgets (such as the production budget), and so has a considerable impact on them. Thus, if the revenue budget is inaccurate, then so too will be the other budgets that use it as source material.

The projected unit sales information in the sales budget feeds directly into the production budget, from which the direct materials and direct labor budgets are created. The revenue budget is also used to give managers a general sense of the scale of operations, for when they create the manufacturing overhead budget, the sales and marketing budget, and the administration budget. The total net sales dollars listed in the revenue budget are carried forward into the revenue line item in the master budget.

EXAMPLE

Quest Adventure Gear is a maker of rugged travel gear. One of its equipment lines is a propane-powered camp stove. Its sales forecast is as follows:

	Quarter 1	Quarter 2	Quarter 3	Quarter 4
Forecasted unit sales	5,500	6,000	7,000	8,000
× Price per unit	$35	$35	$38	$38
= Total gross sales	$192,500	$210,000	$266,000	$304,000
- Sales discounts and allowances	-3,850	-$4,200	-$5,320	-6,080
= Total net sales	$188,650	$205,800	$260,680	$297,920

Quest's sales manager expects that increased demand in the second half of the year will allow it to increase its wholesale unit price from $35 to $38. Also, the sales manager expects that the company's historical sales discounts and allowances percentage of two percent of gross sales will continue through the budget period.

The Detailed Revenue Budget

The very simple revenue budget example in the preceding section only incorporated a single product, which resulted in a very simplistic budget model. Realistically, most companies sell a considerable number of products and services, and must find a way to aggregate them into a revenue budget that strikes a balance between revealing a reasonable level of detail and not overwhelming the reader with a massive list of line-item projections. There are several ways to aggregate information to meet this goal.

One approach is to summarize revenue information by sales territory, as shown below. This approach is most useful when the primary source of information for the revenue budget is the sales managers of the various territories, and is particularly important if the company is planning to close down or open up new sales territories; changes at the territory level may be the primary drivers of changes in sales. In the example, the Central Plains sales territory is expected to be launched midway through the budget year and to contribute modestly to total sales volume by year end.

Sample Revenue Budget by Territory

Territory	Quarter 1	Quarter 2	Quarter 3	Quarter 4
Northeast	$135,000	$141,000	$145,000	$132,000
Mid-Atlantic	200,000	210,000	208,000	195,000
Southeast	400,000	425,000	425,000	395,000
Central Plains	0	0	100,000	175,000
Rocky Mountain	225,000	235,000	242,000	230,000
West Coast	500,000	560,000	585,000	525,000
Totals	$1,460,000	$1,571,000	$1,705,000	$1,652,000

If you aggregate revenue information by sales territory, the various territory managers are expected to maintain additional detail regarding sales in their territories, which is kept separate from the formal budget document.

Another approach is to summarize revenue information by contract, as shown below. This is realistically the only viable way to structure the revenue budget in situations where a company is heavily dependent upon a set of contracts that have definite ending dates. In this situation, you can divide the budget into existing and projected contracts, with subtotals for each type of contract, in order to separately show firm revenues and less-likely revenues. This type of revenue budget is commonly used when a company is engaged in services or government work.

Sample Revenue Budget by Contract

Contract	Quarter 1	Quarter 2	Quarter 3	Quarter 4
Existing Contracts:				
Air Force #01327	$175,000	$175,000	$25,000	$--
Coast Guard #AC124	460,000	460,000	460,000	25,000
Marines #BG0047	260,000	280,000	280,000	260,000
Subtotal	$895,000	$915,000	$765,000	$285,000
Projected Contracts:				
Air Force resupply	$--	$--	$150,000	$300,000
Army training	--	210,000	600,000	550,000
Marines software	10,000	80,000	80,000	100,000
Subtotal	$10,000	$290,000	$830,000	$950,000
Totals	$905,000	$1,205,000	$1,595,000	$1,235,000

Yet another approach for a company having a large number of products is to aggregate them into product lines, and then create a summary-level budget at the product line level. This approach is shown below. However, if you create a revenue budget for product lines, also consider creating a supporting schedule of projected sales for each of the products within that product line, in order to properly account for the timing and revenue volumes associated with the ongoing introduction of new products and cancellation of old ones. An example of such a supporting schedule is also shown below, itemizing the "Alpha" line item in the product line revenue budget. Note that this schedule provides detail about the launch of a new product (the Alpha Windmill) and the termination of another product (the Alpha Methane Converter) that are crucial to the formulation of the total revenue figure for the product line.

Sample Revenue Budget by Product Line

Product Line	Quarter 1	Quarter 2	Quarter 3	Quarter 4
Product line alpha	$450,000	$500,000	$625,000	$525,000
Product line beta	100,000	110,000	150,000	125,000
Product line charlie	250,000	250,000	300,000	300,000
Product line delta	80,000	60,000	40,000	20,000
Totals	$880,000	$920,000	$1,115,000	$970,000

Sample Supporting Schedule for the Revenue Budget by Product Line

	Quarter 1	Quarter 2	Quarter 3	Quarter 4
Alpha product line detail:				
Alpha Flywheel	$25,000	$35,000	$40,000	$20,000
Alpha Generator	175,000	225,000	210,000	180,000
Alpha Windmill	--	--	200,000	250,000
Alpha Methane Converter	150,000	140,000	25,000	--
Alpha Nuclear Converter	100,000	100,000	150,000	75,000
Totals	$450,000	$500,000	$625,000	$525,000

A danger in constructing a supporting schedule for a product line revenue budget is that you delve too deeply into all of the various manifestations of a product, resulting in an inordinately large and detailed schedule. This situation might arise when a product comes in many colors or options. In such cases, engage in as much aggregation at the individual product level as necessary to yield a schedule that is not *excessively* detailed. Also, it is nearly impossible to forecast sales at the level of the color or specific option mix associated with a product, so it makes little sense to create a schedule at that level of detail.

In summary, the layout of the revenue budget is highly dependent upon the type of revenue that a company generates. We have described different formats for companies that are structured around products, contract-based services, and sales territories. If a company engages in more than one of these activities, still create the revenue-specific formats shown in this section in order to provide insights into the sources of revenues, and then carry forward the totals of those schedules to a master revenue budget that lists the totals in separate line items. Users of this master revenue budget can then drill down to the underlying revenue budget schedules to obtain additional information. An example of a master revenue budget that is derived from the last two example revenue budgets is shown below.

Sample Master Revenue Budget

	Quarter 1	Quarter 2	Quarter 3	Quarter 4
Contract revenue	$905,000	$1,205,000	$1,595,000	$1,235,000
Product revenue	880,000	920,000	1,115,000	970,000
Totals	$1,785,000	$2,125,000	$2,710,000	$2,205,000

Responsibility for Revenue Information

The primary responsibility for creating the revenue budget rests with the sales manager, since this is the person who has the best knowledge of how products are selling throughout the company's sales regions, and how competing products impact its sales. However, also gain input from five other sources to obtain a more global view of future sales prospects. They are:

- *Purchasing manager.* The purchasing department can give insights into whether there are going to be significant changes in the cost of the materials that go into the company's products, as well as whether there are likely to be outright supply restrictions that prevent the company from making products at all.

- *Engineering manager.* The engineering manager can give information about the status of new product development, and when those products are likely to be available for sale. Further, if there are problems with products that require their withdrawal from the market, the engineering manager can disclose which items, when they are to be withdrawn, and for how long.
- *Marketing manager.* The marketing department has the best knowledge of exactly when new products are to be rolled out into the marketplace, and so can provide sales start dates with a considerable degree of precision.
- *Financial analyst.* A financial analyst should review the trailing 12-months history of product sales to see if there are trends in unit volume and price points that the sales manager may not be aware of. The result of this analysis may be the discovery of only slight trends of a few percentage points, but incorporating these changes into the revenue budget can still have a considerable impact on profit projections.
- *Chief executive officer (CEO).* The CEO may be considering major strategic moves that will make the sales manager's projections irrelevant, such as selling off or closing down product lines, or opening up entirely new sales regions.

What if the company is primarily in the services business, such as a consulting advisory firm? Then consult with a different group of people. Consider the following:

- *Human resources manager.* In the services business, the primary company resource is its personnel. If a company is engaged in service activities that require a high level of skill by its employees, it is entirely possible that the ability of the company to grow will be constrained by the availability of recruits with the appropriate skill set – and the human resources manager is the best source of information in this area.
- *Contracts manager.* If a company deals with large-scale services contracts, then the contracts manager, who administers the contracts, is the best source of information about how much funding remains on each contract, and may also have knowledge about how likely the contracts are to be renewed. This person serves as a warning flag for a future decline in sales, though he or she may have less knowledge of new service contracts that may be obtained.

In short, the bulk of the responsibility for generating the revenue budget clearly resides with the sales manager. Nonetheless, there are a number of other possible sources of information that can provide input into this budget, so consult with them to refine the sales numbers provided by the sales manager.

Sources of Revenue Information

There are a variety of sources of information related to the sales forecast that are integrated into the revenue forecast, some of which were included in the preceding Responsibility for Revenue Information section. The following bullet points divide this information into primary and secondary sources of revenue information.

Primary sources of revenue information are those that have the highest probability of success in being achieved in the revenue budget, and for which the company has a demonstrated ability to provide products or services. These primary sources are:

- *Historical sales.* While it is certainly true that one cannot manage a business based entirely on extrapolating forward from historical results, it is also true that sales achieved once are fairly likely to be achieved again. This is especially true if the business is situated in a relatively stagnant industry where there are few innovations, so that customers are forced to buy the same products year after year. Historical sales information is least useful when product cycles are extremely short and competition is intense.
- *Contract restrictions.* If a company is selling goods or services under the terms of an existing contract, incorporate into the budget the remaining amount of funding available under the contract, as well as the date when the contract will expire.
- *Sales promotions.* If the marketing department is planning to launch sales promotions at various times during the budget period, then insert the likely impact of these promotions into the budget.
- *Sales of existing products to new regions.* When a company already has an established base of products and services, there is a high likelihood that it knows how to market and support these products. However, the probability of sales prediction declines when you introduce these products into new regions, because there may be new competitors ensconced in those areas that are prepared to defend their turf fiercely.
- *Incremental product sales.* If the company is planning to introduce a new product that is a close derivation of an existing product, then it is quite likely that the company can sell it successfully to its existing customer base and be able to support it properly.

Tip: An excellent source of information about probable sales is the sales staff. However, take into account how they may deliberately skew their forecasts if they believe you will alter their commission structures based on the sales volumes they predict. For example, if the company has a history of setting higher sales goals every year, above which the sales staff will earn a higher commission, it is reasonable to assume that the sales staff will predict lower sales in an effort to influence the setting of a lower sales goal. Thus, the compensation system can influence the sales forecast.

Secondary sources of revenue information are those that have a lower probability of success in being achieved in the revenue budget, and for which the company has little or no demonstrated ability to provide products or services. Examples of these sources are:

- *Sales of new products.* It is vastly more difficult to predict the sales of an entirely new product, especially if the product is situated in a market that is unfamiliar to the company. In this case, the company is faced with multiple problems: uncertainty about suppliers, its production capabilities, price points, competition, regulatory issues, and so forth.
- *Sales in a new country.* Each country has its own permitting system and way of doing business. If a company enters into a new country without a local partner, it will be very difficult to predict sales for several years.

In addition to the revenue sources just noted, apply the following factors to the initial forecast, to see if they will materially modify the forecast:

- *Salesperson replacements.* If a highly experienced salesperson leaves the company, it is quite likely that a less-skilled replacement will generate fewer sales.
- *Salesperson ramp-up period.* If the company's products and services require a fairly high skill level in the sales process, then factor in a lengthy ramp-up period before new sales personnel are capable of maintaining the sales rate of the more experienced sales staff.
- *Commission changes.* If a new commission plan will go into effect during the budget period, how will it impact the willingness of the sales staff to sell? Alternatively, will the compensation structure of the new plan push the sales staff in the direction of selling different products?
- *Product cannibalism.* If the company is expecting to launch a new product during the budget period, will the sales of the new product interfere with the sales of an existing product?
- *Competition.* Have any competitors signaled that they plan to issue competing products or engage in other forms of disruptive behavior (such as changes in pricing, customer service, and warranties) that could impact sales?
- *Supply problems.* Are there any indications that suppliers may alter their prices substantially during the budget period, or that supplies of critical components may be constrained?
- *Product withdrawals.* Do customer complaints indicate that the company may have to withdraw a product from the market? And if so, for what period of time would the product be withdrawn?

Tip: Consider organizing the revenue line items in the revenue budget by probability and providing subtotals by probability range. Doing so gives a reader a ready grasp of the likelihood that the company will achieve its revenue targets. In addition, consider color-coding each probability cluster to make the delineation more obvious.

> **(continued)** For example, to use a stop light color scheme, present all high-probability sales in green, all moderate-probability items in yellow, and low-probability sales in red.

When you assemble sales information for the revenue budget, be sure to concentrate the bulk of the forecasting efforts on the 20% of products or services that make up 80% of all sales. This key 20% will also likely be associated with sales to a relatively small group of customers. By tightly defining what you are going to forecast, you can substantially reduce the amount of budgeting work required.

A final factor to consider when developing the revenue forecast is to compare actual results to the budget for the last period, and see if you can spot the factors that caused the budget to be incorrect. It is entirely possible that those factors still exist, and may cause similar problems in the new budget period. If so, you may be able to mitigate their effects by altering the budget.

The Impact of Pacing on the Revenue Budget

A common trap that companies fall into when budgeting for rapid growth is to account for the delaying effect of pacing. From the perspective of budgeting, pacing is the rate at which an entity can ramp up an operational issue until it can handle a target revenue level. Here are several pacing scenarios to consider:

- *Sales staff.* A company sells a product that requires an intensive hands-on sale by an experienced salesperson. The company must delay budgeted revenues that are associated with new salespeople until such time as they are capable of selling at the same success rate as more experienced salespeople. This is one of the most significant pacing issues.
- *Selling cycle.* In some industries, customers only buy products at a certain pace. This is particularly true for large capital products, where purchases are only considered once a year, and must go through a lengthy review process before a purchase order is issued. In such situations, a company may hire a group of excellent, well-trained sales people, and yet not earn a single new customer order for a long time.
- *Retail roll out.* A company has developed an excellent retail concept store, and can gain sales rapidly if it can roll out the concept into new locations as fast as possible. This is a major pacing issue, since the company likely has only a small number of people who are sufficiently skilled in store openings, and that group can only open a certain number of stores within a given period of time.
- *Production facilities.* If a company can only gain new sales after it builds new production facilities, then it cannot budget for more sales until the facilities are complete and tested, and the new staff hired for the facility is capable of running the facility at the planned level of productivity. The variety of issues involved can mean that new sales cannot begin until a long time after a facility has been constructed.

- *Permits.* A company can only do business in a new sales region after it obtains all necessary government permits. This is a particular problem when a company is attempting to gain entry into a new country where it has few contacts or no local partners.
- *New technology.* A company has created a product that has cutting-edge technology. Such products tend to have a higher failure rate until the engineering and production staffs can figure out the underlying issues. This process of working out the kinks can be extensive and greatly delay revenue generation.

Pacing is an extremely important topic that less seasoned managers tend to completely ignore. The result is a revenue budget that initially appears reasonable, but which a company is not able to meet, due to a lack of attention to underlying factors that exert a natural slowing effect on revenue growth.

The Inherent Variability of the Revenue Budget

No matter how detailed and thorough the analysis of the underlying factors affecting revenue may be, the revenue budget will inevitably depart from actual results after just a few months. This level of inherent variability can be massive if a company's sales cycle is quite short, and it has a small backlog of customer orders. In that situation, a company has to create new sales "from scratch" after just a few months, which makes it very difficult to forecast sales. Conversely, if a company has a massive order backlog that extends beyond the entire forecast period, then the company can probably come fairly close to matching its revenue budget. However, even in this latter case, there will inevitably be production constraints and delays that impact sales, as will cancelled customer orders – and these issues will build over time to cause an increasing level of variability.

There is no way to deal with the inherent variability of the revenue budget, other than to tailor the period covered by the budget to the time period over which a company can predict its revenues with a reasonable degree of certainty. Thus, the company in our first scenario may find that it can only create a budget for the next three months, while the company in the second scenario may be able to comfortably prepare a revenue budget that covers the next two years. An alternative is to intensively review and update the revenue budget over just the period when sales are relatively predictable, while maintaining a longer-term forecast for which little effort is made to compile a detailed operational budget. Doing so reduces the amount of work that goes into the budget, while still presenting an approximate view of the company's revenue direction.

Summary

A key issue when developing the revenue budget is to keep from having an excessively statistical approach to its formulation. This means that you should avoid a preponderance of sales forecasting that is based on time series or correlation analysis, since you are, in effect, basing future sales on a database of past sales. Instead, a better revenue forecast is one that relies on more detailed operational information, such as salesperson reports, marketing schedules for product rollouts, purchasing department estimates of supply problems, and so forth. Though this later approach requires considerably more time to accumulate and analyze information, it also results in a budget that has a much stronger basis in reality.

Chapter 5
The Ending Finished Goods Inventory Budget

Introduction

The ending finished goods inventory budget appears to be a simple declaration of the inventory level that management wants a company to have at the end of each budget period, and which is used as an input to derive the production budget. In reality, management must carefully consider a number of operational and policy issues in determining the correct level of ending inventory. This chapter covers the various assumptions to address when determining the amount of ending inventory, what the impact of inventory levels may be on other parts of the budget, and how to construct this budget.

Ending Inventory Assumptions

The ending inventory budget is not simply the combination of beginning inventory levels, plus production that matches expected sales, minus sales. If that were the case, inventory levels would vary little from the beginning of the first budget period to the end of the last budget period. Instead, consider a variety of assumptions that will alter the amount of inventory that you want to have on hand. These issues are:

- *Customer service.* If management wants to improve customer service, one way to do so is to increase the amount of ending inventory, which allows the company to fulfill customer orders more quickly and avoid backorder situations. This can be accomplished by either a gradual or more forced increase in the planned amount of ending inventory.
- *Inventory record accuracy.* If your inventory record keeping system is inaccurate, then it is necessary to maintain additional amounts of inventory on hand, both of raw materials and finished goods, to ensure that customer orders are fulfilled on time. If you can upgrade the level of inventory accuracy, then there is less need to keep additional stocks on hand.
- *Manufacturing planning.* If you are using a manufacturing resources planning (MRP II) system, then you are producing in accordance with a sales and production plan, which requires a certain amount of both raw materials and finished goods inventory. If you change to the just-in-time (JIT) manufacturing planning system, then you are only producing as required by customers, which tends to reduce the need for inventory. Thus, a switch from an MRP to a JIT system can result in lower inventory levels.
- *Product life cycles.* If there are certain products or even entire product lines that a company is planning to terminate, then factor the related inventory reductions into the amount of planned ending inventory. However, a product termination is frequently coupled with the introduction of a replacement

product, which may require *more* on-hand inventory to meet the higher demand levels that are common with a new product. Thus, there can be offsetting product life cycle issues that can impact inventory levels.

- *Product versions.* If the sales and marketing staff want to offer a product in a number of versions, you may need to keep a certain amount of each type of inventory in stock. Thus, an increase in the number of product versions equates to an increase in ending inventory, and vice versa.
- *Seasonal sales.* If a company experiences very high sales volume at certain times of the year, then it may be more practical to gradually build inventory levels over several months leading up to the prime sales season, rather than attempting to do so over a short period of time. This means that you should plan for a gradual increase in the amount of ending inventory, followed by a sharp decline in inventory levels immediately after the selling season.
- *Supply chain duration.* If you are planning to switch to a supplier located far away from the company, be aware that this calls for having a larger safety stock of finished goods on hand, so that deliveries to customers will not be impacted if there is a problem in receiving goods on time from the supplier. This is a common problem, as many companies have switched to lower-cost foreign suppliers. Conversely, switching to a supplier located nearby can compress the delivery distance so much that you can safely lower the amount of ending inventory to reflect the reduced risk of not receiving deliveries on a timely basis.
- *Working capital reduction.* If you want to increase the amount of inventory turnover, this reduces the amount of cash invested in working capital, but also has the offsetting effect of leaving less inventory in reserve to cover sudden surges in customer orders. There is a general trend toward increased inventory turnover.

All of the preceding factors can have a considerable impact on the amount of planned ending inventory. If more than one factor is impacting your business, you may find that there are conflicting issues that make it more difficult to plan ending inventory levels. For example, a switch to a JIT system would likely reduce inventory, but a management decision to keep more inventory on hand for faster customer order fulfillment would have an opposite effect. Consequently, it can be difficult to sort through the differing issues to arrive at an appropriate level of planned ending inventory.

If you are deliberately altering the ending finished goods inventory level because of any of the preceding issues, be sure to document your reasoning and include it in the notes attached to the budget, so that users of the budget understand the reasons for the change.

Impact of Changes in Ending Inventory

The amount of inventory shown in the ending inventory budget impacts a number of other elements of a company's budget. In particular, be aware of the following issues:

- *Inventory increase.* If the amount of ending inventory is increased, then the production budget must include a ramp-up in production costs, which in turn will require a greater expenditure for direct materials, and possibly an investment in more fixed assets to increase the capacity of the production line. Higher purchasing volumes may allow the procurement staff to obtain some direct materials at a lower cost. The greater investment in inventory will also require more working capital, which can increase the company's need for additional financing.
- *Inventory decrease.* If the amount of ending inventory is reduced, then the planned amount of production will decline. This may require the layoff of some direct labor employees, with attendant severance expenses. Lower purchasing volumes may require the procurement staff to buy goods at higher prices. The reduced investment in inventory will shrink the amount of working capital needed, which may in turn reduce the need for any additional financing. Reducing inventory levels tends to make obsolete inventory items more apparent, so there may be an increased cost of goods sold related to the recognition of obsolete inventory.

The Ending Finished Goods Inventory Budget

The ending finished goods inventory budget states the number of units of finished goods inventory at the end of each budget period. It also calculates the cost of finished goods inventory. The amount of this inventory tends to be similar from period to period, assuming that the production department manufactures to meet demand levels in each budget period. However, and as noted in the "Ending Inventory Assumptions" section, there are a variety of reasons why you may want to alter the amount of ending finished goods inventory. If so, it is useful to create separate layers of ending inventory in the budget that reflect each of the decisions made, so that readers of the budget can see the numerical impact of operational decisions.

In the following example, we assume that changes made in the immediately preceding budget period will continue to have the same impact on inventory in the *next* budget period, so that the adjusted ending inventory in the last period will be the starting point for our adjustments in the next period. We can then make the following adjustments to the unadjusted ending inventory level to arrive at an adjusted ending inventory:

- *Internal systems changes.* Shows the impact of altering the manufacturing system, such as changing from an MRP to a JIT system.
- *Financing changes.* Shows the impact of altering inventory levels in order to influence the amount of working capital used.

- *Product changes.* Shows the impact of product withdrawals and product introductions.
- *Seasonal changes.* Shows the impact of building inventory for seasonal sales, followed by a decline after the selling season has concluded.
- *Service changes.* Shows the impact of changing inventory levels in order to alter order fulfillment rates.

If management is attempting to reduce the company's investment in inventory, it may mandate such a large drop in ending inventory that the company will not realistically be able to operate without significant production and shipping interruptions. You can spot these situations by including the budgeted inventory turnover level in each budget period, as well as the actual amount of turnover in the corresponding period in the preceding year. This is shown in the following example as the historical actual days of inventory, followed by the planned days of inventory for the budget period. Comparing the two measurements may reveal large period-to-period changes, which management should examine to see if it is really possible to reduce inventory levels to such an extent.

EXAMPLE

Quest Adventure Gear has a division that sells electronic signaling devices for lost hikers. Quest wants to incorporate the following changes into its calculation of the ending finished goods inventory:

1. Switch from the MRP to the JIT manufacturing system in the second quarter, which will decrease inventory by 250 units.
2. Reduce inventory by 500 units in the first quarter to reduce working capital requirements.
3. Add 500 units to inventory in the third quarter as part of the rollout of a new product.
4. Build inventory in the first three quarters by 100 units per quarter in anticipation of seasonal sales in the fourth quarter.
5. Increase on-hand inventory by 400 units in the second quarter to improve the speed of customer order fulfillment for a specific product.

The ending finished goods inventory unit and cost calculation follows:

(units)	Quarter 1	Quarter 2	Quarter 3	Quarter 4
Unadjusted ending inventory level	2,000	1,600	1,850	2,450
+/- Internal system changes	0	-250	0	0
+/- Financing changes	-500	0	0	0
+/- Product changes	0	0	500	0
+/- Seasonal changes	100	100	100	-300
+/- Service changes	0	400	0	0
Adjusted ending inventory	1,600	1,850	2,450	2,150
× Standard cost per unit	$45	$45	$45	$45
Total ending inventory cost	$72,000	$83,250	$110,250	$96,750
Historical actual days of inventory	100	108	135	127
Planned days of inventory	92	106	130	114

The days of inventory calculation at the bottom of the table shows few differences from actual experience in the second and third quarters, but the differences are greater in the first and fourth quarters. Management should review its ability to achieve the indicated inventory reductions in those quarters.

The ending finished goods inventory budget shown in the preceding example is quite simplistic, for it assumes that you want to apply the same inventory policies and systems to a company's *entire* inventory. For example, this means that you want to increase inventory levels for all types of inventory in order to increase customer order fulfillment speeds, when in fact you may only want to do so for a relatively small part of the inventory.

If you want to adjust inventory levels at a finer level of detail, then consider creating a budget that sets inventory levels by business unit or product line. It is generally too time-consuming to set inventory levels at the individual product level, especially if demand at this level is difficult to predict.

Summary

The concept of the ending finished goods inventory budget might, on initial viewing, appear to be one of the simplest components of a budget to construct, since it is essentially a single line item. Also, adjusting the ending inventory amount away from its historical level would seem to be a simple way to drive a variety of changes within a company, such as improving the order fulfillment rate or reducing the amount of working capital.

A more detailed analysis reveals that this is an area requiring a considerable amount of thought. An alteration to the ending inventory balance forces changes in the production area, as well as potentially altering the capital budget, modifying the prices at which materials are purchased, and changing the amount of financing needed. Thus, model the impact of alterations to this budget carefully before finalizing the numbers.

A further problem with this budget is that simply budgeting an altered inventory level does not necessarily mean that the actual amount of inventory will change. On the contrary, a manufacturing system will likely continue to require roughly the same amount of inventory to produce a given amount of sales, unless there is a structural change in the way a company produces goods. Consequently, you may find that even the best of intentions to alter the ending finished goods inventory may not result in an actual change.

Chapter 6
The Production Budget

Introduction

The production budget is simply the matching of planned ending inventory levels to estimated sales levels, so that a company manufactures enough units to meet its expected sales requirements and still have the desired amount of inventory in stock at the end of a period. Thus, the budget appears to be a relatively mechanical compilation that requires minimal analysis. The reality is significantly different, since a company may face constraints in such areas as skilled labor, production bottlenecks, and raw materials that may impede its ability to attain the production budget. We address the basic mechanics of the production model in the following sections, as well as cover the issues that can impede its realization.

The Production Budget

The production budget calculates the number of units of products that must be manufactured, and is derived from a combination of the sales forecast and the planned amount of finished goods inventory to have on hand (usually as safety stock to cover unexpected increases in demand). The production budget is typically presented in either a monthly or quarterly format. The basic calculation used by the production budget is:

> \+ Forecasted unit sales
> \+ Planned finished goods ending inventory balance
> = Total production required
>
> \- Beginning finished goods inventory
> = Units to be manufactured

It can be very difficult to create a comprehensive production budget that incorporates a forecast for every variation on a product that a company sells, so it is customary to aggregate the forecast information into broad categories of products that have similar characteristics.

The planned amount of ending finished goods inventory can be subject to a considerable amount of debate, since having too much may lead to obsolete inventory that must be disposed of at a loss, while having too little inventory can result in lost sales when customers want immediate delivery. Unless a company is planning to draw down its inventory quantities and terminate a product, there is generally a need for some ending finished goods inventory. The calculation of the production budget is illustrated in the following example.

EXAMPLE

Quest Adventure Gear plans to produce an array of plastic water bottles for the upcoming budget year. Its production needs are as follows:

	Quarter 1	Quarter 2	Quarter 3	Quarter 4
Forecast unit sales	5,500	6,000	7,000	8,000
+ Planned ending inventory units	500	500	500	500
= Total production required	6,000	6,500	7,500	8,500
- Beginning finished goods inventory	-1,000	-500	-500	-500
= Units to be manufactured	5,000	6,000	7,000	8,000

The planned finished goods inventory at the end of each quarter declines from an initial 1,000 units to 500 units, since the materials manager believes that the company is maintaining too much finished goods inventory. Consequently, the plan calls for a decline from 1,000 units of ending finished goods inventory at the end of the first quarter to 500 units by the end of the second quarter, despite a projection for rising sales. This may be a risky forecast, since the amount of safety stock on hand is being cut while production volume increases by over 30 percent. Given the size of the projected inventory decline, there is a fair chance that Quest will be forced to increase the amount of ending finished goods inventory later in the year.

The production budget deals entirely with unit volumes; it does not translate its production requirements into dollars. Instead, the unit requirements of the budget are shifted into other parts of the budget, such as the direct labor budget and the direct materials budget, which are then translated into dollars.

Other Production Budget Issues

So far, we have only addressed the mechanical formulation of the production budget. In addition, we must consider whether it is even *possible* to achieve the production volumes stated in this budget. As noted in this section, there are several constraints to consider, and which may require some alteration of the planned units of production.

When formulating the production budget, it is useful to consider the impact of proposed production on the capacity of any bottleneck operations in the production area. It is entirely possible that some production requirements will not be possible given the production constraints, so you will either have to scale back on production requirements, invest in more fixed assets, or outsource the work. The following example illustrates the issue.

EXAMPLE

Quest Adventure Gear revises the production budget described in the preceding example to incorporate the usage of a bottleneck machine in its manufacturing area. The revised format follows, beginning with the last row of information from the preceding example:

	Quarter 1	Quarter 2	Quarter 3	Quarter 4
Units to be manufactured	5,000	6,000	7,000	8,000
× Minutes of bottleneck time/unit	15	15	15	15
= Planned bottleneck usage (minutes)	75,000	90,000	105,000	120,000
- Available bottleneck time (minutes)*	110,160	110,160	110,160	110,160
= Remaining available time (minutes)	35,160	20,160	5,160	-9,840

* Calculated as 90 days × 24 hours × 60 minutes × 85% up time = 110,160 minutes

The table reveals that there is not enough bottleneck time available to meet the planned production level in the fourth quarter. However, Quest can increase production in earlier quarters to make up the shortfall, since there is adequate capacity available at the bottleneck in the earlier periods.

Note in the preceding example that the amount of available bottleneck time was set at 85 percent of the maximum possible amount of time available. We make such assumptions because of the inevitable amount of downtime associated with equipment maintenance, unavailable raw materials, scrapped production, and so forth. The 85 percent figure is only an example – the real amount may be somewhat higher or substantially lower.

It is also useful to determine the impact of the production budget on the need for skilled production labor. This is a particular problem in custom-manufacturing environments, where it may take years of training before a person is fully qualified to engage in certain types of production. This issue can seriously constrain a company's production plans. You can model the need for additional production staff using the same model just used for a bottleneck machine, simply by assuming that the bottleneck is staff time, rather than a machine.

The availability of raw materials may keep you from attaining the production level stated in the production budget. This can be an issue where there are few suppliers, or where supplies are located in areas where political issues or customs controls restrict the availability of supplies. If so, you may need to work with the procurement staff to stockpile the necessary materials or find alternative suppliers, or with the engineering staff to redesign products that use other materials. It is also possible that you will be unable to keep raw material constraints from interfering with the production budget.

Yet another issue impacting the production budget is the need to incur step costs when production exceeds a certain volume level. For example, a company may need to open a new production facility, production line, or work shift to accommodate any additional increase in production past a certain amount of volume. It may be possible to adjust the production schedule to accelerate production in slow periods in order to stockpile inventory and avoid such step costs in later periods.

A less common problem is when the planned amount of ending inventory increases to the point where a business must invest an inordinate amount of working capital in the additional inventory. Once management realizes the amount of the extra investment involved, it may elect to plan for less ending inventory than it might consider ideal. This problem may not arise during the initial formulation of the production budget, since financing requirements are compiled later in the budgeting process. If it eventually becomes apparent that there is a problem, you will need to adjust the ending finished goods inventory budget, which feeds into the production budget, to reduce the amount of ending inventory.

All of the factors noted in this section are major concerns, and should be considered when you evaluate the viability of a production budget.

Budgeting for Multiple Products

The production budget shown thus far has centered on the manufacture of a single product. How do you create a production budget if you have multiple products? The worst solution is to attempt to re-create in the budget a variation on the production schedule for the entire budget period – the level of detail required to do so would be inordinately high. Instead, consider one of the following alternatives:

- *Bottleneck focus.* Rather than focusing on the production of a variety of products, only budget for the amount of time that they require at the bottleneck operation. For example, rather than focusing on the need to manufacture every aspect of 20 different products, you could focus on the time that each product needs at a single production operation. If you have multiple production lines or facilities, then only budget for usage of the bottleneck at each location.

- *Product line focus.* In many cases, there are only modest differences in the production activities needed to create any product within a product line. If there are such production commonalities, consider treating the entire production line as a single product with common production requirements.

- *80/20 rule.* It is likely that only a small number of products comprise most of a company's production volume. If this is the case, consider detailed budgeting for the production of the 20 percent of all products that typically comprise 80 percent of all sales, and a vastly reduced (and aggregated) amount of budgeting for the remaining products.

- *MRP II planning.* If a company uses a manufacturing requirements planning (MRP II) system, the software may contain a planning module that allows you to input estimates of production requirements, and generate detailed requirements for machine usage, direct labor, and direct materials. If so, you can input the totals from this module into the budget without also copying in all of the supporting details.

None of the preceding suggestions for multi-product budgeting are perfect (with the possible exception of the MRP II planning module), but one of them or a variation on them should be sufficient to give you a reasonable version of a production budget that can be incorporated into the budget model.

Summary

It may initially appear that formulating the production budget is a mechanical process of matching information in the revenue budget to the ending finished goods inventory budget to arrive at proposed production levels. However, the discussion of additional issues revealed that a key step in creating the production budget is to consider the impact of constraints on the budget, and to modify either the budget or the company's operations or products to deal with these constraints. Consequently, members of the industrial engineering, product design, production, and procurement departments should review this budget to see if it can be achieved.

Chapter 7
The Direct Materials Budget

Introduction

Direct materials are those materials and supplies that are consumed during the manufacture of a product, and which are directly identified with that product. Direct materials can be a large proportion of the total costs of a company, so it is critical to be especially careful when constructing the direct materials budget. This chapter presents three ways to compile a direct materials budget – either by rolling up costs based on production estimates and bills of material, or by extrapolating historical costs into the budget period, or by a combination of the two. We also address several anomalies to be aware of when you create this budget.

The Direct Materials Budget (Roll up Method)

The direct materials budget calculates the materials that must be purchased, by time period, in order to fulfill the requirements of the production budget, and is typically presented in either a monthly or quarterly format. The basic calculation for the roll up method is to multiply the estimated amount of sales (in units) in each reporting period by the standard cost of each item to arrive at the standard amount of direct materials cost expected for each product. Standard costs are derived from the bill of materials for each product. A bill of materials is the record of the materials used to construct a product. A sample calculation is:

Sample Calculation of the Cost of Direct Materials

	Quarter 1	Quarter 2	Quarter 3	Quarter 4
Product A				
Units	100	120	110	90
Standard cost/each	$14.25	$14.25	$14.25	$14.25
Total cost	$1,425	$1,710	$1,568	$1,283
Product B				
Units	300	350	375	360
Standard cost/each	$8.40	$8.40	$8.40	$8.40
Total cost	$2,520	$2,940	$3,150	$3,024
Grand total cost	$3,945	$4,650	$4,718	$4,307

Note that the preceding example only addressed the direct materials *expense* during the budget period. It did not address the amount of materials that should be purchased during the period; doing so requires that you also factor in the planned amounts of beginning and ending inventory. The calculation used for direct material purchases is:

+ Raw materials required for production
+ Planned ending inventory balance
= Total raw materials required

- Beginning raw materials inventory
= Raw materials to be purchased

The presence or absence of a beginning inventory can have a major impact on the amount of direct materials needed during a budget period – in some cases, there may be so much inventory already on hand that a company does not need to purchase any additional direct materials at all. In other cases, and especially where management wants to build the amount of ending inventory (as arises when a company is preparing for a seasonal sales surge), it may be necessary to purchase far more direct materials than are indicated by sales requirements in just a single budget period. The following example illustrates how beginning and ending inventory levels can alter direct material requirements.

EXAMPLE

Quest Adventure Gear plans to produce a variety of large-capacity water coolers for camping, and 98% of the raw materials required for this production involve plastic resin. Thus, there is only one key commodity to be concerned with. The production needs of Quest for the resin commodity are shown in the following direct materials budget:

	Quarter 1	Quarter 2	Quarter 3	Quarter 4
Product A (units to produce)	5,000	6,000	7,000	8,000
× Resin/unit (lbs)	2	2	2	2
= Total resin needed (lbs)	10,000	12,000	14,000	16,000
+ Planned ending inventory	2,000	2,400	2,800	3,200
= Total resin required	12,000	14,400	16,800	19,200
- Beginning inventory	1,600	2,000	2,400	2,800
= Resin to be purchased	10,400	12,400	14,400	16,400
Resin cost per pound	$0.50	$0.50	$0.55	$0.55
Total resin cost to purchase	$5,200	$6,200	$7,920	$9,020

The inventory at the end of each quarter is planned to be 20% of the amount of resin used during that month, so the ending inventory varies over time, gradually increasing as production requirements increase. The reason for the planned increase is that Quest has some difficulty receiving resin in a timely manner from its supplier, so it maintains a safety stock of inventory on hand.

The purchasing department expects that global demand will drive up the price of resin, so it incorporates a slight price increase into the third quarter, which carries forward into the fourth quarter.

It is impossible to calculate the direct materials budget for every component in inventory, since the calculation would be massive. Instead, it is customary to either calculate the *approximate* cost of direct materials required, or else at a somewhat more detailed level by commodity type (see the later discussion of the 80/20 method). It is possible to create a reasonably accurate direct materials budget by either means, if you have a material requirements planning software package that has a planning module. If you enter the production budget into the planning module, the software can generate the expected direct materials budget for future periods. Otherwise, you will have to calculate the budget manually.

If you use the roll up method, you are basing the unit volume of materials on the quantities listed in the bill of materials for each item. It is a fundamental principle of materials management that the information in bills of material be as accurate as possible, since the materials management department relies on this information to purchase materials and schedule production. However, what if the bill of materials information is incorrect, even if only by a small amount? Then, under the roll up method, that incorrect amount will be multiplied by the number of units to be produced in the budget period, which can result in quite a large error in the amount of materials used in the budget. If you are intent upon using the roll up method, it is difficult to avoid this problem, other than by scheduling periodic audits of the bills of material to verify their accuracy.

The Direct Materials Budget (Historical Method)

In a typical business environment, there may be a multitude of factors that impact the amount of direct materials as a percentage of sales, including scrap, spoilage, rework, purchasing quantities, and volatility in commodity prices. Many companies are unable to accurately capture these factors in their bills of material, which makes it nearly impossible for them to create a reliable direct materials budget using the roll up method that was described in the last section.

In such cases, an alternative budget calculation is the historical method, under which you assume that the historical amount of direct materials, as a percentage of revenues, will continue to be the case during the budget period. This approach means that you simply copy forward the historical percentage of direct material costs, with additional line items to account for any budgeted changes in key assumptions.

Under the historical method, you must adjust the projected amount of sales for any increase or decrease in production that is required for planned changes in the amount of ending inventory, and express the result as adjusted revenue. You can then multiply the adjusted revenue figure by the historical percentage of direct materials to arrive at the total direct materials cost required to achieve the production budget. Despite the need for these adjustments, it is still much easier to create a direct materials budget using the historical method than by using the roll up method.

EXAMPLE

Quest Adventure Gear finds that its last direct materials budget, which was created using the roll up method, did not come anywhere near actual results. This year, Quest wants to use the historical method instead, using the historical direct materials rate of 32% of revenues as the basis for the budget. To avoid having the company become complacent and not work toward lower direct material costs, the budget also includes several adjustment factors that are expected from several improvement projects. There is also an adjustment factor that addresses a likely change in the mix of products to be sold during the budget period. The budget model is:

	Quarter 1	Quarter 2	Quarter 3	Quarter 4
Projected revenue	$4,200,000	$5,000,000	$5,750,000	$8,000,000
+/- planned ending inventory change	-400,000	+100,000	+250,000	-350,000
Adjusted revenue	$3,800,000	$5,100,000	$6,000,000	$7,650,000
Historical direct materials percentage	27.1%	27.1%	27.1%	27.1%
+ / - Adjustment for product mix	+3.4%	+4.0%	+1.8%	-0.9%
- Adjustment for scrap reduction	0.0%	0.0%	-0.2%	-0.2%
- Adjustment for rework reduction	0.0%	-0.1%	-0.1%	-0.1%
= Adjusted direct materials percentage	30.5%	31.0%	28.6%	25.9%
Total direct materials cost	$1,159,000	$1,581,000	$1,716,000	$1,981,350

The problem with the historical method is that it is based on a certain mix of products that were sold in the past, each possibly with a different proportion of direct materials to sales. It is unlikely that the same mix of products will continue to be sold through the budget period; thus, applying an historical percentage to a future period may yield an incorrect direct materials cost. You can mitigate this issue by including an adjustment factor in the budget (as was shown in the preceding example), which modifies the historical percentage for what is expected to be the future mix of product sales.

The Direct Materials Budget (80/20 Method)

The Pareto principle holds that about 80 percent of the effects come from 20 percent of the causes. Or, stated in terms of direct materials, you can expect that 80 percent of all direct material costs come from 20 percent of the materials that you use in your products. You can use the Pareto principle as the basis for engaging in the detailed budgeting of 20 percent of all materials, and then cluster the remaining 80 percent of materials used into a lump sum that you estimate in a more general manner, such as by an historical average. We call this the 80/20 method.

The 80/20 method is derived from the two preceding methods, because you use the roll up method to derive the amount of those direct materials comprising 80 percent of costs, and the historical method to estimate the remaining amount of materials. It is common to find that commodity purchases are heavily represented in the roll up portion of this budget, since these items typically comprise a large part of the cost of a product.

The effort required to create the direct materials budget using this method is about midway between the requirements of the other two models, since it includes elements of both. The 80/20 method is used in the following example.

EXAMPLE

Quest Adventure Gear has created a new division that produces lightweight equipment for extreme adventure racers. Quest is using the 80/20 method to derive the direct materials budget for this division. Rip stop nylon and webbing are the key commodities used in the products of this division, and so are included in the roll up portion of the budget. There are a large number of other materials whose cost is calculated in a lump sum, using the historical percentage method. The purchasing department expects to be able to centralize purchases with a smaller number of suppliers as the year progresses, thereby achieving a 0.1% reduction in non-commodity costs in each quarter after the first quarter.

	Quarter 1	Quarter 2	Quarter 3	Quarter 4
Adjusted revenue	$451,500	$471,600	$503,850	$506,250
Direct materials – roll up method				
Rip stop nylon (square yards)	10,000	10,250	10,000	9,900
Rip stop nylon unit price	$8.00	$8.00	$9.00	$9.00
Rip stop nylon total cost	$80,000	$82,000	$90,000	$89,100
Webbing (feet)	10,250	10,625	10,250	10,125
Webbing unit price	$4.00	$4.00	$4.00	$4.00
Webbing total cost	$41,000	$42,500	$41,000	$40,500
Total direct materials – roll up method	$121,000	$124,500	$131,000	$129,600
Direct materials – historical method				
Historical direct materials percentage	6.7%	6.7%	6.7%	6.7%
+/- Adjustments	0.0%	-0.1%	-0.2%	-0.3%
= Adjusted direct materials percentage	6.7%	6.6%	6.5%	6.4%
Total direct materials – historical method	$30,250	$31,125	$32,750	$32,400
Grand total direct materials	$151,250	$155,625	$163,750	$162,000

Note in the budget how the purchasing manager of Quest estimates a commodity price change for rip stop nylon as of the beginning of the third quarter, and notes this change in a separate line item. Also, note that the historical direct materials percentage in the historical method section of the budget does not include the cost of the materials already estimated above it in the roll up portion of the budget.

Anomalies in the Direct Materials Budget

In this section, we discuss how to handle two issues in the direct materials budget – how to budget for changes in commodity prices, and for the cost of materials lost by various means.

If commodity prices tend to change by large amounts and at irregular intervals, it will be difficult to reflect these changes in a full-year budget. This is a particular problem when a certain commodity comprises a large part of the raw materials of a business, as is the case with corn syrup for candy manufacturers and resin for the manufacturers of plastic products. In these situations, you have the following choices:

- *Probability basis.* If there are several possible changes in commodity prices and you can assign a probability of occurrence to each one, multiply the probability of occurrence by each pricing scenario and then add the results together to arrive at a probability-adjusted commodity price.
- *Rolling forecast.* If commodity prices have a large impact on a company's financial results, then consider revising the budget once a quarter to reflect your best estimates of commodity prices. Not doing so might result in a budget that is not even remotely achievable, if commodity prices head in an unexpected direction.
- *Multiple versions.* You could create several versions of the budget, each using a different commodity price. Though this approach is good for providing management with models of different scenarios, it will result in an unwieldy budget.
- *Budget vs. actual adjustment.* When creating budget versus actual reports, the accounting department can segregate the commodity expense in a different line item and always show a budget that matches actual results, so that management can view the results of the company, excluding the impact of the commodity prices over which it has no control.

You can select any of the preceding alternatives to match your specific circumstances. We prefer the rolling forecast approach, since it preserves the integrity of the budget over the short term and relies on a single budget version that is relatively easy to maintain.

There are a variety of additional costs that are sometimes included in the cost of direct materials, such as scrap, spoilage, rework, and inventory obsolescence. These costs are usually included in a lump sum in the cost of goods sold, because there are no systems in place to track them individually. This can present a problem when constructing a budget, because there are both normal (expected) and abnormal (unexpected) amounts of these costs, and some of them may not recur in the future. Thus, not tracking them separately will result in the inclusion of abnormal expenses in the budget. Consequently, if you have tracking systems in place to monitor scrap, spoilage, rework, and obsolete inventory, use them to report these items separately. With this additional information available, it should be possible to budget for normal expenses, while avoiding the inclusion of abnormal expenses.

The Role of the Direct Materials Budget

It is important to understand that the direct materials budget is not used by the procurement department for its daily purchasing tasks. The department uses a combination of the production schedule, on-hand inventory balances, and bills of material to determine its purchasing needs. If the company uses a material requirements planning (MRP) system, then the computer derives exact purchasing quantities from these information sources for the procurement staff. In some cases, the MRP system may even automatically place orders with suppliers.

This means that the procurement department is *not* relying on the direct materials budget in any way to conduct its daily business. Thus, it is not necessary to include an inordinate amount of cost or unit detail in the budget – no one is going to use it. Instead, it is much more efficient to aggregate information in the direct materials budget, probably at the level of a few key commodities and then a subtotal for all other direct materials. If it is necessary to engage in detailed calculations in order to derive the aggregated amounts, then restrict these calculations to a subsidiary-level document that a typical user of the budget will not see.

Summary

The direct materials budget contains a large proportion of a company's total expenses, and so is worthy of considerably more detailed compilation work than many other parts of the budget. Because of the amount of costs involved, we have presented three possible ways to compile the cost of direct materials – select the one that best fits your circumstances. If you have highly accurate and comprehensive bills of materials, the roll up method may provide the best information. Conversely, if you lack faith in the bills of material, then the historical method may be a better alternative. The 80/20 method is a blend of the two alternatives, with an emphasis on detailed analysis of commodity costs, and so may also be useful.

To develop the best possible information, consider two or even all three of the methods described here to create multiple models of the direct materials budget. You can then compare actual results to each of the budget models to determine which one works best for you.

Chapter 8
The Direct Labor Budget

Introduction

Direct labor is the wages and associated benefits and payroll taxes incurred to produce goods or provide services to customers. The direct labor budget is used to create an estimated cost of labor for the budget period, which is then incorporated into the cost of goods sold budget. The direct labor budget is unique in that the traditional derivation of it is fundamentally flawed, yielding results that could differ substantially from what a company may actually experience. In this chapter, we show the traditional method for deriving this budget, as well as an alternative approach that is likely to yield more realistic information.

The Direct Labor Budget (Traditional Method)

The direct labor budget is used to calculate the number of labor hours that will be needed to produce the units itemized in the production budget, as well as their cost. A more complex direct labor budget will calculate not only the total number of hours needed, but will also break down this information by labor category. The direct labor budget is useful for anticipating the number of employees who will be needed to staff the manufacturing area throughout the budget period. This allows management to anticipate hiring needs, as well as when to schedule overtime, and when layoffs may be needed.

The direct labor budget is typically presented in either a monthly or quarterly format. The basic calculation used by this budget is to import the number of units of production from the production budget, and to multiply this by the standard number of labor hours for each unit. This yields a subtotal of the direct labor hours needed to meet the production target. You can also add more hours to account for production inefficiencies, which increases the amount of direct labor hours. Then multiply the total number of direct labor hours by the fully burdened direct labor cost per hour, to arrive at the total cost of direct labor.

If you have a material requirements planning software package that includes a planning module, you may be able to load the production budget into the planning module and have it calculate the required number of direct labor hours, by position. Otherwise, you will have to calculate this budget manually.

EXAMPLE

Quest Adventure Gear plans to produce a number of titanium camp stoves during the budget period. The labor routing for each stove is 0.1 hours per stove for the machine operator, and 0.05 hours per stove for all other labor. The labor rates for machine operators and other staff

---

are substantially different, so they are recorded separately in the budget. Quest's direct labor needs are budgeted as follows:

	Quarter 1	Quarter 2	Quarter 3	Quarter 4
Product A (units)	5,000	6,000	7,000	8,000
× Machine operator hours per unit	0.1	0.1	0.1	0.1
= Total machine operator hours	500	600	700	800
× Other labor hours per unit	0.05	0.05	0.05	0.05
= Total other labor hours	250	300	350	400
Machine operator cost/hour	$25	$25	$25	$25
Other labor cost/hour	$15	$15	$15	$15
Total machine operator cost	$12,500	$15,000	$17,500	$20,000
Total other labor cost	$3,750	$4,500	$5,250	$6,000
Grand total direct labor cost	$16,250	$19,500	$22,750	$26,000

The budget contains two types of labor that are compiled separately, since they have different costs. There are 0.1 machine hours of time required for each product manufactured, which costs the company $25 per hour. Additionally, there are 0.05 other hours of time required for each product manufactured, which costs the company $15 per hour. The table shows the hours required for each labor category by quarter, as well as the cost of each type of labor.

The traditional approach to developing a direct labor budget relies upon labor routing information at the unit level. A labor routing is a document showing the work steps required to manufacture a product, and which includes the time required for each work step. If there is even a minor error in a labor routing, it will be multiplied by all of the units expected to be produced, possibly creating substantially inaccurate budget results. Because of this issue, be sure to include in the direct labor budget a comparison to current crewing levels for the existing rate of production, and compare this information to the budget for reasonableness.

Another verification issue to consider is to budget for considerably less than the 2,080 hours of work per year that would be expected if a full-time employee were to work 40 hours per week for all 52 weeks of a year. Instead, use a considerably smaller number that factors in the amount of work lost to vacations, holidays, and other issues, and match the result against the headcount figures suggested in the budget. The following table shows the derivation of what the actual number of hours might be that would be available for productive work.

Derivation of Usable Hours per Year

Hours per Year	Derivation
2,080	40 hours per week × 52 weeks per year
- 80	2 weeks per year of vacation × 40 hours per week
- 80	2 weeks per year of holidays × 40 hours per week
- 384	20% utilization reduction × remaining 1,920 hours
= 1,536	

The 1,536 figure noted in the preceding derivation of usable hours may vary from a company's actual experience; it only serves to highlight the extent to which the direct labor staff may actually be available for work.

The Direct Labor Budget (Crewing Method)

The preceding presentation of the calculation of this budget makes it appear as though the cost of direct labor is entirely variable. If this was the case, the production manager would only hire people for the exact period of time needed to produce whatever was called for in the daily production schedule, and then send everyone home. Such an unstable work environment would make it very unlikely that a company could retain a production staff for long. And if a company is constantly hiring new employees to replace those unwilling to work in this uncertain environment, then it will have inexperienced employees who are very inefficient. Instead, the production manager must retain experienced employees, which calls for paying them irrespective of the vagaries of the production schedule.

Further, a production operation usually calls for a certain minimum number of employees in order to crew the production lines or work cells – it is not possible to operate the equipment with fewer people. Because of this crewing requirement, a company must spend a certain minimum amount for direct labor personnel, irrespective of the actual quantity of items being manufactured.

Another consideration is the concept of labor efficiency. Under an old-style production environment, it was considered a best practice to keep the direct labor staff working diligently, manufacturing goods all day long. This practice drove down the cost of labor on a per-unit basis. However, it eventually became apparent that lowering the cost of labor on a per-unit basis came at the cost of creating more inventory than was needed for immediate sale – and having too much inventory introduced a variety of other costs that greatly exceeded the cost savings from having an efficient direct labor staff. This realization led to the creation of the just-in-time manufacturing system, where the direct labor staff is only allowed to produce goods as they are needed. Doing so greatly reduced the amount of inventory, while also reducing the efficiency of the direct labor staff; instead, it is now acceptable if these employees are not working at all if there are no products to be produced.

In a just-in-time environment, management hires for direct labor positions based on an expected range of production volume. If the expected range changes, then management adjusts the number of direct labor positions accordingly. Thus, the expenditure for direct labor tends to be relatively fixed. This results in a much simpler direct labor budget, known as the *crewing method*, which is illustrated in the following example.

EXAMPLE

Quest Adventure Gear has used a direct labor budget model in previous years that was based on labor routing information, and found that actual results differed substantially from what was indicated in the budget. For the next budget year, Quest managers decide to experiment with a new approach, where they determine the fixed labor cost needed to crew an entire production line, and then make adjustments to the budget for those periods in which they expect production volumes to require the use of staff overtime. It uses this method with its titanium backpack production line. This production line is staffed by eight people, and can produce 1,000 backpacks per quarter with no overtime. The company expects to require additional production during the second quarter that will call for the addition of two temporary workers to the production line. There are also plans for a 6% pay raise at the beginning of the fourth quarter. The direct labor budget for this production line is:

	Quarter 1	Quarter 2	Quarter 3	Quarter 4
Backpack line:				
Staffing headcount	8	10	8	8
× Quarterly pay per person	$10,400	$10,400	$10,400	$11,024
= Total direct labor cost	$83,200	$104,000	$83,200	$88,192

Note the considerably simpler budget needed for the crewing method, rather than the more detailed traditional method that was described earlier. Not only is the crewing method simpler, but it is also likely to be more accurate than the results obtained from the traditional method. This is because the traditional method is based upon the false assumption that labor levels vary at the unit level, when they usually vary only at the level of the production line.

The Direct Labor Budget for Manufacturing Cells

A company may use a large number of manufacturing cells in its production process. A manufacturing cell is one or more machines that are manned by a small number of employees. Employees walk individual units of production through the various processing steps in their cells, and then hand them off to the next cell in the production sequence. If there is no work to be done, then employees are not authorized to build additional units.

The manufacturing cell concept is extremely useful for minimizing inventory levels and keeping scrap and spoilage at a minimum. A side effect of the cell is that labor efficiency per person is much lower than would be found in a production line, since there are many machine setups to handle, and it is acceptable to not produce units at all if there is no need for them.

Given the focus of a manufacturing cell system on materials, rather than labor, it is best to use the crewing method to compile the direct labor budget. Doing so results in a fairly accurate portrayal of the cost of manning the various manufacturing cells. If you were to instead use the traditional method, where you derive labor costs from the number of units produced, the budget could be significantly different from actual results.

The Cost of Direct Labor

It is not efficient or even practical to break down the direct labor budget into a direct labor rate for each labor category, especially in an environment where any of the following factors can make it more difficult to estimate costs:

- There are many labor classifications, all at different pay levels
- Employees regularly shift between labor classifications
- Overtime occurs on an irregular basis
- The mix of labor classifications on work crews changes repeatedly

In such an environment, it is nearly impossible to attain a high degree of precision in calculating the cost of labor per hour. Instead, use the historical average rate of pay for the entire production department or product line, adjusted for any changes in overtime and pay rates that are anticipated during the budget period. Such an approach is vastly easier and may prove to be reasonably accurate.

Anomalies in the Direct Labor Budget

This section addresses a number of issues that may apply to your company, and which you may need to consider when constructing a direct labor budget.

If you use the traditional method noted earlier in this chapter for determining the expected amount of direct labor for the budget period, be aware that not all of the costs associated with an hour of direct labor actually vary on a per-hour basis. Those costs that accrue on a per-hour basis are:

- *Payroll taxes*. Both social security and Medicare taxes vary on a per-hour basis, since they are both calculated as a percentage of wages earned.
- *Vacation and sick pay*. The amount of vacation and sick pay earned by an employee is usually earned based on a percentage of hours worked, though the formula can vary by company, and may simply be granted based on weeks or months of continuing employment.

There are a number of benefits that *do not* vary on a per-hour basis. Instead, these benefits are paid in a fixed amount to benefit suppliers once a month, irrespective of the actual amount of hours worked. Benefits of this type include:

- *Medical insurance*. The company and/or the employee pays a fixed amount each month for medical insurance, where the key variable is not the number of hours worked, but rather the number of dependents who will be covered by the insurance.

- *Life insurance.* The company and/or the employee pays a fixed amount each month for life insurance, with the amount paid being a function of the employee's age and pay. Thus, this benefit may be partially associated with pay on a per-hour basis.

Because of the non-variable nature of the employee benefits just described, structure the direct labor budget to show the cost of such benefits as a fixed period cost, rather than a component of the cost per hour.

If a company conducts a layoff, it will likely lay off direct labor staff in the reverse order of their hiring, so that the more experienced personnel are retained. When this happens, the average pay rates used in the direct labor budget will be too low, since the people retained are paid at a higher average rate. Thus, if there is any expectation of a layoff during a budget period, the budget should reflect an increased labor cost per hour that is coincident with the timing of a layoff, and extending until such time as employees are hired back.

If a company pays its direct labor staff either entirely or partially on a piece rate plan (where pay is based on the number of units produced), then the direct labor budget must be more closely aligned with the planned rate of production. This calls for use of the traditional method of constructing the direct labor budget, as explained earlier. However, payroll regulations require that employees must receive at least the minimum wage, so it may be necessary to build into the budget model a verification that at least the minimum wage is being paid.

If a company plans to expand its direct labor staffing rapidly during the budget period, it may mean that the new employees will be less efficient during the time period required for them to learn the necessary skills and gain experience. If so, the budget model should factor in this reduced efficiency level, perhaps through the need for additional staff. However, if staffing levels are expected to remain relatively constant through the budget period, with new employees only being hired to replace normal numbers of employees lost to turnover, then the historical efficiency level can be used in the budget.

Summary

We have shown two alternative methods for deriving the direct labor budget. The traditional method requires you to calculate the amount of direct labor from the bottom up, based on the exact amounts of inventory to be produced and the standard labor usage rates for each product.

In most cases, it is much easier and may very well be more accurate to use the crewing method, where you determine the amount of labor to operate an entire production facility within certain volume constraints. The concept of the crewing method is based on the assumption that "direct" labor does not really exist, and so should be portrayed as indirect labor. This concept is accurate in a manufacturing environment where employees are on-site and being paid irrespective of production volume levels. We strongly recommend the crewing method, not only because of its simplicity, but because it more accurately reflects the reality of how the production department is staffed.

Chapter 9
The Manufacturing Overhead Budget

Introduction

The manufacturing overhead budget is one of the larger sources of expenses in the budget of a manufacturing firm, and includes many types of expenses. If you assume that these costs are largely fixed, then constructing the budget is a relatively simple matter. If, alternatively, there are points at which step costs may arise, or where costs may change with production volumes, or where sales are seasonal, then you might want to consider changing the basic model. We will discuss these issues and more in the following sections.

The Manufacturing Overhead Budget

The manufacturing overhead budget contains all manufacturing costs other than the costs of direct materials and direct labor (which are itemized separately in the direct materials budget and the direct labor budget). Expenses normally considered part of manufacturing overhead include:
- Depreciation
- Facilities maintenance
- Factory rent
- Factory utilities
- Indirect materials, such as supplies
- Insurance on the factory and inventory
- Materials management staff compensation
- Personal property taxes on manufacturing equipment
- Production employee fringe benefits
- Production employee payroll taxes
- Production supervisor compensation
- Quality assurance staff compensation

It is also possible to include the cost of idle time in manufacturing overhead, but this is usually too difficult to track, and so is not recommended.

The information in the manufacturing overhead budget becomes part of the cost of goods sold line item in the master budget.

EXAMPLE

Quest Adventure Gear owns a division that produces camping furniture for car campers. Quest budgets all raw materials and direct labor in the direct materials budget and direct labor budget, respectively. Its manufacturing overhead costs are stated in the manufacturing overhead budget as follows:

	Quarter 1	Quarter 2	Quarter 3	Quarter 4
Production management salaries	$142,000	$143,000	$144,000	$145,000
Management payroll taxes	10,000	10,000	11,000	11,000
Depreciation	27,000	27,000	29,000	29,000
Facility maintenance	8,000	7,000	10,000	9,000
Rent	32,000	32,000	32,000	34,000
Personal property taxes	6,000	5,000	7,000	6,000
Quality assurance expenses	3,000	3,000	3,000	3,000
Utilities	10,000	10,000	10,000	12,000
Total manufacturing overhead	$238,000	$237,000	$236,000	$237,000

The production management salaries line item contains the wages paid to the manufacturing supervisors, the purchasing staff, and production planning staff, and gradually increases over time to reflect changes in pay rates. The depreciation expense is relatively fixed, though there is an increase in the third quarter that reflects the purchase of new equipment. Both the freight and supplies expenses are closely linked to actual production volume, and so their amounts fluctuate in conjunction with planned production levels. The rent expense is a fixed cost, but does increase in the fourth quarter to reflect a scheduled rent increase.

Several of the larger expense line items in this budget are step costs, so they tend to be incurred when a certain production volume is reached, and then stay approximately the same until production volumes change to a significant extent. This means that some line items can be safely copied from the actual expenditures in the preceding year with only minor changes. For example, if the current production level requires a second shift, and a production supervisor for that shift, then the manufacturing overhead budget for the next year should include the salary of that supervisor as long as there is going to be a second shift. Examples of situations giving rise to step costs are:

- *Additional production line.* If an entire production line is added, then expect to incur step costs for all supporting staff, including materials management, supervision, and quality assurance personnel. There will also likely be an increase in the cost of utilities.
- *Additional shift.* If the facility is to be kept open for a second or third shift, then expect to incur step costs for additional supervisors, as well as for a jump in the cost of utilities needed to power the facility during the extra time period.

Other expenses in this budget will require more analysis than the step costs just described. In particular, expenditures for the maintenance of machines and buildings can vary over time, depending upon the age of the assets being maintained and the need for large maintenance overhauls from time to time. For example, the expenditure for machinery maintenance may have been $100,000 in the preceding year, but can now be dropped to $50,000 in the new budget period because the company has replaced much of the equipment that had been requiring the bulk of the maintenance.

It is very difficult to run a facility at close to 100% of capacity. In this situation, equipment tends to break down more frequently, so a high utilization level requires additional overhead expenditures for parts, supplies, and maintenance labor.

In summary, the basic manufacturing overhead model is a relatively simple one, though it can involve a considerable amount of money. We will now address a more complicated method of budgeting for manufacturing overhead.

Overhead Allocation between Periods

The discussion thus far has assumed that you should charge all manufacturing overhead to expense in the period incurred. It is possible to instead create an allocation methodology, and allocate the overhead to both the cost of goods sold within each budget period and the amount of finished goods inventory on hand at the end of each period. Doing so defers some overhead recognition until a later period when the inventory is used. We do not recommend allocating overhead between periods for the following reasons:

- *Complexity*. You need to allocate manufacturing overhead based on a calculated overhead rate, which can add some additional complexity to the budget model.
- *Results*. If sales levels are relatively steady, then using an overhead allocation will not result in a significant difference in the reported amount of overhead charged to expense in different periods.

The one application in which overhead allocation may be needed is when sales are seasonal. For example, if you are building inventory for the Christmas selling season, then allocate manufacturing overhead to inventory produced, so that you can charge it to expense when the inventory is eventually sold. If you elect to allocate overhead for this or a similar reason, keep the allocation methodology as simple as possible. The following example demonstrates the concept:

EXAMPLE

To continue with the preceding example, Quest Adventure Gear finds that its sales of camping furniture for car campers is highly seasonal, with most sales being to retailers in the second quarter of the calendar year. To more accurately simulate its recognition of manufacturing overhead, Quest redesigns the preceding budget, so that the overhead is allocated to each unit based on the number of units produced during the period. The following table assumes the presence of some inventory that was manufactured in the preceding year.

	Quarter 1	Quarter 2	Quarter 3	Quarter 4
Total manufacturing overhead	$238,000	$237,000	$236,000	$237,000
Allocation per unit	$20	$20	$19	$22
Units produced	11,900	11,850	12,400	10,750
Units sold	3,000	41,000	2,000	500
Units added to inventory	8,900	0	10,400	10,250
Amount charged to expense	$60,000	$820,000	$38,000	$11,000
Amount recorded in ending inventory	$178,000	$0	$198,000	$226,000

The table shows that most of the manufacturing overhead incurred during the year is charged to expense during the second quarter, which is when most products are sold.

The preceding example of overhead allocation simplifies how overhead is charged to expense as products are sold. The example assumes that all 41,000 units sold in the second quarter had $20 of overhead charged to each unit. In reality, those units were mostly produced in prior quarters when the allocation per unit might have been different. Consequently, if you want to include overhead allocation in the budget model, be prepared for a considerable amount of complexity in modeling how much overhead is allocated into inventory, and how much overhead is relieved from inventory over time.

Additional Issues

This section addresses two additional issues related to manufacturing overhead – an alternative presentation format and the use of detailed expense allocations. The issues are:

- *Fixed/variable format.* A less common format for the manufacturing overhead budget is to group the line items into fixed and variable expenses. It can be difficult to determine the fixed or variable status of a cost, in which case you can add a third cost grouping for mixed costs. Ascertaining the variability of a cost can be difficult, so most manufacturing overhead costs are usually clustered under the fixed expenses heading.
- *Detailed allocations.* There may be a temptation to engage in extremely detailed overhead allocations within the budget model, where you assign costs to specific products, projects, and so forth. The budget is not a good place to engage in such detailed allocations, since (as you will see in the Budgeting Efficiencies chapter), it is extremely useful to keep the budget model as streamlined as possible. If you want to engage in allocations at such an extreme level of detail, use an activity-based costing model to assign overhead as actual costs are incurred.

Summary

As noted in this chapter, some of the largest expenses in the manufacturing overhead budget are step costs, and so will not be expected to change significantly from period to period – as long as production volumes do not change. However, if significant production changes are anticipated, then expect to review this budget in detail to ascertain whether any large step costs should be added to or subtracted from the budget.

Some elements of the manufacturing overhead budget will vary with the level of production volume, such as maintenance expense. If so, consider modifying the budget model so that fixed overhead costs are unchanged through the entire budget period, while more variable costs reflect changes in the amount of production. This issue is addressed in detail in the Flexible Budgeting chapter.

Chapter 10
The Cost of Goods Sold Budget

Introduction

The cost of goods sold budget is one of the simplest budgets to construct, since it contains nothing but inputs from other budgets. Nonetheless, it is also the first place in the overall budget where all elements of the cost of goods sold are brought together, so this is a good place to test the various expense line items for consistency. We explore the construction of the budget and its testing in the following section.

The Cost of Goods Sold Budget

The cost of goods sold budget is derived from the direct labor budget, direct materials budget, and manufacturing overhead budget. The budget itself is quite simple, since it is comprised of nothing more than the inputs from these three other budgets. Also include the total sales (from the revenue budget), so that you can derive the gross margin and gross margin percentage within the budget. Also, add the actual prior year gross margin in a separate line item. Being able to compare the gross margin percentage to actual prior year results is useful for ascertaining whether the cost of goods sold is reasonable. An example follows.

EXAMPLE

The controller of Quest Adventure Gear compiles the following cost of goods sold budget based on expense totals carried forward from the direct labor, direct materials, and manufacturing overhead budgets.

	Quarter 1	Quarter 2	Quarter 3	Quarter 4
Revenue	$400,000	$425,000	$460,000	$410,000
Cost of goods sold:				
Direct labor expense	28,000	29,000	31,000	28,500
Direct materials expense	112,000	114,000	147,000	161,500
Manufacturing overhead	80,000	82,000	84,000	81,000
Total cost of goods sold	$220,000	$225,000	$262,000	$271,000
Gross margin	$180,000	$200,000	$198,000	$139,000
Gross margin percentage	45%	47%	43%	34%
Prior year actual gross margin	43%	46%	45%	44%

Since there are both fixed and variable cost elements in the cost of goods sold, it is reasonable to expect some variation in the gross margin percentage from period to period. Nonetheless, the sudden decline in the gross margin in the fourth quarter of the example is certainly worthy of investigation.

When you review the cost of goods sold budget for reasonableness, consider the following points:

- *Direct labor issues.* Direct labor does not change much, since it generally requires a certain crew size to staff the production area, irrespective of the actual amount of production. The only time when the cost of direct labor should change is when there is a step cost, such as adding a second shift.
- *Direct materials issues.* This is the only element of the cost of goods sold that should vary directly with revenue. If it does not vary in such a manner, there may be a change in the product mix or altered product prices that cause the proportion of direct materials to revenue to vary. If there is no such change, then review the direct materials budget for an error.
- *Manufacturing overhead issues.* As was the case with direct labor, there should be little variation in the amount of manufacturing overhead from period to period. A significant change in this area is probably caused by a step cost. If there is a change but no corresponding step cost, investigate whether your method of allocating overhead is causing the problem.

Reasonableness testing might involve a separate line item for direct materials as a percentage of revenue. As just noted, this is the one truly variable expense in the cost of goods sold budget, and so should fluctuate in a predictable manner, unless the product mix or product prices change.

Summary

The cost of goods sold budget may seem like a simple one that you can quickly construct, test, and subsequently ignore. However, consider that this budget contains a very large proportion of the total expenses that a company incurs. Thus, a one percent change in the gross margin in this budget may equate to the entire budget of a department elsewhere in the company. Given the volume of expenses flowing through this budget, it is prudent to spend extra time examining it, particularly in regard to how it compares to the actual results of the preceding year.

Chapter 11
The Sales and Marketing Budget

Introduction

The sales and marketing budget is linked to the revenue budget, since changes in this budget directly impact revenue. Consequently, this is a closely-reviewed budget that may attract a large amount of company resources. In this chapter, we address the various expenses normally found in the sales and marketing budget, how to aggregate the information into different types of budget formats, and various issues that impact the productivity of the sales and marketing department.

Types and Timing of Sales and Marketing Expenses

Selling expenses are those costs incurred to demonstrate products to customers and obtain orders from them, while marketing expenses involve the positioning, placement, and advertising of a company's products and services. More specifically, the following expenses fall within the general category of sales and marketing expenses:

- *Sales compensation.* This is the cost of paying base salaries, wages, bonuses, and commissions to the sales staff.
- *Other compensation.* This is the cost of the salaries and wages paid primarily to the marketing staff.
- *Order entry compensation.* This is the wages paid to the order entry staff and its management.
- *Advertising and promotions.* This is the set of activities managed by the marketing staff, and may include print advertising, Internet advertising, radio and television advertisements, billboards, coupons, catalogs, direct mail solicitations, one-time promotions, samples, and so forth.
- *Research.* This covers the expenses incurred by the marketing department to discover the optimal ways to promote products and services.
- *Office expenses.* These are the usual expenses incurred to run an office, including rent, utilities, and supplies.

Depending on the size of the department, it may be necessary to further subdivide the preceding expenses by functional area within the department. Specifically, consider separately tracking the performance of the following areas:

- Direct selling to customers
- Sales promotions
- Market research
- Customer service

- Customer warranties
- Selling activities by region

We do not consider the transport or storage of goods to be part of the sales and marketing budget. These expenses should be included within either the direct materials budget or the manufacturing overhead budget. See the chapters addressing those topics for more information.

Most of the expenses just noted are relatively fixed for the duration of the budget period, and can be estimated with considerable accuracy. However, there are four timing exceptions to be aware of:

- *Promotion feedback loop.* If the marketing manager schedules a promotion, such as a short-term advertising campaign for a specific product, then this will (hopefully) increase the sales figure in the revenue budget. Consequently, part of the budget preparation process is to match sales to promotion periods.
- *Commission plans.* If the sales manager has authorized a boost in the commission rate for the sales staff if they reach a certain sales volume, then you need to include in the budget model the estimated date on which the increased commission rate is triggered. This can be a complex calculation, based on sales volumes by sales person, the timing of promotions, and the introduction and termination of products.
- *Product introduction marketing.* The marketing manager is responsible for making the marketplace aware of any new products released by the engineering department. However, this means that the timing of these product-specific expenditures depends upon the release dates of products – which are the responsibility of the engineering manager. Thus, you need to match the product release dates in a different part of the budget to these marketing expenditures.
- *Travel.* If the nature of the business requires that the sales staff make a large number of sales calls, then be sure to include a sufficient travel expense. In particular, if you are planning to add a large number of new sales staff, then assume that they will be less efficient for the first few months of their employment, and so will require more travel expense in exchange for fewer sales than more experienced sales personnel. There may also be special travel expenditures related to trade shows.

Structure of the Sales and Marketing Budget

This section describes several formats in which you can organize the sales and marketing budget. The format you select will likely depend upon the number of sales territories, or whether a large proportion of sales are derived from a few customers. If there are no sales territories and sales are spread among many customers, then the most appropriate budget layout is likely to be by expense type.

The most common type of sales and marketing budget is one that itemizes expenses by type. This is a simple design that shows budgeted compensation, promotions, travel, office expenses, and so forth. An example of this budget format follows:

Sales and Marketing Budget by Expense Type

Expense Type	Quarter 1	Quarter 2	Quarter 3	Quarter 4
Salaries and wages	$270,000	$275,000	$320,000	$380,000
Commissions	10,000	70,000	120,000	140,000
Payroll taxes	22,000	27,000	35,000	41,000
Promotions	0	50,000	85,000	42,000
Advertising	20,000	22,000	22,000	28,000
Research	0	0	35,000	0
Travel and entertainment	40,000	20,000	80,000	70,000
Office expenses	15,000	15,000	21,000	21,000
Other	5,000	5,000	5,000	5,000
Totals	$382,000	$484,000	$723,000	$727,000

It is particularly advisable to break out the commission expense in the sales and marketing budget, since it can vary considerably over time and may be quite a large proportion of the total department expense. The line items used for marketing expenses can vary substantially, depending on the types and timing of marketing activities the company engages in. If the portion of the budget assigned to advertising is substantial, it may make sense to break out this item in a finer degree of detail to show expenditures by type of media, sales campaign, region, and so forth. All other expense line items in this budget are typical for any type of department.

Though the budget format by expense type is the most common, it also tends to hide what may be very important information at the sales region and customer level. Ideally, your primary sales and marketing budget should be by expense type, with additional budgeting at the territory and customer levels if you feel that the additional amount of budgeting investigation creates valuable information.

If a company is organized by sales territory, recast the sales and marketing budget to determine the projected level of expenditures by territory. This is particularly important if most of the sales staff is assigned to specific territories, since this means that most of the cost structure of the company is oriented toward the territory format. You can then match territory gross margins with territory sales and marketing costs to determine earnings by territory. A typical format for such a budget is:

Sales and Marketing Budget by Territory

Sales Territory	Quarter 1	Quarter 2	Quarter 3	Quarter 4
Department overhead	$250,000	$255,000	$255,000	$260,000
Northeast region				
Compensation	400,000	410,000	430,000	450,000
Promotions	65,000	0	75,000	0
Travel	23,000	23,000	25,000	25,000
Other	18,000	19,000	19,000	19,000
Subtotal	$506,000	$452,000	$549,000	$494,000
North central region				
Compensation	450,000	600,000	620,000	630,000
Promotions	75,000	0	80,000	0
Travel	31,000	33,000	35,000	39,000
Other	20,000	24,000	26,000	26,000
Subtotal	$576,000	$657,000	$761,000	$695,000
Totals	$1,332,000	$1,364,000	$1,565,000	$1,449,000

If there are many sales territories, then the preceding format will require some compression of expenses in order to keep the report down to a manageable size. The format just shown itemizes the major expenses and clusters all other expenses into an "other" category.

There may be a small number of dominant customers with whom a company does most of its business. If so, it is entirely possible that one or more of these customers is demanding special discounts or free services that greatly reduce the amount of profit that the company earns. If so, it is imperative that the company be aware of this profit pressure, and plan for it appropriately in its budget. By engaging in advance planning, the sales manager knows how much profit margin he can give up if a customer makes additional demands. This level of preparation tells management where it is making money, and when to walk away from an overly aggressive customer. An example of such a budget is shown in the following example.

Sales and Marketing Budget by Customer

Customer	Quarter 1	Quarter 2	Quarter 3	Quarter 4
Anatolian Designs				
Revenue	$150,000	$175,000	$180,000	$150,000
Cost of goods	75,000	80,000	90,000	75,000
Sales and marketing	30,000	32,000	35,000	30,000
Profit	$45,000	$63,000	$55,000	$45,000
Bosworth Inc.				
Revenue	200,000	210,000	250,000	235,000
Cost of goods	170,000	180,000	220,000	200,000
Sales and marketing	25,000	28,000	40,000	35,000
Profit	$5,000	$2,000	-$10,000	$0
All other customers				
Revenue	250,000	220,000	210,000	200,000
Cost of goods	150,000	130,000	125,000	130,000
Sales and marketing	65,000	71,000	73,000	65,000
Profit	$35,000	$19,000	$12,000	$5,000
Total contribution	$85,000	$84,000	$57,000	$50,000

The preceding exhibit shows that one customer, Anatolian Designs, generates a considerable amount of profit for the company, but that the other customer, Bosworth Inc., appears to have driven prices so low and demands so much sales and marketing funding that there is little room for a profit. Thus, the budget reveals that there is no additional room for concessions for Bosworth; indeed, the sales manager may need to reevaluate the entire relationship with that customer.

Note that the preceding analysis of sales and marketing expense by customer is really an enhanced form of gross margin analysis, which encompasses additional information about revenues and the cost of goods sold. As such, it is a complex document that requires a considerable amount of time to assemble. Thus, only create it for the very largest customers who are responsible for a large part of a company's total sales. If instead there are many small customers, all generating roughly the same profit percentage, it is not necessary to prepare this type of budget.

There may be situations where some salespeople incur much greater expenses than others. This can arise when the sales staff is segmented into an in-house staff and one that travels to customer locations. It may also arise when a sales territory covers a large geographical area. In these situations, it may be necessary to budget expenses by individual salesperson. However, this is an excessive level of detail for most companies, so we do not advise creating a budget structure for it, and do not provide an example of it. In nearly all cases, it is quite sufficient to track salesperson expenses after-the-fact with a trend line analysis report.

Sources of Sales and Marketing Expense Information

Primary responsibility for the sales and marketing expense budget resides with the manager of that department. There may be a separate marketing manager within the department, who will be responsible for the amount and timing of any expenses related to marketing. Cross-check the information provided by these people with the following group, in order to ensure that the budget is achievable in relation to activities elsewhere in the company:

- *Human resources manager.* If the company is continually hiring sales staff, and sales headcount is a key driver of sales, then check with the human resources manager to see if the company has a history of hiring sufficient sales staff, and whether he or she believes that this hiring pace can be maintained for the budgeted salesperson headcount.
- *Materials manager.* The materials manager is responsible for creating a distribution network to supply products to customers within any new sales territories. If the sales manager is planning to commence sales activities in a new territory as of a certain date, that needs to follow the construction of a distribution system for that area.
- *Engineering manager.* The engineering staff has to complete its testing of new products and release them to production before the marketing staff can schedule a promotional campaign, so the product release dates must coincide with the marketing budget.
- *Production manager.* The production manager knows when new products will first be available for delivery, which should coincide with the start of any marketing campaigns for those products.

Given the nature of the cross-checks needed for the sales and marketing budget, it should be apparent that it is easier to construct this budget *after* most of the other departments have completed their preliminary budgets. Thus, the sales and marketing budget contains a number of activities that are dependent upon the completion of tasks by other departments.

Analysis of the Sales and Marketing Budget

When reviewing the sales and marketing budget, there are three areas in particular that call for detailed analysis. The first is the relationship between the expenditures *for* the sales staff and corresponding revenues generated *by* the sales staff. Consider the following factors when deciding whether this expenditure is reasonable:

- *Appropriate sales channels.* Strip away from the revenue figure all sales derived from sales channels that do not require the use of sales staff. You are only interested in sales specifically generated by the sales staff.
- *Historical trend.* If the sales staff has historically been able to generate a certain amount of sales per person, it should be quite difficult for them to exceed this productivity level in the new budget year, so be wary of large presumed productivity increases.

- *Diminishing returns.* It is increasingly difficult to extract more sales from existing markets, so question such revenue increases where the sales and marketing budget does not increase to an even greater extent. See the Diminishing Returns Analysis section for more information.

The second area to investigate in detail is the justification for advertising expenditures. The marketing staff should provide an analysis of the estimated number of target customers reached, the conversion rate for those customers, and the projected margin from the incremental sales generated by the advertising. This is a difficult analysis area, since projections are difficult to verify. You can derive rough estimates of appropriate advertising expenditures by comparing the company's advertising to:

- *Competitor expenditures.* If key competitors are expending a certain amount, then you may feel it necessary to maintain a similar expenditure level to be competitive.
- *Percentage of sales.* This approach is based on an assumption that the company should re-invest in its branding continually by expending a consistent percentage of sales on advertising. However, this approach ignores the probability of advertising overload in some distribution channels. A more targeted approach to advertising could likely result in a more cost-effective method of allocating funds.
- *Cost per unit.* Divide total units sold by the advertising expense in previous periods, and use the same relationship to derive the expenditure for the budget period. This approach assumes that expenditure levels in the past were appropriate, and should be continued into the future.
- *Cost per thousand.* This is the advertising cost divided by the number of customers reached (expressed in thousands). It is more a measure of the cost-effectiveness of dissemination of the advertising message than it is of contacting the correct customers.

Realistically, none of the preceding methods are adequate for determining the "correct" amount of advertising expenditure. A more detailed analysis includes reviewing the advertising for specific product launches and ongoing branding advertising, coupled with research into advertising effectiveness. This can involve a historical analysis of how sales changed before, during, and after an advertising campaign, as well as customer usage of coupons and discount codes. However, even this more detailed level of analysis will only result in a better guesstimate of the most appropriate amount of advertising expenditure.

The third area to investigate is the source of new sales. If new sales are expected to come from existing customers (as occurs when a new product is introduced to the market), it is possible to increase sales without a corresponding increase in the sales staff. However, this is a rarity, for new product sales typically cannibalize the sales of existing products. Conversely, if new sales are expected to come entirely from new customers, then sales and marketing expenditures will need to be unusually large in order to absorb the incremental cost of contacting and selling to these new customers.

Diminishing Returns Analysis

A company will find that, after it achieves a certain amount of sales volume, the cost of generating additional sales goes up. This is caused by a variety of factors, such as having to offer more product features, ship products into more distant sales regions, increase warranty coverage, and so forth. Thus, the cost of obtaining each incremental sale will eventually reach the point where there is no further profit to be gained.

The concept of diminishing returns analysis is a useful one for the sales manager, since he or she should realize that it requires a gradual proportional increase in the sales and marketing budget over time in order to continue to increase sales. You cannot simply assume that the costs incurred in the preceding year to generate a certain sales volume can be applied to the next tranche of projected sales growth.

The concept of diminishing returns is difficult to calculate precisely, since it can appear in varying degrees throughout the budget. Here are some areas to be aware of:

- *Incremental sales staff.* If you add a sales person to an existing sales territory, it is likely that the existing sales staff is already handling the easiest sales, which means that the new hire will have to work harder to gain a smaller amount of sales than the average salesperson. You can estimate this reduced amount and build it into the budget.
- *Incremental advertising.* If you launch a new advertising campaign designed to bring in new customers, does the campaign target a smaller group than had been the case with previous campaigns, or is the targeted group one with less income to spend? Has research shown that increasing amounts of advertising result in incrementally fewer sales? If so, is there an optimal advertising expenditure level beyond which the return on funds expended declines?
- *Incremental region.* When you add a new geographic area, consider how the new region varies from the company's existing sales territories. If it has a less dense population, then it may be more expensive to contact them regarding a sale. If there is entrenched competition, expect a lower market share than normal. If products must be converted for use in a different language, how does the cost of doing so alter the product profit?
- *Incremental product.* If you add a product to an existing product line, will the new addition cannibalize the sales of other products in the product line?
- *Incremental sales channel.* When you add a new sales channel, does it cannibalize the sales of an existing channel? What is the cost of the infrastructure required to maintain the new channel? Will the new channel damage the company's relations with distributors or retailers?

This discussion does not mean that the sales manager should not push for continual sales growth, only that a detailed analysis is needed to clarify the diminishing returns that will be generated from the increased sales, and to ensure that those returns are noted in the budget.

Sales and Marketing Pacing

Pacing is the rate at which an entity can ramp up an operational issue until it can handle a target revenue level. It is a particular concern when a company wishes to grow fast, and depends on its sales staff to handle complex sales presentations and closing activities. In these situations, the ability of a company to hire and train sales personnel may be the single most important factor interfering with revenue growth. To highlight this issue, it is useful to insert into the budget model the number of salespeople expected to be on staff during each month or quarter of the budget period, and divide this number into the sales expected for the same period. If the budgeted sales-per-person figure is higher than the historical average, then it is quite likely that the company will not achieve its revenue budget. There are three additional factors that make this an even larger problem than may at first be apparent:

- *Salesperson training cycle.* Depending upon the complexity of the sale, it may take quite a long time for new salespeople to reach the efficiency level of more experienced personnel. If so, the revenue budget should reflect an appropriate interval for sales to increase, as well as an assumed dropout rate for those new salespeople who leave partway through the ramp-up process.
- *Sales cycle.* Depending on the type of product and industry, it may take quite a long time for a salesperson to follow a new sale through to its conclusion. Thus, even hiring a perfectly competent salesperson may still yield no new sales until the salesperson works through the sales cycle. If customers only buy in accordance with their annual budget authorizations, it may be an entire year before a new salesperson records a single sale.
- *Overloaded sales territories.* What if the company is already selling into all of the sales regions that it wants? Does adding even more sales people to the existing sales territories really result in a reasonable increase in sales? More than likely, the additional sales staff will find that they are chasing after the more difficult and less creditworthy customers, and will not come anywhere near historical sales levels on a per-person basis.

The pacing concept is addressed in more detail in the Revenue Budget chapter.

The Impact of Bottlenecks on the Sales and Marketing Budget

Where there is a bottleneck in a process, it represents a chokepoint through which work cannot proceed at a faster rate. Solutions include increasing the capacity of the bottleneck and routing work around it. This concept has been applied to the production area for many years, but is also applicable to the sales area. If there is a bottleneck in the sales department, then additional sales will not occur, so there is a direct impact on profits if you cannot locate and correct the problem.

The sales process varies widely, depending on the industry, the nature of the products sold, price points, and sales automation. Nonetheless, let us assume the following steps in the sales process to illustrate the bottleneck issue:

1. The junior sales staff conducts cold calls of prospective customers and arranges for meetings.
2. The senior sales staff meets with the prospective customers and evaluates their needs.
3. The sales engineering team conducts product demonstrations.
4. The quote staff compiles quotes and forwards them to customers.
5. The senior sales staff negotiates contracts with customers.
6. The order entry staff enters orders into the company's order-taking software.

In the admittedly complex sales process just described, there are a number of specialists – junior sales staff to prospect for customers, a senior sales team to meet with customers, a quote specialist, and sales engineers to demonstrate the product. A bottleneck can arise at any point in this process, creating a tight restriction on the ability of the company to achieve an increase in sales. It is very common for this problem to arise in the areas of quote compilation and product demonstrations, since these two areas require more experience and so are more difficult to staff.

There are two ways to detect a bottleneck in the sales area. One is to compare the capacity of each step in the sales process flow to the activity level. The bottleneck is located wherever the capacity level and actual activity level are approximately the same. An alternative method is to measure the backlog of work in front of each process. A large backlog indicates a bottleneck. The second measurement method is typically the easiest to measure, since a brief discussion of who is working overtime will usually highlight which area is causing the problem.

EXAMPLE

Grubstake Brothers manufactures backhoes for use by construction companies. Grubstake's management team has set a goal of doubling sales within the next five years. To do so, it has doubled the size of the sales force, primarily in the area of cold calling customers, but sales have not increased. The controller investigates the issue and uncovers the following facts:

Sales Activity	Monthly Activity	Backlog	Overtime Percentage
1. Cold calling	425 initial leads	0	0%
2. Initial meeting / request for demo	75 requests for demo	0	0%
3. Product demonstration	35 demos conducted	82 demos	28%
4. Quote generation	20 quotes issued	2	5%
5. Contract finalization	15 contracts signed	0	0%

The table clearly shows that the investment in junior sales staff to conduct cold calls is not paying off, because all of the leads generated by this group are piling up in the work queue of the product demonstration team (for which management had not invested in additional personnel).

The controller recommends the immediate doubling of the product demonstration staff in order to clear away the backlog that has built up. This will likely shift the backlog to the quote generation team, which does not appear to have sufficient staff to handle what will likely be a substantial increase in requests for quote after the product demonstration bottleneck has been resolved. Consequently, Grubstake needs to hire more people in the quoting area, as well.

This issue is of particular concern in the situation just described, where there are multiple specialists involved in the sales process. When there is only a single person involved in the entire sales process, there is no question about where the bottleneck lies, or how to resolve it – just add more trained sales personnel.

The bottleneck issue is a key one during the compilation of the budget, because the sales manager has to estimate where there may be a bottleneck among the staff during the budget period, and plan to resolve it with appropriate hiring.

Sales and Marketing Metrics

There are several metrics that may be useful for tracking the ability of the sales and marketing managers to meet their budgeted targets. They are:

- *Selling expense as a percentage of sales.* This is the most aggregate-level metric, and is best used on a trend line to see if the cost of selling is changing over time (see the Diminishing Returns Analysis section). If the trend line reveals that there is an issue, then use the following additional metrics to delve into the reasons for the change.
- *Sales per salesperson.* In a selling environment that requires a sales staff, the ultimate driver of new revenue is sales per salesperson. It reflects the experience level, training, contacts, and sales region assigned to a salesperson. Track it on a trend line and monitor it closely, especially for newer salespeople who are still gaining experience in their jobs. It is perhaps the best tool for deciding whether to continue to retain a sales trainee or to let the person go.
- *Sales and margin by sales channel.* A company may have a variety of distribution methods for selling its products and services to customers. If so, the company may have different price points and costs for each sales channel, which may call for an analysis of not only sales by channel but (more importantly) margin by channel. It is quite possible that a lesser distribution channel yields far larger margins than a company's primary sales channel, and so is worth expanding. The reverse may also be the case.
- *Sales calls.* If the nature of the business requires that the sales staff engage in a certain number of sales calls, either by phone or in person, then it certainly makes sense to track this information on a per-person basis.

- *Customer turnover*. Customer turnover has a major impact on the sales department, since high turnover equates to more sales and marketing expenditures to create additional sales from new customers. Such issues as product quality and customer service are primary drivers of customer turnover.
- *Profit per customer*. If there are a few large customers who demand lower prices and/or special services, then subtract all direct costs of doing business with those customers from their revenues to see if the company is losing money by dealing with them. This may result in the rejection of a few customers or a revision in pricing. The following grid is useful for categorizing customers by profit and volume level. Ideally, you should minimize sales to those customers in the lower left corner of the grid, and work to push all other customers into the high-volume high-profit quadrant in the upper right corner of the grid.

Customer Profitability Grid

High Volume - Low Profit	High Volume - High Profit
Avian Supply	Highway Presentations
Beatrice Acquisitions	Illustrious Cleaners
Carroll Manufacturing	Jingo Products
Dork Designs	Killer Company
Enough Supply	Lingo Linguistics
Franklin Marbles	Morton Sugar
Gorilla Suit Rentals	Nana Supply Company
Low Volume - Low Profit	**Low Volume - High Profit**
Ortho Products	Verity Copy Review
Pippa Plumbing	Wilson Tires
Quandary Location Services	Xenon Lighting
Rudolph Delivery Service	Yampa Culinary
Stevens Legal Services	Zorro Fencing Tutelage
Torrent Gutter Cleaning	Arbor Tree Pruning
Unbelievable Delivery	Boris Private Eye

- *Cost per sales call*. If the sales staff spends a large amount of its time on the road, consider tracking either the travel cost per sales call or the travel cost per month for each salesperson. The intent is to see if any salespeople are less efficient in their travel arrangements or are spending significantly more on travel than the other sales staff. Use this measure with caution, since it may be worthwhile to spend considerably more time and money dealing with a small number of customers who place unusually large orders.

- *Direct mail effectiveness.* This calculation is direct mail sales divided by the total direct mail expense. It is a particularly effective measurement if a company invests heavily in direct mail advertising.

It may be useful to include estimated amounts for these metrics in the budget, since they have an impact on assumptions regarding how many sales staff will be required to reach a certain targeted level of sales. For example, if there is a budgeted decline in customer turnover, this may mean that fewer salespeople will be required (though there should be budgeted expenditures to improve the odds of achieving the reduced turnover). As another example, if a company engages in a large amount of direct mail advertising, you can incorporate the direct mail effectiveness ratio into the budget to estimate projected sales levels.

Subsequent reporting for the department should include the standard budget versus actual analysis for all line items. In addition, it may be useful to generate a detailed analysis of the types of expenses incurred in the area of *field sales*, where the sales staff is traveling to customers and engaging in other promotional activities. It is useful for gaining an understanding of the types of costs that are incurred by the sales staff. However, it may require an inordinate amount of time to collect the information needed for this report (since the typical chart of accounts does not segregate information at this level of detail), which means that it may not be cost effective to compile. The following sample is in aggregate for the entire field sales staff, but can also be generated at the sales region or salesperson level.

Field Sales Expense Detail Report

Expense Item	Month Actual	Month Budget	Month Variance	Y-T-D Actual	Y-T-D Budget	Y-T-D Variance
Field Sales						
Air travel	$14,500	10,000	-$4,500	$98,000	$92,750	-$5,250
Reimbursed mileage	2,500	2,000	-500	12,800	11,000	-1,800
Lodging	4,750	3,500	-1,250	37,650	35,000	-2,650
Meals	1,750	1,500	-250	18,900	17,000	-1,900
Other	550	500	-50	4,500	7,000	2,500
Subtotal	$24,050	$17,500	-$6,550	$171,850	$162,750	-$9,100
Promotions						
Trade show fees	$8,000	$7,500	-$500	$45,000	$45,000	$0
T&E for promotions	4,500	4,000	-500	10,000	8,500	-1,500
Other	2,200	2,500	300	5,800	5,000	-800
Subtotal	$14,700	$14,000	-$700	$60,800	$58,500	-$2,300
Grand total	$38,750	$31,500	-$7,250	$232,650	$221,250	-$11,400

It may also be useful to engage in subsequent reporting for advertising campaigns, to see how actual expenditures compare to the budget. It is not necessary to include a monthly or year-to-date analysis in this type of report; instead, conduct the analysis for the period of each campaign, which may cover just one month or extend over many periods. The following report format shows a "Campaign Complete" flag to indicate when all expenditures have been completed for a specific advertising campaign.

Advertising Campaign Expense Report

Campaign Name	Campaign Actual	Campaign Budget	Campaign Variance	Campaign Complete
Winter promotion	$42,000	$40,000	-$2,000	√
Spring promotion	36,000	35,000	-1,000	√
July 4th promotion	15,000	18,000	3,000	√
Summer promotion	55,000	50,000	-5,000	√
Fall promotion	30,000	27,000	-3,000	√
Thanksgiving promotion	2,000	16,000	14,000	×
Totals	$180,000	$186,000	$6,000	

A variation on the concept of reporting on cost by advertising campaign is to instead report on expenditures by brand. Brand-level advertising tends to be consistently applied over a long period of time in order to build brand awareness with customers. Consequently, tracking budget versus actual information for individual months does not yield useful information. Instead, track the expense on a trend line over multiple years.

Summary

The sales and marketing budget is closely tied to the revenue budget, since it is a prime driver of sales. Accordingly, this budget should attract more analysis than other parts of the budget, particularly in regard to whether the designated expenditures are sufficient to support the sales noted in the revenue budget, not only in regard to revenue totals but also the timing of those revenues.

The sales and marketing functions are assumed to be a single department for the purposes of constructing the budget shown in this chapter. In reality, many larger companies separate the two functions, so they would have different budgets. If so, the concepts illustrated in this chapter are still relevant – they are just addressed in two budget documents rather than one.

Chapter 12
The Research and Development Budget

Introduction

Research and development (R&D) includes basic research, the application of the results of research to specific products, and the design and testing of prototypes and pilot production facilities. In some industries, R&D forms the core of a business' ability to expand and provide consistent profitability over a long period of time. It may not be a direct contributor to revenues in the current year (which is more a matter of production and marketing execution), but will provide the engine for growth in later years. Thus, if a company wants to earn a large profit in the current year, it could conceivably cut deep into its R&D budget, but at the cost of obliterating its growth in later years.

This chapter gives an overview of the research and development budget, and discusses how much funding to allocate, how to select projects, and how to oversee them.

General Funding for Research and Development

The amount of funds to allocate to the R&D budget can be an extraordinarily difficult discussion, for there is no correct answer – a small amount carefully invested can have an enormous payback, while a large investment can be frittered away among a variety of ho-hum projects. Still, there are several ways to generate a general estimate of how much funding to assign to R&D. They are:

- *Historical*. If a certain funding level has worked for the company in the past, then consider using it again – adjusted for inflation.
- *Industry benchmark*. If the industry as a whole spends a certain proportion of sales on R&D, this at least gives an indication of the level of spending required to compete over the long term. Better yet, isolate the same metric for just the top-performing competitors, since their level of R&D spending is more likely to be your target.
- *Best in class benchmark*. Look outside of the industry for companies that do a very good job on their R&D, and match their spending level as a proportion of sales. This is a particularly important approach when your company is in a moribund industry where R&D spending is minimal, and you want to take a different approach.
- *Percent of cash flow*. Management may be willing to spend a certain proportion of its available cash on R&D on an ongoing basis, irrespective of what competitors are spending. This is a much better approach than apportioning a percentage of net income to R&D, since net income does not nec-

essarily equate to cash flow, and a commitment to spend a certain proportion of net income could lead to a cash shortage.

No matter what method is used to derive the appropriate funding level, senior management should settle upon the *minimum* R&D funding level that must be maintained over the long term in order to remain competitive in the industry, and be sure never to drop below that figure.

Research and Development Funding Decisions

Research and development is a difficult area in which to decide how to allocate funds. One possibility is to create a return on investment analysis, and fund the projects with the highest projected return. However, managers can easily skew this sort of analysis by altering their models in the direction of whichever project they favor. Another possibility is that project funding is slanted in favor of extensions to existing product lines, which results in no entirely new products ever being created. Either approach tends to lead to product stagnation.

An alternative that tends to avoid skewed funding is to allocate the available funding into different sets of investment funds, with each fund having different investment criteria. These funds may also be administered by people having different agendas. For example:

- *High-risk fund.* This fund is only for projects that have a high risk of failure, but also a correspondingly high return on investment. The fund administrators cannot be managers of existing product lines.
- *Existing product fund.* This fund is intended only for the extension of existing product lines, and the fund administrators are the managers of those product lines.

There will likely need to be a significant amount of funding apportioned to the existing product fund in order to keep the managers of the company's product lines happy, but try to reserve as much cash as possible for the high-risk fund, so that it has a good chance of achieving breakthrough products in other areas.

Expected Commercial Value

Even if a company takes the step of creating separate investment funds for its research and development program (as just described), it still needs a way to determine which projects will receive funding from each of its investment funds. A good method for doing so is to use the expected commercial value formula (ECV), which includes all of the key factors that impact a project.

The formula is:

	Net present value
×	Probability of commercial success
-	Cost of commercialization
×	Probability of technical success
-	Development cost
=	Expected commercial value

Or, stated as a formula:

(((Project net present value × probability of commercial success) – commercialization cost) × (probability of technical success)) – product development cost

---

EXAMPLE

Quest Adventure Gear is evaluating the prospect of creating a portable fuel cell that provides electricity for a camping trip. Quest collects the following information about the project:

Project net present value	$2,000,000
Probability of commercial success	80%
Commercialization cost	$250,000
Probability of technical success	40%
Product development cost	$500,000

Based on the information it has collected, Quest computes the following ECV for the portable fuel cell product:

((($2,000,000 project net present value × 80% probability of commercial success) - $250,000 commercialization cost) × 40% probability of technical success)) - $500,000 product development cost

Expected commercial value = $40,000

The expected commercial value of the project is extremely low, primarily because the probability of technical success is so low that it is dragging down the overall value of the project. The Quest management team elects to fund a small feasibility study to see if the probability of technical success can be improved. If so, the results of the formula may change dramatically, and justify funding the full project at a later date.

Project Risk

It is extremely difficult to quantify the risk of a prospective R&D project, since many factors can impact its ultimate success. If you can break down risk into specific categories and analyze each one, you can more easily determine which risks can be managed or tolerated, and which ones are so intractable that the company would do better to expend its funds elsewhere. Here are the more important risk categories:

- *New product in a new market.* This is a high-risk endeavor, because there is no certainty that the company can build the product or sell it in a new market about which it has no knowledge.
- *New product in an existing market.* This is a moderate-risk endeavor, because there is a mix of uncertainty about being able to build the product, but the company is knowledgeable about the market.
- *Incremental product.* A project that incrementally builds on an existing product has low risk, since the company likely has the skill to complete the project, there is an existing market into which you can sell it, and the company can service the product.
- *Project duration.* The longer it takes to bring a project to market, the greater the risk that either the project will fail or the market will change.
- *Legal protections.* Will a project come close to the restrictions imposed by a competing patent? If so, there is a risk that a successfully completed project will go to market and promptly be assailed by a legal attack by a competitor.
- *Skill level.* Does the company have enough in-house skill to engage in the project, or does it have a relationship with a qualified research firm that is willing to handle the work? If the company has essentially no skill in this area, its risk is extremely high.

You can quantify these risks to some extent by assigning each project (along with its funding) to one of the first three of the preceding risk categories. The result is the following table, which shows the risk levels to which funds are assigned. The table presents information both in terms of dollar funding and the proportion of funds in each category over a multi-year time period.

Sample R&D Investment Risk Report

	Year 1 ($)	Year 2 ($)	Year 3 ($)	Year 1 (%)	Year 2 (%)	Year 3 (%)
New product, new market	$1,500,000	$1,250,000	$1,100,000	25%	21%	18%
New product, existing market	3,750,000	4,000,000	4,200,000	63%	66%	68%
Incremental product	750,000	800,000	850,000	12%	13%	14%
Totals	$6,000,000	$6,050,000	$6,150,000	100%	100%	100%

The sample report shows an ongoing trend into more conservative investments, primarily by shifting funding away from new products that would be launched in new markets.

Project Selection Issues

The bulk of the projects that are assigned to the R&D department are concepts for entirely new products or for extensions of existing products. These projects are then added to the existing group of R&D projects, are assigned a certain amount of funding, and gradually work their way through the R&D process, hopefully resulting in commercially-viable products. However, there are some additional considerations that can alter the mix of products that the R&D department works on. They are:

- *Review existing projects.* You may be currently funding a research project based on an initial analysis of its prospects that is no longer valid. Consequently, the budgeting process should include frequent reviews of all current projects to see if they are still worth funding. This is a critical issue, since any funds spent thus far on a project are sunk costs, and so should not be considered when deciding whether to continue funding. A sunk cost is a cost that has been incurred, and which can no longer be recovered by any means. However, many managers continue investing in projects because of the sheer size of the amounts already invested. They do not want to "lose the investment" by curtailing a project that is proving to not be profitable, so they continue pouring more cash into it.

- *Review shelved ideas.* It is entirely possible that you reviewed and rejected projects in previous years. As circumstances change over time, it is possible that one of those earlier projects, or an idea contained within a project, may finally be a potentially profitable product. Consequently, maintain a database of information about shelved ideas and review it on a regular basis.

- *Design internal systems.* There is a presumption that funding allocated to R&D will be spent on the development of new products. While this is likely true in most cases, there are other uses for the funds, particularly in the area of internal processes. For example, an entirely new production technique may result in vastly lower manufacturing costs that give a company a large competitive advantage. Or, a software redesign may allow customers to configure products online that they have ordered, thereby building customer loyalty. These are internal systems that can drastically improve a company's competitive position, and are reasonable targets for the R&D staff to pursue.

- *Analyze future trends.* Research and development is the one area in a business where you should certainly spend time projecting how the convergence of technology, industry shifts, and consumer spending patterns can yield new product opportunities. Even in this area, managers tend to be too focused on incremental product changes that do not give a business the opportunity to grow in new directions.

Tip: Part of the review process for new R&D projects is whether a product, component, or process already exists elsewhere, and can be purchased as a commercial off-the-shelf product. If so, it is an inappropriate project for the R&D department, which should be focused on activities that *do not* currently exist.

- *Integrate target costing analysis.* It is inherently impossible to determine the probable price point, costs, and gross margin of a product that is still in the R&D department, since the staff is trying to determine whether the product can even be built. However, you *can* consider the impact of target costing at a very general level when deciding whether to engage in an R&D project in a specific area. Target costing describes the costs that you expect to incur to create a new product, and how this will impact product profitability levels. By addressing costs before a product design has been finalized, you can alter the design before it enters the manufacturing process to ensure that you earn a reasonable profit.

    If a company is considering developing a product line in a new area, it is very worthwhile to first estimate the unit costs being incurred by competitors, and therefore the profits they are likely earning. If this review reveals an unusually low profitability level in the target area, then the R&D staff should be mostly concerned with whether any R&D activities can reduce costs sufficiently to produce reasonable profits. If not, curtail funding in that area and allocate it to areas where the prospects for a reasonable amount of profitability are higher.

If you pay attention to all of the issues noted in this section, you can avoid a rote acceptance of projects submitted to the R&D department, and instead create a mix of projects from a variety of sources that have the potential to create maximum returns for the company.

The Project Failure Rate

One of the basic rules of R&D budgeting is to *fail fast and fail cheap*. The concept is to review projects with sufficient rapidity and rigor to be able to kill those that appear to be substandard. By doing so, you preserve capital for other, more likely projects. Taking this approach calls for a fundamentally different attitude in the department, so that managers are more willing to walk away from existing investments before they become massive sunk costs.

You can take the "fail fast and fail cheap" concept one step further and treat the R&D department as an angel investor that doles out small amounts of cash to fund initial "proof of concept" projects. If the concept fails, the amount of funds lost is minimal, and the company gains some knowledge about an area in which it probably does not want to invest additional funds.

Tip: When someone insists that only a major additional investment will truly prove a product concept, treat it as a warning flag to thoroughly review the status of the project, and be more prepared than usual to kill it. The reason is that the person making this demand should have been able to prove the concept already for a small up-front investment, and is now so tied up with the project (perhaps due to ego, fear of job loss, or office politics) that he is imposing his will on the budgeting process, rather than letting the information gathered about the project thus far drive the decision to continue funding it.

The "fail fast and fail cheap" concept can be hard for some managers to stomach, especially when there appear to be a large number of new products being abandoned prior to their release into the market. However, the reverse situation, where *no* products fail, is actually a sign of excessive conservatism. The latter situation means that a company is not investing in a sufficient number of risky products. The ideal situation is to achieve a proper balance where there is a modest amount of project failure and an equally modest number of products making it past the company's review hurdles and into the marketplace. This balance calls for an ongoing review by management to determine whether it is investing in too many or too few risky projects.

You can measure the proportion of project failure with a measure called *R&D waste*, which is the total amount of expenditures on cancelled projects during a designated measurement period, divided by the total amount expended on all projects during the measurement period. The measurement period should be fairly lengthy, such as a rolling 12-month period, and is most effective when you track it on a trend line over several years. The result is a measure of changes in the riskiness of the R&D projects that a company undertakes.

EXAMPLE

The camping equipment market is cluttered with "me too" products, so Quest Adventure Gear decides to reapportion more of its annual $2 million in R&D funding to attempt to create breakthrough products that it can protect with patents. The five-year result of this effort appears in the following table:

	20x1	20x2	20x3	20x4	20x5
Total expenditure	$2,000,000	$2,000,000	$2,000,000	$2,000,000	$2,000,000
Cancelled project expenditures	100,000	400,000	250,000	800,000	500,000
R&D waste percentage	5%	20%	12.5%	40%	25%

The waste percentage was quite low in the first year, since the R&D department was just starting and did not have enough information to properly evaluate its initial set of products. The percentage was generally in the vicinity of 20% in subsequent years, except for one year where it rose to 40%; the cause of this one-time increase was the failure of a heavily-funded project that was backed by the company president. Quest may need to re-evaluate its project review system in light of that project failure to see if it is cancelling projects soon enough.

The R&D waste metric should be used with some caution, since the failure of a single, well-funded project can skew the results, as could the cancellation of several projects at once. Thus, investigate the details of any sudden changes in the metric to understand what happened.

There is no right or wrong amount for the R&D waste percentage. It simply reflects the riskiness of the projects that management is willing to undertake. If management is unhappy with the amount of expenditures for cancelled projects and the return on investment of the projects that were brought to market, then clearly it needs to address its system for allocating funds to projects.

Structure of the Research and Development Budget

Given the volume of discussion about R&D funding thus far, it is clear that the emphasis in the R&D budget is on where to invest funds, and much less on the format of the R&D budget. This is not an especially difficult budget to formulate, since it contains fewer than the usual number of expense line items. The budget is typically comprised of the following expense categories:

- *Compensation and benefits*. Compensation tends to be the largest R&D expenditure.
- *Contract services*. It is quite common to shift some research work to independent laboratories that specialize in particular types of work. In some cases, virtually all R&D work may be contracted out, in which case this becomes the largest R&D expenditure category.
- *Consumable supplies*. In some types of R&D, the staff may use (or destroy) a significant amount of supplies as part of its work. Depending on the situation, this can be quite a significant expense.
- *Office expenses*. These are the standard operational costs of running a department, such as utilities and office rent.
- *Depreciation on equipment*. There will be recurring depreciation charges for any fixed assets used by the R&D staff.
- *Amortization of acquired intangible assets*. If a company has acquired a patent or other intangible asset from another entity, it will likely have to amortize the asset over its useful life.

There are three general formats you can use to construct an R&D budget. They are:

- *Integrated into engineering department*. If the amount of funds expended on R&D is minor, then you do not have to budget for it separately. Instead, include it within the budget for the engineering department, either aggregated into a single line item or spread among the various expense line items attributable to that department.
- *Treated as a separate department*. If the expenditures associated with specific projects are relatively minor, and the R&D staff is occupied with several projects at the same time, it may be sufficient to simply aggregate all expenses into a department-level budget for R&D, and not attempt to further assign expenses to specific projects.
- *Treated as projects within a department*. If there are significant expenditures that can be traced to individual projects, consider creating an R&D budget that clearly shows which projects are expected to consume funds.

The following two examples show the budget reporting format for treating R&D as a separate department with no further subdivision by project, and for revealing projects within the department.

Sample R&D Budget at the Department Level

	Quarter 1	Quarter 2	Quarter 3	Quarter 4	Total
Compensation	$150,000	$150,000	$160,000	$165,000	$625,000
Contract services	320,000	180,000	450,000	250,000	1,200,000
Consumable supplies	25,000	25,000	25,000	25,000	100,000
Office expenses	8,000	8,000	9,000	9,000	34,000
Depreciation	10,000	10,000	10,000	10,000	40,000
Amortization	15,000	15,000	15,000	15,000	60,000
Totals	$528,000	$388,000	$669,000	$474,000	$2,059,000

Sample R&D Budget at the Project Level

	Quarter 1	Quarter 2	Quarter 3	Quarter 4	Total
Department overhead	$23,000	$24,000	$24,000	$26,000	$97,000
Project Alpha					
Compensation	82,000	82,000	84,000	84,000	332,000
Contract services	65,000	65,000	75,000	70,000	275,000
Other	15,000	18,000	18,000	20,000	71,000
Project subtotal	162,000	165,000	177,000	174,000	678,000
Project Beta					
Compensation	40,000	60,000	60,000	60,000	220,000
Contract services	35,000	30,000	30,000	30,000	125,000
Other	5,000	7,000	7,000	10,000	29,000
Project subtotal	80,000	97,000	97,000	100,000	374,000
Totals	$265,000	$286,000	$298,000	$300,000	$1,149,000

Note in the second example that not all expenses could be assigned to a specific project, so they were instead listed separately from the projects under the "department overhead" designation.

Ongoing Project Analysis

Unlike most other departments, the research and development staff deals with a multitude of discrete projects that have beginning and ending dates, and specific amounts of allocated funds. This means that R&D is one of the few areas in which a budgeted funding status report is worthwhile. This report shows the amount expended to date on a project, the amount of authorized funding remaining, and (most importantly) the amount of funding that the R&D manager estimates will be required to complete the project. It also contains the original and revised completion date. The report is designed to show managers which projects are in trouble, either from a funding or completion date perspective. A sample report follows.

Sample Project Analysis Report

Project Description	Funds Expended	Funds Remaining	Funds to Finish	Funds Needed	Scheduled Completion	Estimated Completion
Project 1054	$69,000	$201,000	$230,000	$29,000	05/2014	08/2015
Project 1055	58,000	150,000	150,000	0	06/2014	Same
Project 1056	52,000	48,000	120,000	72,000	07/2014	12/2015
Project 1057	49,000	127,000	120,000	0	08/2014	Same
Project 1058	23,000	83,000	90,000	7,000	09/2014	10/2015
Project 1059	10,000	490,000	490,000	0	10/2014	Same
Totals	$261,000	$1,099,000	$1,200,000	$108,000		

The sample report reveals that Project 1054 is somewhat over budget and will require three additional months to complete, while Project 1056 is far over budget in terms of both funding and the completion date.

Project managers should also submit a more detailed report on each project at regular intervals that summarizes both accomplishments and remaining hurdles. Managers can then use the preceding project analysis report to spot those projects that appear to be in trouble, and then use the following project status report to delve more deeply into the underlying problems.

Sample Project Status Report

Project name: Portable hydrogen fuel cell
Project number: 1056
Start date: 01/2014
Estimated completion date: 12/2016
Completion date overrun: 5 months
Project budget: $100,000
Projected overrun: $72,000
Accomplishments to date: Completed initial design
Issues to date: ABC Competitor has filed a patent on a similar design, so we need to redesign the product to avoid the patent.
Recommendations: Treat funds expended thus far as a sunk cost, and continue with the project. We do not foresee any problems with the redesign at this time.

Research and Development Measurements

It can be extremely difficult to measure the effectiveness of the R&D function, since there can be quite a separation in time between the expenditure of funds and the arrival of any corresponding benefits. Any measurement must necessarily cover multiple years, and will be particularly ineffective for the first few years after the department is initially established, since it takes so long to achieve a return on R&D.

With these caveats in mind, here are several measurements you can use to measure R&D:

- *Revenue from new products.* This measurement should be on at least a rolling 12-month basis, and can be subdivided into revenues from new products in new markets, new products in existing markets, and incremental products.
- *Contribution margin from new products.* Contribution margin is the margin that results when variable production costs are subtracted from revenue. This information may be more difficult to gather than the revenue metric just noted, but it reveals the real profit contribution of each new product, and so is more valuable information than the revenue metric.
- *Proportion of sales from new products.* This metric is useful in situations where senior management sets a target of constantly replenishing sales with new products, and so wants to see a high proportion of sales being generated from R&D projects every year.
- *Time period to commercial production.* How long does it take the R&D staff to convert a concept into a commercial product? This figure can vary considerably, depending on many factors, and will likely cover a broad range of time periods. Thus, an average time period for many projects may hide a few substantial project overruns. Instead, consider a report that itemizes this figure for each individual project, so that management can spot those requiring an inordinate amount of time, and delve into the reasons for the delays.

Over what period of time should these metrics be measured? It depends on the average time period to complete a project. If the nature of a company's products is so simple that the R&D department can churn out new products after just a few months, then there is a close association between R&D expenditures and new revenues, and there is less need to measure over a lengthy historical period. However, if products are complex and require multiple years to reach fruition, then R&D expenditures made several years in the past will correlate to new sales in the current year. In this latter case, you may need to match up expenditures with sales over quite a long period.

Treatment of Cancelled Projects

Earlier, we noted that you should periodically review projects that had been shelved at an earlier date. In order to do this, you need to properly document projects when they are cancelled, so that the information is available for review at the start of the next budgeting cycle. Consequently, consider adopting a standard project archiving format that includes the following information:

- Commentary on technical viability
- Competing products and key differences from those products
- Customer surveys
- Discussion of what key factors must occur in order to make the project commercially viable

- Expected commercial value calculation
- Product cost information
- Project notes regarding research and tests conducted

Part of this documentation is simply a compilation of all the information assembled over the course of a project, while the ECV, technical viability, and discussion of key success factors should be included in a summary report. The summary report will be the key review document when the project is periodically examined in the future to see if it should be reactivated.

Summary

Research and development is one of the most interesting components of the corporate budget, because management must deal with multiple issues for which there are no correct answers – how much to invest in the department, which general categories of projects to fund, and then which projects to select within those categories. To a considerable extent, proper management of the R&D budget is a key driver of the long-term success of a business, and so is worthy of considerable ongoing attention.

Chapter 13
The Administration Budget

Introduction

The administration budget contains those expenses attributable to a variety of support functions, including accounting, treasury, human resources, and corporate. It also includes expenses that are not easily allocated elsewhere, such as the cost of directors and officers insurance. In this chapter, we address the layout of the administration budget, its contents, and how administration costs may vary in response to certain activities.

The Administration Budget

The administration budget contains all of the expenses that are not directly involved in the provision of products or services to customers, or their sale to customers. This usually means that the following departments are included in the administration budget:

Accounting	Human resources	Public relations
Corporate	Information technology	Risk management (insurance)
Facilities	Internal auditing	Treasury
	Legal	

In a larger company, there may be individual budgets for each of these departments, rather than an administration department.

The expense line items included in the administration budget generally include the following:

Audit fees	Director fees	Payroll taxes
Bank fees	Dues and subscriptions	Property taxes
Charitable contributions	Employee benefits	Rent
Compensation	Insurance	Supplies
Consulting fees	Legal fees	Travel and entertainment
Depreciation		Utilities

The information in the administration budget is not directly derived from any other budgets. Instead, managers use the general level of corporate activity to determine the appropriate amount of expenditure (see a further discussion of cost variability later in this chapter). When creating this budget, consider the following issues:

- *Compensation.* The largest item in this budget is usually employee compensation, so pay particular attention to the formulation of this amount and test it for reasonableness.

- *Historical basis*. The amounts in this budget are frequently carried forward from actual results in the preceding year. This may be reasonable, but some costs may disappear due to the termination of a contract, or increase due to contractually scheduled price increases. Be sure to verify these items.
- *Step costs*. Determine when any step costs may be incurred, such as additional staff to support reporting requirements when a company goes public, and incorporate them into the budget.
- *Zero-base analysis*. It may be useful to occasionally re-create the administration budget from the ground up, justifying the need for each expense. This is a time-consuming process, but may uncover a few expense items that can be eliminated.

The following example illustrates the basic layout of an administration budget.

EXAMPLE

Quest Adventure Gear compiles the following administration budget, which is organized by expense line item:

	Quarter 1	Quarter 2	Quarter 3	Quarter 4
Audit fees	$35,000	$0	$0	$0
Bank fees	500	500	500	500
Insurance	5,000	5,500	6,000	6,000
Payroll taxes	10,000	10,500	10,500	11,000
Property taxes	0	25,000	0	0
Rent	11,000	11,000	11,000	14,000
Salaries	140,000	142,000	144,000	146,000
Supplies	2,000	2,000	2,000	2,000
Travel and entertainment	4,500	8,000	4,000	4,000
Utilities	2,500	3,000	3,000	4,000
Other expenses	1,500	1,500	1,500	2,000
Total expenses	$212,000	$209,000	$182,500	$189,500

The CEO of Quest likes to restate the administration budget by department, so that he can assign responsibility for expenditures to the managers of those departments. This results in the following variation on the same budget:

	Quarter 1	Quarter 2	Quarter 3	Quarter 4
Accounting department	$130,500	$102,500	$102,000	$108,000
Corporate department	30,000	30,000	30,000	30,000
Human resources department	19,500	19,500	18,000	19,000
IT department	25,000	25,000	25,000	25,000
Treasury department	7,000	7,000	7,500	7,500
Unassigned expenses	0	25,000	0	0
Total expenses	$212,000	$209,000	$182,500	$189,500

The reconfigured administration budget contains an "unassigned expenses" line item for property taxes, since management does not believe that expense is specifically controllable by any of the administrative departments.

The preceding example reveals a common characteristic of most line items in the administration budget, which is that most costs are fixed over the short term, and so only vary slightly from period to period. The exceptions are pay increases and scheduled events, such as audits. Otherwise, the main reason for a sudden change in an administrative expense is a step cost, such as increasing the headcount. This type of minimal cost variability is typical for the administration budget (see the next section for further discussion of cost variability).

If you simply carry forward administration costs into the budget from the previous year, you will not know if the company is being efficient in its expenditures. To find out, consider separating the administration costs into their constituent parts, such as the cost of the accounting, treasury, and human resources departments, and calculate each of these costs as a percentage of company revenues. Then compare these percentages to the industry average or a best-in-class benchmark. The comparison may reveal that some parts of the administration budget are operating at excessively high cost levels.

> **Tip:** Rather than reviewing the information technology budget as an unconsolidated mass that will be approved as a whole, consider segmenting the budget for more detailed analysis. One part is associated with the administrative cost of running the department, another part supports the company's legacy infrastructure, and part is allocated to growing the business. Pay particular attention to the cost of the legacy infrastructure, which can be reduced by shifting to commercially-available applications.

Cost Variability in the Administration Budget

We have indicated so far that most of the expenditures in the administration budget are relatively fixed. This is not precisely the case, since nearly every part of the administration budget varies *somewhat* with the overall level of activity of a business. For example:

- *Accounting department.* This department must alter its payroll staffing in proportion to company headcount, as well as its accounts receivable and accounts payable staff to match the amount of billing and purchasing volume.
- *Human resources department.* This department may need to increase its staffing level if the rest of the company needs assistance with either a large layoff or an extended period of hiring. Also, as overall headcount increases, the human resources staff must also increase in order to recruit replacements caused by normal amounts of staff turnover.

- *Information technology (IT) department.* A key function of the IT department is to provide support for the desktop computers of employees. Thus, as the number of employees changes, so too does the amount of IT support staff.
- *Risk management department.* The amount of insurance charged is closely associated with either the amount of sales, assets, or personnel; all three are derived from the overall level of corporate activity.
- *Treasury department.* As a company branches out into new geographic locations, and especially when it buys and sells internationally, this department must be expanded to deal with additional bank accounts and foreign exchange issues.

The preceding examples show that administration expenses can indeed change approximately in step with the volume of activity. A more accurate assessment of cost variability is that the administration budget contains expenditure levels that are fixed within a certain range of activity. For example, if there are no more than 500 customer billings per month, the accounting department needs one collections person; if billings exceed that amount, then a second collections person will be needed, and that expenditure will be sufficient until such time as the company reaches 1,000 customer billings per month – and so on.

Allocation of Administration Expenses

There is an argument favoring the allocation of all administration expenses to the profit centers of a business, on the grounds that those profit centers will increase their prices in order to offset this cost allocation, resulting in greater overall profits for the company. We do not recommend the allocation of administration expenses for the following reasons:

- *Responsibility.* The manager of a profit center usually has no control over the allocated amount of administration expense. If the manager has no way to influence the amount of the allocation, he or she has no responsibility for it, and so should not be charged for it. This would not be the case if the manager could enter into a service agreement with the administrative staff for services or be able to outsource this work; in that situation, the manager has control over the costs, and should be charged the amount stated under the service agreement.
- *Altered prices.* If a profit center manager wants to show a profit after absorbing the allocation of administration expenses, it will probably be necessary to raise prices. This can be a problem in a price-sensitive market, or where the manager occasionally is asked for the lowest and best price for short-term customer purchasing queries. In these situations, the profit center will be more likely to set a higher price than normal, and therefore lose business to competitors.

Instead of allocating administration expenses, a better alternative is a combination of encouraging profit centers to maximize their profitability (which should be happening already) and keeping administration expenses as low as possible. This approach avoids the price inflation issue just noted, while keeping local managers focused on those costs over which they have direct control. The following section presents a variation on the concept of allocating administrative costs, where the allocation is being done by service centers.

Service-Based Costing

Serviced-based costing is the concept of having a service center within a business charge out its services to other parts of the business, using a charge for services rendered. This charge should be based on at least the direct costs associated with providing services, and can ramp up to a more rounded concept of cost, where an overhead charge and even a profit is added to the service charge. Examples of service centers that might use service-based costing are information technology (IT), janitorial services, and facilities maintenance.

By using service-based costing, "client" departments can decide upon the volume of services that they want to receive, based on the budgeted price, or whether they want to go outside of the company to obtain services for a lower price elsewhere. This has the effect of putting downward pricing pressure on the service department, which must now compete with the prices offered by outside service providers.

When exposed to outside competition, a service center is more likely to re-evaluate its cost structure. For example, an IT service center may be more inclined to switch away from legacy computer systems and toward off-the-shelf software, or a cloud-based solution.

In some cases, the manager of a service center may realize that it is impossible to compete with an outside supplier of the same service, and so may voluntarily agree to outsource the department. A more likely circumstance is that the manager will constantly compare internal and external costs to ensure that his or her department remains competitive.

A caution when using service-based costing is that an outside provider might lower its prices sufficiently to cause an internal service department to be disbanded, after which the provider raises its prices when there is no longer any internal competition.

Summary

As just noted in the discussion of cost variability, there are linkages between the administration budget and other parts of a company's budget that can result in changes to the administration budget. This means that you should not initially create the administration budget and then consider it settled. Instead, continue to examine it as part of the review iterations for the rest of the budget; this may result in incremental alterations to the administration budget that are caused by changes in the level of activity elsewhere in the system of budgets.

Chapter 14
The Capital Budget

Introduction

Capital budgeting is a series of analysis steps followed to justify the decision to purchase an asset, usually including an analysis of the costs, related benefits, and impact on capacity levels of the prospective purchase. In this chapter, we will address a broad array of issues to consider when deciding whether to recommend the purchase of a fixed asset, including constraint analysis, the lease versus buy decision, and post-acquisition auditing.

> **Related Podcast Episodes:** Episodes 45, 144, 145, and 147 of the Accounting Best Practices Podcast discuss throughput capital budgeting, evaluating capital budgeting proposals, capital budgeting with minimal cash, and net present value analysis. You can listen to them at: **accountingtools.com/podcasts** or **iTunes**

Overview of Capital Budgeting

The normal capital budgeting process is for the management team to request proposals to acquire fixed assets from all parts of the company. Managers respond by filling out a standard request form, outlining what they want to buy and how it will benefit the company. The financial analyst or accountant then assists in reviewing these proposals to determine which are worthy of an investment. Any proposals that are accepted are included in the annual budget, and will be purchased during the next budget year. Fixed assets purchased in this manner also require a certain number of approvals, with more approvals required by increasingly senior levels of management if the sums involved are substantial.

These proposals come from all over the company, and so are likely not related to each other in any way. Also, the number of proposals usually far exceeds the amount of funding available. Consequently, management needs a method for ranking the priority of projects, with the possible result that some proposals are not accepted at all. The traditional method for doing so is net present value (NPV) analysis, which focuses on picking proposals with the largest amount of discounted cash flows.

The trouble with NPV analysis is that it does not account for how an investment might impact the profit generated by the entire system of production; instead, it tends to favor the optimization of specific work centers, which may have no particular impact on overall profitability. Also, the results of NPV are based on the future projections of cash flows, which may be wildly inaccurate. Managers may even tweak their cash flow estimates upward in order to gain project approval, when they know that actual cash flows are likely to be lower. Given these issues, we favor constraint analysis over NPV, though NPV is also discussed later in this chapter.

A better method for judging capital budget proposals is constraint analysis, which focuses on how to maximize use of the bottleneck operation. The bottleneck operation is the most constricted operation in a company; if you want to improve the overall profitability of the company, concentrate all attention on the management of that bottleneck. This has a profound impact on capital budgeting, since a proposal should have some favorable impact on that operation in order to be approved.

There are two scenarios under which certain project proposals may avoid any kind of bottleneck or cash flow analysis. The first is a legal requirement to install an item. The prime example is environmental equipment, such as smokestack scrubbers, that are mandated by the government. In such cases, there may be some analysis to see if costs can be lowered, but the proposal *must* be accepted, so it will sidestep the normal analysis process.

The second scenario is when a company wants to mitigate a high-risk situation that could imperil the company. In this case, the emphasis is not on profitability at all, but rather on the avoidance of a situation. If so, the mandate likely comes from top management, so there is little additional need for analysis, other than a review to ensure that the lowest-cost alternative is selected.

A final scenario is when there is a sudden need for a fixed asset, perhaps due to the catastrophic failure of existing equipment, or due to a sudden strategic shift. These purchases can happen at any time, and so usually fall outside of the capital budget's annual planning cycle. It is generally best to require more than the normal number of approvals for these items, so that management is made fully aware of the situation. Also, if there is time to do so, they are worthy of an unusually intense analysis, to see if they really must be purchased at once, or if they can be delayed until the next capital budgeting approval period arrives.

Once all items are properly approved and inserted into the annual budget, this does not end the capital budgeting process. There is a final review just prior to actually making each purchase, with appropriate approval, to ensure that the company still needs each fixed asset.

The last step in the capital budgeting process is to conduct a post-implementation review, in which you summarize the actual costs and benefits of each fixed asset, and compare these results to the initial projections included in the original application. If the results are worse than expected, this may result in a more in-depth review, with particular attention being paid to avoiding any faulty aspects of the original proposal in future proposals.

Bottleneck Analysis

Under constraint analysis, the key concept is that an entire company acts as a single system, which generates a profit. Under this concept, capital budgeting revolves around the following logic:

1. Nearly all of the costs of the production system do not vary with individual sales; that is, nearly every cost is an operating expense; therefore,
2. You need to maximize the throughput of the *entire* system in order to pay for the operating expense; and

3. The only way to increase throughput (which is revenues minus totally variable costs) is to maximize the throughput passing through the bottleneck operation.

Consequently, give primary consideration to those capital budgeting proposals that favorably impact the throughput passing through the bottleneck operation. See the author's *Constraint Management* book for more information.

This does not mean that all other capital budgeting proposals will be rejected, since there are a multitude of possible investments that can reduce costs elsewhere in a company, and which are therefore worthy of consideration. However, throughput is more important than cost reduction, since throughput has no theoretical upper limit, whereas costs can only be reduced to zero. Given the greater ultimate impact on profits of throughput over cost reduction, any non-bottleneck proposal is simply not as important.

Net Present Value Analysis

Any capital investment involves an initial cash outflow to pay for it, followed by a mix of cash inflows in the form of revenue, or a decline in existing cash flows that are caused by expense reductions. We can lay out this information in a spreadsheet to show all expected cash flows over the useful life of an investment, and then apply a discount rate that reduces the cash flows to what they would be worth at the present date. This calculation is known as *net present value*.

Net present value is the traditional approach to evaluating capital proposals, since it is based on a single factor – cash flows – that can be used to judge any proposal arriving from anywhere in a company.

EXAMPLE

Milford Sound, a manufacturer of audio equipment, is planning to acquire an asset that it expects will yield positive cash flows for the next five years. Its cost of capital is 10%, which it uses as the discount rate to construct the net present value of the project. The following table shows the calculation:

Year	Cash Flow	10% Discount Factor	Present Value
0	-$500,000	1.0000	-$500,000
1	+130,000	0.9091	+118,183
2	+130,000	0.8265	+107,445
3	+130,000	0.7513	+97,669
4	+130,000	0.6830	+88,790
5	+130,000	0.6209	+80,717
		Net Present Value	-$7,196

The net present value of the proposed project is negative at the 10% discount rate, so Milford should not invest in the project.

In the "10% Discount Factor" column, the factor becomes smaller for periods further in the future, because the discounted values of cash flows are reduced as they progress further from the present day. The discount factor is widely available in textbooks, or can be derived from the following formula:

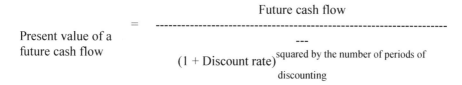

$$\text{Present value of a future cash flow} = \frac{\text{Future cash flow}}{(1 + \text{Discount rate})^{\text{squared by the number of periods of discounting}}}$$

To use the formula for an example, if we forecast the receipt of $100,000 in one year, and are using a discount rate of 10 percent, then the calculation is:

$$\text{Present value} = \frac{\$100,000}{(1+.10)^1}$$

Present value = $90,909

A net present value calculation that truly reflects the reality of cash flows will likely be more complex than the one shown in the preceding example. It is best to break down the analysis into a number of sub-categories, so that you can see exactly when cash flows are occurring and with what activities they are associated. Here are the more common contents of a net present value analysis:

- *Asset purchases.* All of the expenditures associated with the purchase, delivery, installation, and testing of the asset being purchased.
- *Asset-linked expenses.* Any ongoing expenses, such as warranty agreements, property taxes, and maintenance, that are associated with the asset.
- *Contribution margin.* Any incremental cash flows resulting from sales that can be attributed to the project.
- *Depreciation effect.* The asset will be depreciated, and this depreciation shelters a portion of any net income from income taxes, so note the income tax reduction caused by depreciation.
- *Expense reductions.* Any incremental expense reductions caused by the project, such as automation that eliminates direct labor hours.
- *Tax credits.* If an asset purchase triggers a tax credit (such as for a purchase of energy-reduction equipment), then note the credit.
- *Taxes.* Any income tax payments associated with net income expected to be derived from the asset.
- *Working capital changes.* Any net changes in inventory, accounts receivable, or accounts payable associated with the asset. Also, when the asset is eventually sold off, this may trigger a reversal of the initial working capital changes.

By itemizing the preceding factors in a net present value analysis, you can more easily review and revise individual line items.

We have given priority to bottleneck analysis over net present value as the preferred method for analyzing capital proposals, because bottleneck analysis focuses on throughput. The key improvement factor is throughput, since there is no upper limit on the amount of throughput that can be generated, whereas there are only so many operating expenses that can be reduced. This does not mean that net present value should be eliminated as a management tool. It is still quite useful for operating expense reduction analysis, where throughput issues are not involved. However, before using net present value, consider the following issues that may limit its use:

- *Cash inflows association.* Is it possible to trace incoming cash flows to a specific piece of equipment? In many cases, it is not possible to do so. Instead, revenues can only be associated with a cluster of equipment, such as an entire production line.
- *Imprecise discount rate.* The discount rate used in a net present value analysis is generally considered to be the corporate cost of capital. However, if a company is privately held and most funding comes from equity, it can be quite difficult to derive the discount rate; and if the discount rate is imprecise, then so too will be the resulting net present values.
- *Estimate fudging.* All too many managers are willing to adjust their projected cash flows just enough to ensure that a net present value analysis will yield a guaranteed project approval, irrespective of what the actual result should be.

In short, net present value is based on nothing but forecasted information, and the information can be wrong. There are ways to mitigate these effects. Consider the following solutions, which essentially confine the use of net present value to a reduced set of situations:

1. *Avoid for small purchases.* Do not use net present value analysis for small purchases. Below a certain cutoff level, it is not worth the time to develop cash forecast information – if it is even available. Instead, give managers a pool of cash that they can invest, using their best judgment. This will not represent a massive percentage of the company's available cash, but it should make the purchasing process more efficient for smaller acquisitions.
2. *Use throughput analysis.* Use throughput analysis to the greatest extent possible, since it does a better job of tracing incremental changes in cash inflows to the entire system of production.
3. *Employ scenario analysis.* For those scenarios to which net present value should still be applied, develop high-medium-low scenarios of possible cash flows. Pay particular attention to the worst-case scenario, to see if the company can still earn a return on a prospective investment.

The Payback Method

The simplest and least accurate evaluation technique is the payback method. This approach is still heavily used, because it provides a very fast "back of the envelope" calculation of how soon a company will earn back its investment. This means that it provides a rough measure of how long a company will have its investment at risk, before earning back the original amount expended. There are two ways to calculate the payback period, which are:

1. *Simplified.* Divide the total amount of an investment by the average resulting cash flow. This approach can yield an incorrect assessment, because a proposal with cash flows skewed far into the future can yield a payback period that differs substantially from when actual payback occurs.
2. *Manual calculation.* Manually deduct the forecasted positive cash flows from the initial investment amount, from Year 1 forward, until the investment is paid back. This method is slower, but ensures a higher degree of accuracy.

EXAMPLE

Quest Adventure Gear has received a proposal from a manager, asking to spend $1,500,000 on equipment that will result in cash inflows in accordance with the following table:

Year	Cash Flow
1	+$150,000
2	+150,000
3	+200,000
4	+600,000
5	+900,000

The total cash flows over the five-year period are projected to be $2,000,000, which is an average of $400,000 per year. When divided into the $1,500,000 original investment, this results in a payback period of 3.75 years. However, the briefest perusal of the projected cash flows reveals that the flows are heavily weighted toward the far end of the time period, so the results of this calculation cannot be correct.

Instead, the accountant runs the calculation year by year, deducting the cash flows in each successive year from the remaining investment. The results of this calculation are:

Year	Cash Flow	Net Invested Cash
0		-$1,500,000
1	+$150,000	-1,350,000
2	+150,000	-1,200,000
3	+200,000	-1,000,000
4	+600,000	-400,000
5	+900,000	0

The table indicates that the real payback period is located somewhere between Year 4 and Year 5. There is $400,000 of investment yet to be paid back at the end of Year 4, and there is $900,000 of cash flow projected for Year 5. The accountant assumes the same monthly amount of cash flow in Year 5, which means that he can estimate final payback as being just short of 4.5 years.

The payback method is not overly accurate, does not provide any estimate of how profitable a project may be, and does not take account of the time value of money. Nonetheless, its extreme simplicity makes it a perennial favorite in many companies.

Capital Budget Proposal Analysis

Reviewing a capital budget proposal does not necessarily mean passing judgment on it exactly as presented. You can attach a variety of suggestions to your analysis of the proposal, which management may incorporate into a revised proposal. Here are some examples:

- *Asset capacity.* Does the asset have more capacity than is actually needed under the circumstances? Is there a history of usage spikes that call for extra capacity? Depending on the answers to these questions, consider using smaller assets with less capacity. If the asset is powered, this may also lead to reductions in utility costs, installation costs, and floor space requirements.
- *Asset commoditization.* Wherever possible, avoid custom-designed machinery in favor of standard models that are readily available. By doing so, it is easier to obtain repair parts, and there may even be an aftermarket for disposing of the asset when the company no longer needs it.
- *Asset features.* Managers have a habit of wanting to buy new assets with all of the latest features. Are all of these features really needed? If an asset is being replaced, then it is useful to compare the characteristics of the old and new assets, and examine any differences between the two to see if they are really needed. If the asset is the only model offered by the supplier, would the supplier be willing to strip away some features and offer it at a lower price?
- *Asset standardization.* If a company needs a particular asset in large quantities, adopt a policy of always buying from the same manufacturer, and preferably only buying the same asset every time. By doing so, the maintenance staff becomes extremely familiar with maintenance requirements, and only has to stock replacement parts for one model.
- *Bottleneck analysis.* As noted earlier in this chapter, assets that improve the amount of throughput in a production operation are usually well worth the investment, while those not impacting the bottleneck require substantially more justification, usually in the direction of reducing operating expenses.
- *Comprehensiveness of expenditures.* Are all of the expenditures associated with a capital purchase actually included in the proposal? There may be additional costs for preparing the site, wiring and plumbing, pouring a concrete pad, testing the equipment, permits, training, and working capital.
- *Expenditure reduction.* A capital proposal likely includes a projection of reduced costs. Verify that these costs are of a sufficiently incremental nature

that the cash flows will actually be realized. For example, eliminating 10% of the workload of a salaried employee does not reduce any cost.

- *Extended useful life.* A manager may be applying for an asset replacement simply because the original asset has reached the end of its recommended useful life. But is it really necessary to replace the asset? Consider conducting a formal review of these assets to see if they can still be used for some additional period of time. There may be additional maintenance costs involved, but this will almost certainly be lower than the cost of replacing the asset.

- *Facility analysis.* If a capital proposal involves the acquisition of additional facility space, consider reviewing any existing space to see if it can be compressed, thereby eliminating the need for more space. For example, shift storage items to less expensive warehouse space, shift from offices to more space-efficient cubicles, and encourage employees to work from home or on a later shift. If none of these ideas work, then at least consider acquiring new facilities through a sublease, which tends to require shorter lease terms than a lease arranged with the primary landlord.

- *Monument elimination.* A company may have a large, fixed asset around which the rest of the production area is configured; this is called a monument. If there is a monument, consider adopting a policy of using a larger number of lower-capacity assets. By doing so, you avoid the risk of having a single monument asset go out of service and stopping all production, in favor of having multiple units, among which work can be shifted if one unit fails.

The sponsors of capital proposals frequently do *not* appreciate this additional review of their proposals, since it implies that they did not consider these issues themselves. Nonetheless, the savings can be substantial, and so are well worth the aggravation of dealing with annoyed managers.

If the additional review indicates some promising alternatives that may substantially reduce the cost of a proposal, if not eliminate it entirely, then it may be politically wise to route the proposed changes through the controller or chief financial officer, who may have the clout to force a serious review of the alternatives by the project sponsor.

The Outsourcing Decision

It may be possible to avoid a capital purchase entirely by outsourcing the work to which it is related. By doing so, the company may be able to eliminate all assets related to the area (rather than acquiring more assets), while the burden of maintaining a sufficient asset base now shifts to the supplier. The supplier may even buy the company's assets related to the area being outsourced. This situation is a well-established alternative for high technology manufacturing, as well as for information technology services, but is likely not viable outside of these areas.

If you are in a situation where outsourcing is a possibility, then the likely cash flows resulting from doing so will be highly favorable for the first few years, as your capital expenditures vanish. However, the supplier must also earn a profit and pay for its own infrastructure, so the cost over the long term will probably not vary dramatically from what a company would have experienced if it had kept a functional area in-house. There are three exceptions that can bring about a long-term cost reduction. They are:

- *Excess capacity*. A supplier may have such a large amount of excess capacity already that it does not need to invest further for some time, thereby potentially depressing the costs that it would otherwise pass through to its customers. However, this excess capacity pool will eventually dry up, so it tends to be a short-term anomaly.
- *High volume*. There are some outsourcing situations where the supplier is handling such a massive volume of activity from multiple customers that its costs on a per-unit basis decline below the costs that a company could ever achieve on its own. This situation can yield long-term savings to a company.
- *Low costs*. A supplier may locate its facility and work force in low-cost countries or regions within countries. This can yield significant cost reductions in the short term, but as many suppliers use the same technique, it is driving up costs in all parts of the world. Thus, this cost disparity is useful for a period of time, but is gradually declining as a long-term option.

There are also risks involved in shifting functions to suppliers. First, a supplier may go out of business, leaving the company scrambling to shift work to a new supplier. Second, a supplier may gradually ramp up prices to the point where the company is substantially worse off than if it had kept the function in-house. Third, the company may have so completely purged the outsourced function from its own operations that it is now completely dependent on the supplier, and has no ability to take it back in-house. Fourth, the supplier's service level may decline to the point where it is impairing the ability of the company to operate. And finally, the company may have entered into a multi-year deal, and cannot escape from the arrangement if the business arrangement does not work out. These are significant issues, and must be weighed as part of the outsourcing decision.

The cautions noted here about outsourcing do not mean that it should be avoided as an option. On the contrary, a rapidly growing company that has minimal access to funds may cheerfully hand off multiple operations to suppliers in order to avoid the up-front costs associated with those operations. Outsourcing is less attractive to stable, well-established companies that have better access to capital.

In summary, outsourcing is an attractive option for rapidly growing companies that do not have sufficient cash to pay for capital expenditures, but also carries with it a variety of risks involving shifting key functions to a supplier over which a company may not have a great deal of control.

The Capital Budgeting Application Form

Most companies require managers to fill out a standardized form for all capital budgeting proposals. The type of information that you include in the form will vary, depending on whether you are basing the approval decision on bottleneck considerations or the results of a net present value analysis. However, the header section of the form will likely be the same in all circumstances. It identifies the project, its sponsor, the date on which it was submitted, and a unique project identification number that is filled in by the recipient. A sample header is:

Sample Application Header

Project name:	50 Ton plastic injection molder
Project sponsor:	E. R. Eddison
Submission date:	May 28 Project number: 2015-10

If a proposal is for a legal requirement or a risk mitigation issue, then it is absolved from most analysis, and will likely move to the top of the approved project list. Consequently, the form should contain a separate section for these types of projects, and should involve a different set of approvers. The corporate attorney may be involved, as well as anyone involved in risk management. A sample block in the application form for legal and risk mitigation issues is:

Sample Legal and Risk Mitigation Block

			Required Approvals
Initial cash flow:	-$250,000	All proposals	*Susan Lafferty*
Year 1 cash flow:	-10,000		Attorney
Year 2 cash flow:	-10,000		
Year 3 cash flow:	-10,000	< $100,000	*George Mason*
			Risk Officer
Describe legal or risk mitigation issue:			
Replanting of pine forest on southern property, with annual forestry review, per new zoning requirements		$100,000+	*Fred Scurry* President

If you elect to focus on bottleneck considerations for capital budgeting approvals, then include the following block of text in the application form. This block focuses on the changes in cash flow that are associated with a capital expenditure. The block requests an itemization of the cash flows involved in the purchase (primarily for finance planning considerations), followed by requests for information about how the investment will help the company – via an improvement in throughput, a reduction in operating costs, or an increase in the return on investment. In the example, note that the primary improvement used as the basis for the proposal is the improvement in throughput. This also leads to an enhancement of the return on investment. There is an increase in the total net operating cost, which represents a reduction in the positive effect of the throughput, and which is caused by the annual $8,000 maintenance cost associated with the investment.

The approvals for a bottleneck-related investment change from the ones shown previously for a legal or risk mitigation investment. In this case, a process analyst should verify the information include in the block, to ensure that the applicant's claims are correct. The supervisor in whose area of responsibility the investment falls should also sign off, thereby accepting responsibility for the outcome of the investment. A higher-level manager, or even the board of directors, should approve any really large investment proposals.

Sample Bottleneck Approval Block

		Required Approvals	
Initial cash flow:	-$125,000	All proposals	*Monica Byers*
Year 1 cash flow:	-8,000		Process Analyst
Year 2 cash flow:	-8,000		
Year 3 cash flow:	-8,000	< $100,000	*Al Rogers*
			Responsible Supervisor
Net throughput change:*	+$180,000		
		$100,000+	*Fred Scurry*
Net operating cost change:*	+$8,000		President
Change in ROI:*	+0.08%		

* On an annual basis

If you do not choose to use a bottleneck-oriented application, then the following block may be useful in the application. It is based on the more traditional analysis of net present value. You may also consider using this block as a supplement to the bottleneck block just noted, in case some managers prefer to work with both sets of information.

Sample Net Present Value Information Block

Year	Cash Out (payments)	Cash In (Revenue)	Incremental Tax Effect	Totals
0	-$1,000,000			-$1,000,000
1	-25,000	+$200,000	+$8,750	+183,750
2	-25,000	+400,000	-61,250	+313,750
3	-25,000	+400,000	-61,250	+313,750
4	-25,000	+400,000	-61,250	+313,750
5	-25,000	+400,000	-61,250	+313,750
Totals	-$1,125,000	+$1,800,000	-$236,250	+$438,750
			Tax Rate:	35%
			Hurdle Rate:	12%
			Net Present Value:	+$13,328

The net present value block requires the presentation of cash flows over a five-year period, as well as the net tax effect resulting from this specific transaction. The tax

113

effect is based on $25,000 of maintenance expenses in every year shown, as well as $200,000 of annual depreciation, and a 35% incremental tax rate. Thus, in Year 2, there is $400,000 of revenue, less $225,000 of depreciation and maintenance expenses, multiplied by 35%, resulting in an incremental tax effect of $61,250.

The block then goes on to state the corporate hurdle rate, which is 12% in the example. We then discount the stream of cash flows from the project at the hurdle rate of 12%, which results in a positive net present value of $13,328. Based on just the net present value analysis, this appears to be an acceptable project.

A variation on the rather involved text just shown is to shift the detailed cash flow analysis to a backup document, and only show the resulting net present value in the application form.

The text blocks shown here contain much of the key information that management should see before it decides whether to approve a capital investment. In addition, there should be a considerable amount of supporting information that precisely describes the nature of the proposed investment, as well as backup information that supports each number included in the form.

The Post Installation Review

It is very important to conduct a post installation review of any capital expenditure project, to see if the initial expectations for it were realized. If not, then the results of this review can be used to modify the capital budgeting process to include better information.

Another reason for having a post installation review is that it provides a control over those managers who fill out the initial capital budgeting proposals. If they know there is no post installation review, then they can wildly overstate the projected results of their projects with impunity, just to have them approved. Of course, this control is only useful if it is conducted relatively soon after a project is completed. Otherwise, the responsible manager may have moved on in his career, and can no longer be tied back to the results of his work.

It is even better to begin a post installation review while a project is still being implemented, and especially when the implementation period is expected to be long. This initial review gives senior management a good idea of whether the cost of a project is staying close to its initial expectations. If not, management may need to authorize more vigorous management of the project, scale it back, or even cancel it outright.

If the post implementation review results in the suspicion that a project proposal was unduly optimistic, this brings up the question of how to deal with the responsible manager. At a minimum, the proposal reviews can flag any future proposals by this reviewer as suspect, and worthy of especially close attention. Another option is to tie long-term compensation to the results of these projects. A third possibility is to include the results of these project reviews in personnel reviews, which may lead to a reduction in employee compensation. A really catastrophic result may even be grounds for the termination of the responsible party.

EXAMPLE

Quest Adventure Gear has just completed a one-year project to increase the amount of production capacity at its primary equipment manufacturing center. The original capital budgeting proposal was for an initial expenditure of $290,000, resulting in additional annual throughput of $100,000 per year. The actual result is somewhat different. The accountant's report includes the following text:

> **Findings:** The proposal only contained the purchase price of the equipment. However, since the machinery was delivered from Germany, Quest also incurred $22,000 of freight charges and $3,000 in customs fees. Further, the project required the installation of a new concrete pad, a breaker box, and electrical wiring that cost an additional $10,000. Finally, the equipment proved to be difficult to configure, and required $20,000 of consulting fees from the manufacturer, as well as $5,000 for the materials scrapped during testing. Thus, the actual cost of the project was $350,000.

> Subsequent operation of the equipment reveals that it cannot operate without an average of 20% downtime for maintenance, as opposed to the 5% downtime that was advertised by the manufacturer. This reduces throughput by 15%, which equates to a drop of $15,000 in throughput per year, to $85,000.

> **Recommendations:** To incorporate a more comprehensive set of instructions into the capital budgeting proposal process to account for transportation, setup, and testing costs. Also, given the wide difference between the performance claims of the manufacturer and actual results, to hire a consultant to see if the problem is caused by our installation of the equipment; if not, we recommend not buying from this supplier in the future.

The Lease versus Buy Decision

Once the asset acquisition decision has been made, management still needs to decide if it should buy the asset outright, or lease it. In a leasing situation, a lessor buys the asset and then allows the lessee to use it in exchange for a monthly fee. Depending on the terms of the lease, it may be treated in one of two ways:
- *Capital lease*. The lessee records the leased asset on its books as a fixed asset and depreciates it, while recording interest expense separately.
- *Operating lease*. The lessor records the leased asset on its books as a fixed asset and depreciates it, while the lessee simply records a lease payment.

The decision to use a lease may be based on management's unwillingness to use its line of credit or other available sources of financing to buy an asset. Leases can be easier to obtain that a line of credit, since the lease agreement always designates the asset as collateral.

There are a multitude of factors that a lessor includes in the formulation of the monthly rate that it charges, such as the down payment, the residual value of the asset at the end of the lease, and the interest rate, which makes it difficult to break out and examine each element of the lease. Instead, it is much easier to create separate net present value tables for the lease and buy alternatives, and then compare the results of the two tables to see which is the better alternative.

EXAMPLE

Quest Adventure Gear is contemplating the purchase of an asset for $500,000. It can buy the asset outright, or do so with a lease. Its cost of capital is 8%, and its incremental income tax rate is 35%. The following two tables show the net present values of both options.

Buy Option

Year	Depreciation	Income Tax Savings (35%)	Discount Factor (8%)	Net Present Value
0				-$500,000
1	$100,000	$35,000	0.9259	32,407
2	100,000	35,000	0.8573	30,006
3	100,000	35,000	0.7938	27,783
4	100,000	35,000	0.7350	25,725
5	100,000	35,000	0.6806	23,821
Totals	$500,000	$175,000		$360,258

Lease Option

Year	Pretax Lease Payments	Income Tax Savings (35%)	After-Tax Lease Cost	Discount Factor (8%)	Net Present Value
1	$135,000	$47,250	$87,750	0.9259	$81,248
2	135,000	47,250	87,750	0.8573	75,228
3	135,000	47,250	87,750	0.7938	69,656
4	135,000	47,250	87,750	0.7350	64,496
5	135,000	47,250	87,750	0.6806	59,723
Totals	$675,000	$236,250	$438,750		$350,351

Thus, the net purchase cost of the buy option is $360,258, while the net purchase cost of the lease option is $350,351. The lease option involves the lowest cash outflow for Quest, and so is the better option.

Capital Budgeting with Minimal Cash

This chapter has addressed a number of analysis techniques that can be used to determine whether to buy a fixed asset, and which financing choice to select. But what if the company has very little money to spend? If so, the capital budgeting choices may be entirely different. The primary target is to obtain the maximum return on investment as fast as possible, while spending a minimum amount of cash. Here are some options:

- *Repairs*. Evaluate the extent to which the lives of existing equipment can be prolonged, and see if there is old, unused equipment that can be brought back to workable condition with a modest investment in repairs. The cost of these repairs should be limited to a level well below the cost of investing in new equipment. The result may be equipment that is not overly efficient, but this is acceptable as long as the amount of funds invested is low.
- *Operating hours*. See if it is possible to extend the operating hours of the existing equipment. It may be much less expensive to have a few people work overtime or on an additional shift than to buy new equipment. The result could be equipment that runs for all three shifts, though be aware that the cost of maintenance will increase when usage levels go up.
- *Outsource*. It may save cash to outsource work to a third party, even if the cost is higher on a per-unit basis than producing in-house. To keep options open for bringing work back to the company in the future, only sign short-term agreements to outsource work.
- *Buy used equipment*. Place a major emphasis on purchasing used equipment. The market prices of used equipment can be so much less than for new equipment that it may be worthwhile to institute a rule that new equipment can only be acquired with the prior approval of senior management. However, consider the availability of spare parts before acquiring older equipment. If parts are in short supply, it may be inordinately expensive to repair the equipment.
- *Lease assets*. Be sure to institute the lease versus buy analysis that was covered in the last section. A lease may carry a relatively high implicit interest rate, but has the particular advantage of deferring the payment of cash to later periods.
- *Cash inflow analysis*. When cash is in short supply, only invest in equipment that will generate an immediate return. This means equipment that can produce verifiable cash flows within a few weeks is much better than equipment that is only intended to provide spare capacity, and which may not be needed immediately. Also, do not acquire equipment for which the associated cash inflows are speculative.

In short, being in survival mode changes the orientation of the capital budgeting process to one where you try to get by with what you have, scrounge for used equipment, and only invest when the offsetting cash inflows are certain. With the orientation on day-to-day survival, there is no long-term analysis of return on investment.

There are some issues with the recommendations noted here. First, older equipment is likely to be less efficient, and may require additional maintenance time. Also, the result could be a clutter of equipment that does not work together very well. These points are acceptable in the short term, but should be addressed over the long term, assuming the company has emerged from its cash-poor situation and can afford better equipment.

Summary

This chapter addressed a variety of issues to consider when deciding whether to recommend the purchase of a fixed asset. We put less emphasis on net present value analysis, which has been the primary capital budgeting tool in industry for years, because it does not take into consideration the impact on throughput of a company's bottleneck operation. The best capital budgeting analysis process is to give top priority to project proposals that have a strong favorable impact on throughput, and then use net present value to evaluate the impact of any remaining projects on cost reduction.

Chapter 15
The Compensation Budget

Introduction

A key component of any budget is the derivation of the compensation to be paid to employees. It is not usually itemized as a separate budget. Instead, it is integrated into the various departmental budgets, so that managers can more easily see the compensation information pertaining to their areas of responsibility. We have segregated it in this chapter in order to delve into the various technical aspects of its construction. We also address the issue of linking bonus compensation to budget performance.

The Compensation Budget

The key goals of a compensation budget are to itemize the pay rates of all employees, the dates on which you expect to alter their pay, and all associated payroll taxes. Bonus payments and their associated payroll taxes are generally handled separately, or may not be included in the budget at all if it is unlikely that employees will earn them.

The compensation budget in the following example separates the calculation of compensation, social security taxes, Medicare taxes, and federal unemployment taxes. The separate calculation of these items is the only way to achieve a reasonable level of accuracy in the calculation of payroll taxes, since there are different tax rates and wage caps associated with each of the taxes. The pertinent information related to each of the indicated payroll taxes is:

Tax Type	Tax Rate	2014 Wage Cap
Social security	6.20%	$117,000
Medicare	1.45%	No cap
Federal unemployment	0.80%	$7,000

In a lower-wage environment, there may be few employees whose pay exceeds the social security wage cap, which makes the social security tax budget quite simple to calculate. However, in situations where compensation levels are quite high, expect to meet social security wage caps within the first two or three quarters of the year. Given the size of the social security match paid by employers, it is especially important to budget for the correct amount of tax; otherwise, the compensation budget could be inaccurate by a significant amount.

The simplest of the tax calculations is for the Medicare tax, since there is no wage cap for it. We have presented its calculation in the following example as a table in which we calculate it for each individual employee. However, given the lack of a wage cap, you can more easily create a budget for it with a single line item that multiplies total compensation in every budget period by the Medicare tax rate.

Given the size of the social security and Medicare expenses, the paltry amount of the federal unemployment tax may seem like an afterthought. However, since it is based on a very low wage cap, nearly all of the expense is incurred in the first calendar quarter of each year, where it represents a modest expense bump. Some companies create a separate budget schedule for this expense, just to ensure that the correct amount is included in the first quarter of each year. Others find the cost to be so insignificant that they do not track it.

These concepts are noted in the following example, where we present separate budgets for base pay, social security, Medicare, and federal unemployment taxes, and then aggregate them into a master compensation budget.

EXAMPLE

Quest Adventure Gear is starting up a small group that will deal with research into advanced materials. The company decides to create a separate compensation budget for the group, which includes five employees. The compensation budget is as follows, with quarters in which pay raises are scheduled being highlighted. Note that the annual salary is stated in each calendar quarter.

Base Pay Budget

	Quarter 1	Quarter 2	Quarter 3	Quarter 4
Erskin, Donald	$75,000	$75,000	$79,500	$79,500
Fells, Arnold	45,000	46,250	46,250	46,250
Gainsborough, Amy	88,000	88,000	88,000	91,500
Harmon, Debra	68,500	68,500	70,000	70,000
Illescu, Adriana	125,000	125,000	125,000	125,000
Annual compensation	$401,500	$402,750	$408,750	$412,250
Quarterly compensation	$100,375	$100,688	$102,188	$103,063

Social Security Budget (6.2% tax, $117,000 wage cap)

	Quarter 1	Quarter 2	Quarter 3	Quarter 4
Erskin, Donald	$1,163	$1,163	$1,232	$1,232
Fells, Arnold	698	717	717	717
Gaisborough, Amy	1,364	1,364	1,364	1,418
Harmon, Debra	1,062	1,062	1,085	1,085
Illescu, Adriana	1,938	1,938	1,938	1,440
Totals	$6,225	$6,244	$6,336	$5,892

Medicare Budget (1.45% tax, no wage cap)

	Quarter 1	Quarter 2	Quarter 3	Quarter 4
Erskin, Donald	$272	$272	$288	$288
Fells, Arnold	163	168	168	168
Gaisborough, Amy	319	319	319	332
Harmon, Debra	248	248	254	254
Illescu, Adriana	453	453	453	453
Totals	$1,455	$1,460	$1,482	$1,495

Federal Unemployment Tax Budget (0.8% tax, $7,000 wage cap)

	Quarter 1	Quarter 2	Quarter 3	Quarter 4
Erskin, Donald	$56	$0	$0	$0
Fells, Arnold	56	0	0	0
Gaisborough, Amy	56	0	0	0
Harmon, Debra	56	0	0	0
Illescu, Adriana	56	0	0	0
Totals	$280	$0	$0	$0

Quest then shifts the summary totals from each of the preceding tables into a master compensation budget, as follows:

Master Compensation Budget

	Quarter 1	Quarter 2	Quarter 3	Quarter 4
Total base pay	$100,375	$100,688	$102,188	$103,063
Total social security	6,225	6,244	6,336	5,892
Total Medicare	1,455	1,460	1,482	1,495
Total unemployment	280	0	0	0
Grand totals	$108,335	$108,392	$110,006	$110,450

In the preceding example, compensation is shown in each quarter on an annualized basis, since it is easier to review the budget for errors when the information is presented in this manner. The information is then stepped down to a quarterly basis, which is used to calculate taxes in the tax budgets.

In the model, any change in pay is assumed to occur as of the first day of an accounting period. If this is not the case, then listing the full amount of the revised compensation level will result in an excessively high budgeted compensation level in that period. This may be a minor issue if the amount of compensation changes is small. Alternatively, you can enter a reduced amount of pay change in that period and the full amount of the change in compensation in the next period.

The Treatment of Hourly Pay and Overtime

In the preceding example, we assumed that all employees were paid salaries. In environments where employees are paid an hourly wage, you can alter the format of the budget to instead list the hourly pay rate for each employee, and then multiply it by the standard number of working hours in the year to arrive at annual compensation. This is useful when you need the hourly rate information to verify it against payroll records. However, we recommend itemizing pay based on an annual rate of pay, rather than an hourly rate of pay, because employees may be expected to work more or fewer hours than the standard number of hours in a year. Doing so also creates more consistency within the budget model, so that the compensation of both salaried and hourly employees are presented in terms of their annual compensation.

Overtime is difficult to predict at the level of an individual employee, but can be estimated at a more aggregated level. It is easiest to use the historical proportion of overtime hours, adjusted for expectations in the budget period. This means that you can multiply an overtime percentage by the aggregate amount of employee compensation to derive the amount of budgeted overtime pay. The following example illustrates the concept.

EXAMPLE

Quest Adventure Gear operates a production line for titanium sleds for which the sales season is November through January. Quest prefers to deactivate the production line for the first half of the calendar year and then run it with substantial employee overtime during the third quarter and a portion of the fourth quarter of the year. This results in the following overtime budget, which also assumes that a production crew is still working during the first half of the year – they just happen to be working on other production lines.

	Quarter 1	Quarter 2	Quarter 3	Quarter 4
Total wage expense	$250,000	$255,000	$270,000	$240,000
Overtime percentage	0%	2%	28%	12%
Overtime pay	$0	$5,100	$75,600	$28,800
Social security for overtime pay	$0	$316	$4,687	$1,786
Medicare for overtime pay	0	$74	$1,096	$418
Total overtime compensation	$0	$390	$5,783	$2,204

There is no calculation of the federal unemployment tax in the overtime budget, since that amount has such a low wage cap that the maximum amount would already have been included in the compensation budget.

The trouble with the overtime calculation format just presented is that it does not account for the social security wage cap, which is calculated at the level of the individual employee. It is easiest to simply assume that the wage cap is never reached, which may result in some excess amount of social security tax being budgeted. Realistically, few employees who are paid on an hourly basis will exceed the wage cap, so this should be a minor issue for most companies.

The Benefits Budget

A key part of employee compensation is the benefits paid to each employee, since benefits can comprise a large part of total compensation. Budgeting for benefits can be a problem under the following combination of circumstances:

- The company-paid portion is significant; and
- The amount of the expense varies based on the number of dependents covered by the benefits; and
- Employees may opt into or out of the coverage.

If you are faced with this much variability, it may be necessary to create the benefits budget with line items for each employee. However, if there are many benefits, this can result in an inordinately large budget that is difficult to update.

An alternative approach is to avoid compiling the benefits budget at the level of the individual employee. Instead, create a moderate level of detail for those few benefits that cost the most (usually medical insurance), and aggregate the cost of all other benefits in a few line items. This approach is easy to maintain and provides a reasonably accurate picture of benefit expenses. The following example illustrates the concept.

EXAMPLE

The controller of Quest Adventure Gear is compiling the budgeted amount of benefits for the corporate headquarters staff. This budget provides additional detail for medical insurance, since it is the key benefit provided by the company, and the amount of the expense varies markedly, depending on the number of dependents. The cost of dental and life insurance is much lower, so these expenses are only shown in aggregate, and based on total headcount. The calculation of the total amount of 401(k) pension matching is based on the following factors:

- 85% of the headquarters staff will enroll in the pension plan
- The company will match employee pension deductions up to a maximum of $3,000 per year
- The company's payment of the pension match will be distributed over the four quarters in proportions of 35%, 25% 20%, and 20%. This distribution is based on some employees having more than $3,000 deducted from their pay, so that the pension match is completed earlier in the year for those employees.

	Quarter 1	Quarter 2	Quarter 3	Quarter 4
Total headquarters compensation	$705,000	$726,000	$767,000	$767,000
Medical insurance headcount:				
Single coverage	12	12	14	14
Married coverage	17	16	16	16
Family coverage	5	7	7	7
No coverage	10	10	10	10
Total headcount	44	45	47	47
Medical insurance employer cost				
Single coverage ($1,050/qtr each)	$12,600	$12,600	$14,700	$14,700
Married coverage ($1,575/qtr each)	26,775	25,200	25,200	25,200
Family coverage ($2,500/qtr each)	12,500	17,500	17,500	17,500
Total medical employer cost	$51,875	$55,300	$57,400	$57,400
Total employer dental expense	$9,250	$9,500	$10,000	$10,000
Total employer life insurance expense	2,380	2,450	2,590	2,590
401(k) pension assumptions:				
Proportion enrolled in pension plan	85%	85%	85%	85%
Matching cap	$3,000	$3,000	$3,000	$3,000
Matching distribution	35%	25%	20%	20%
401(k) pension matching*	$39,270	$28,688	$23,970	$23,970
Total benefits expense	$102,775	$95,938	$93,960	$93,960

* Calculated as the quarterly total headcount × proportion enrolled in the pension plan × matching cap × matching distribution percentage

The Headcount Budget

It may be useful to compile a headcount budget as part of the overall corporate budget. This budget is entirely non-monetary – it simply lists the number of employees, either by department, location, or position. This information may be used by the human resources staff to plan for hiring or layoffs, or by the facilities manager to determine the amount of square footage needed to house all employees.

The information in the headcount budget is usually derived from all other budgets that involve headcount (which is nearly all budgets other than the financing budget). As such, it is typically populated automatically through the budget model. A sample headcount budget follows.

Sample Headcount Budget

	Quarter 1	Quarter 2	Quarter 3	Quarter 4
Accounting department	5	5	6	6
Corporate staff	8	7	7	7
Customer service department	4	4	6	6
Engineering department	11	12	13	13
Production department	83	87	90	90
Sales and marketing department	6	8	8	8
Total headcount	117	123	130	130
Total non-production headcount	34	36	40	40
Square feet per non-production person	250	250	250	250
Total non-production square footage needed	8,500	9,000	10,000	10,000

The sample budget multiplies total headcount by a standard amount of square footage per person, which is useful for estimating the amount of space needed to house the budgeted number of employees.

The Link between Budgets and Bonus Compensation

Some companies like to budget for bonuses that employees earn if they reach certain performance targets. This presents a budgeting conundrum – what if you budget for a bonus that does *not* occur, or you elect not to budget for a bonus that *does* occur? For example, if you budget for a bonus that does not occur, this creates a favorable compensation expense variance, since the company spent less than expected. However, not paying the bonus also meant that the employee to whom it would normally have been paid did not achieve his objectives, which presumably translated into reduced financial performance by the company. Thus, budgeting for a bonus can result in offsetting performance results.

This is not an issue that has an easy solution. How you choose to budget for a bonus may be impacted by the following factors:

- *Historical-basis bonus.* If a bonus is essentially a roll-forward of the company's performance from the preceding period into the budget period, the recipient of the bonus plan presumable only has to copy existing performance to achieve the bonus. In this case, the payment is probable, so budget for the bonus expense.
- *Attainable bonus.* If the bonus is based on an improvement in the company's present performance, base the decision to record the bonus on a qualitative estimate of how difficult it will be to attain the bonus. If it is more likely than not that the recipient of the bonus plan will be paid the bonus, then budget for the bonus expense.
- *Theoretically attainable bonus.* If the bonus is only paid if one or more extremely difficult targets are met, then do not budget for the bonus expense. In these cases, the bonus is based on the achievement of targets that may only be theoretically possible, such as running a production facility at 100% of its capacity. Given the low probability of success, there is no reason to budget for the bonus expense.

If there are several possible payouts under a bonus plan, then budget for the amount that is more likely than not to be attained. An alternative is to calculate the most likely payout based on probabilities, and add this expected bonus amount to the budget. However, be aware that doing so means that the actual bonus payment will never match the exact amount budgeted. The following example illustrates the concept.

EXAMPLE

The board of directors of Quest Adventure Gear negotiates a bonus plan with the company's president, under which he will be paid $100,000 if he meets several goals that will be difficult to attain or $50,000 if he meets several more easily attainable goals or $10,000 if he meets a few easily achievable targets. The controller of Quest assigns a probability to each of the payouts and calculates the following expected bonus:

Bonus Payout		Probability		Probability-Adjusted Payout
$100,000	×	10%	=	$10,000
$50,000	×	30%	=	$15,000
$10,000	×	60%	=	$6,000
		100%		$31,000

The trouble with this probability-based calculation is that Quest may budget for a bonus of $31,000, but none of the alternatives pay out that amount. In fact, there is a more than 50% chance that the bonus will only be $10,000, thereby leaving a variance of $21,000.

An alternative to this decision process flow is to restructure the bonus plan itself, so that the bonus is paid on a sliding scale, rather than as a binary (yes or no) solution. This means that the bonus payment is set at a specific percentage of the goal, such as two percent of sales or three percent of net profits – no matter what the total amount of sales or profits may be. Further, try to avoid imposing an upper boundary on the amount paid. Instead, the bonus is a simple percentage of the goal. By doing so, you budget for the amount of bonus that matches the goals listed in the budget. If the employee responsible for the goal achieves the target amount, then the budgeted bonus amount is paid. If the employee achieves a slightly lower amount, then he is paid a slightly lower bonus. The following example illustrates the concept.

EXAMPLE

Quest Adventure Gear is considering a new bonus plan for its sales manager. In the previous year, the bonus plan was for a $125,000 payout only if the sales department achieved a difficult target of $50 million in revenue. The target was not met, and the sales manager essentially gave up on it at mid-year, once it became clear that the target could not be achieved. For the next budget year, Quest implements a simple bonus plan that awards a ½% bonus to the sales manager for all sales above $25 million. The $25 million minimum sales level is the company's breakeven point, and the president does not want to award bonuses if the company is losing money. If the sales manager achieves sales of $50 million, he still earns the $125,000 bonus that was stated in the plan from the previous year. However, the new bonus plan awards him the ½% bonus at *any* point above the initial $25 million starting point. This approach should ensure that the sales manager remains motivated throughout the year, irrespective of the sales level.

The example presents the use of a sliding scale for a bonus. Essentially, the method of calculation of that bonus is the same as for a commission, which is a percentage of sales. This type of arrangement is easily incorporated into a budget model.

Summary

Compensation is one of the more difficult areas to budget, since it involves not only base pay, but also overtime, payroll taxes, benefits, and (possibly) bonuses. A considerable amount of precision is needed to create a budget that simulates what actual compensation is likely to be, so compensation modeling should comprise a significant amount of the total time spent in constructing a budget.

The budget models shown in this chapter have been quite detailed, and could potentially become massive documents in organizations that employ hundreds or thousands of people. To avoid an unwieldy budget, consider aggregating employees by department or type of job, as described in the Budgeting Efficiencies chapter.

Chapter 16
The Master Budget

Introduction

The master budget is the aggregation of all lower-level budgets produced by a company's various functional areas, which results in a budgeted income statement. There may also be a budgeted balance sheet, though the derivation of that document requires additional work. In this chapter, we will discuss the compilation of the income statement and balance sheet, as well as the additional documentation that usually accompanies a budget.

The Budgeted Income Statement

The core of the master budget is the budgeted income statement. It is derived from nearly all of the budgets that we have already discussed, and looks quite a bit like a standard income statement. This is a sufficient summarization of the budget for many companies, because they are primarily concerned with *financial performance*. However, some companies may still have an interest in their projected *financial position* (especially cash), which is contained in the balance sheet. Since the balance sheet is more difficult to derive than the income statement, they may be content to use a rough calculation of ending cash position whose components are mostly derived from information already in the budget. The following sample income statement contains this rough estimation of the ending cash balance in each period.

Sample Budgeted Income Statement

	Quarter 1	Quarter 2	Quarter 3	Quarter 4
Revenue	$2,200,000	$2,425,000	$2,500,000	$2,545,000
Cost of goods sold:				
Direct labor expense	220,000	253,000	253,000	253,000
Direct materials expense	767,000	838,000	831,000	840,000
Manufacturing overhead	293,000	293,000	309,000	310,000
Total cost of goods sold	1,280,000	1,384,000	1,393,000	1,403,000
Gross margin	$920,000	$1,041,000	$1,107,000	$1,142,000
Sales and marketing	315,000	351,000	374,000	339,000
Administration	453,500	452,500	435,000	447,000
Research and development	50,000	52,000	54,000	55,500
Profits before taxes	$101,500	$185,500	$244,000	$300,500
Income taxes	35,500	65,000	85,500	105,000
Profits after taxes	$66,000	$120,500	$158,500	$195,500

	Quarter 1	Quarter 2	Quarter 3	Quarter 4
Cash flow:				
Beginning cash	$50,000	-$52,500	$77,500	$7,000
+ Net profit	66,000	120,500	158,500	195,500
+ Depreciation	19,500	17,500	18,000	18,000
- Capital purchases	-38,000	-8,000	-47,000	-28,000
- Dividends	-150,000	0	-200,000	0
Ending cash	-$52,500	$77,500	$7,000	$192,500

The calculation of ending cash is appended to the budgeted income statement because it is partly derived from the net income figure located directly above it in the budget. Also, if a company does not intend to create a balance sheet, it is practical to include a cash calculation on the same page as the income statement.

The trouble with the ending cash measurement presented in the sample is that it is not complete. It does not incorporate any timing delays for when cash may be received or issued, and it also does not factor in the impact of changes in working capital. Thus, it can present inaccurate estimates of cash flow. For a more detailed derivation of ending cash, we need a balance sheet. The compilation of that document is discussed in the next section.

Components of the Budgeted Balance Sheet

The balance sheet is difficult to derive as part of the budgeting process, because little of the information derived through the budgeting process is designed for it. Instead, you need to make a variety of estimates to approximate the amounts of various asset and liability line items as of the end of each budgeted reporting period. The key elements of the balance sheet that require estimation are:
- Accounts receivable
- Inventory
- Fixed assets
- Accounts payable

We will address the derivation of these items below.

Accounts Receivable

Accounts receivable is the amount of sales made on credit that have not yet been paid by customers. It is closely correlated with sales, with a delay measured using days sales outstanding (DSO). DSO is calculated as:

$$\frac{\text{Accounts receivable}}{\text{Annual sales} \div 365 \text{ days}}$$

If sales vary significantly by quarter, then alter the denominator in the formula to be quarterly sales divided by the number of days in the quarter. This version of the formula is:

129

Accounts receivable
Quarterly sales ÷ 91 days

You then apply the DSO figure to projected credit sales during the budget period to determine the amount of accounts receivable outstanding at any given time.

EXAMPLE

Quest Adventure Gear has a division whose annual sales are $10 million. Its accounts receivable balance at the end of the most recent month was $1,400,000. Its DSO is calculated as:

$1,400,000 accounts receivable
$10,000,000 annual sales ÷ 365 days

= 51 days sales outstanding

Thus, it takes an average of 51 days for Quest to collect an account receivable. In its balance sheet budget, Quest would record as accounts receivable the current month's sales plus 21/30ths of the sales budgeted in the immediately preceding month. Thus, Quest's budgeted receivables would be calculated as follows for a four-month sample period:

	December (prior year)	January	February	March
Credit sales	$790,000	$810,000	$815,000	$840,000
Receivables for month	--	810,000	815,000	840,000
Receivables from prior month	--	553,000	567,000	571,000
Total receivables in balance sheet	--	$1,363,000	$1,382,000	$1,411,000

An alternative approach for calculating the amount of accounts receivable is to calculate the percentage of credit sales that are collected within the month of sales and then within each of the next 30-day time buckets, and apply these layers of collections to a calculation of the ending accounts receivable in each budget period. The following example illustrates the concept.

EXAMPLE

The controller of Quest Adventure Gear decides to use an alternative method for deriving the ending accounts receivable balance for the division described in the preceding example.

The controller finds that, historically, the following percentages of credit sales are paid within the stated time periods:

	Percent Paid	Percent Unpaid
In month of sale	10%	90%
In following month	65%	25%
In 2nd month	18%	7%
In 3rd month	5%	2%
In 4th month	2%	0%
Total	100%	

The controller then uses the following table to derive the ending accounts receivable balance for the month of January, which is part of the budget period. The information from the preceding three months is needed to derive the ending accounts receivable balance in January.

	October (prior year)	November (prior year)	December (prior year)	January
Credit sales	$815,000	$820,000	$790,000	$810,000
90% of January sales				729,000
25% of December sales				198,000
7% of November sales				57,000
2% of October sales				16,000
Total ending accounts receivable				$1,000,000

A truly detailed model would assume an even longer collection period for some receivables, which may extend for twice the number of months shown in the model. If you choose to use this method, the increased accuracy from adding more months to the model does not appreciably improve the accuracy of the ending accounts receivable figure. Thus, restrict the accounts receivable layering to no more than three or four months.

The receivables layering method is clearly more labor intensive than the DSO method, though it may result in slightly more accurate results. In the interests of modeling efficiency, we prefer the DSO method. It requires much less space in the budget model, is easy to understand, and produces reasonably accurate results.

There are a number of concerns regarding the estimation of accounts receivable to be aware of. They are:

- *Credit policy*. If the company alters its credit policy, then estimate its impact on DSO. For example, if management wants to loosen credit in order to increase sales, expect DSO to increase. Conversely, a tighter credit policy should reduce the DSO figure.
- *Arbitrary DSO changes*. Do not arbitrarily alter the historical DSO rate used in the budget. A common practice by senior managers is to assume that cash flow can be improved with more aggressive collection practices, so they

budget for a reduced amount of DSO. This does not happen in practice, because the collections staff is presumably already engaged in the optimum level of collection activities.

- *Large receivables.* If there will be large individual invoices outstanding during the budget period, the collection of these specific invoices can dramatically alter the DSO. If you suspect that this will be the case, adjust the DSO for your historical collection experience with the customers who will owe you the large invoices.
- *General economic conditions.* Your customers are subject to general economic conditions, so if there is a general worsening in the business environment, expect their customers to pay late, which will cause your customers to pay late. The reverse is not necessarily true; if economic conditions improve and customers are flush with cash, they may be paying in accordance with an internal payment policy, and so will *not* pay any sooner.

In general, our recommendation is to maintain the historical DSO through the budget period; it is rarely good practice to assume a reduction in DSO. If anything, DSO is more likely to increase.

Inventory

There should be a relatively constant relationship between the level of sales and the amount of inventory on hand. Thus, if you can calculate the historical number of days of inventory on hand and then match it against the budgeted amount of cost of goods sold through the budget period, you can estimate the amount of inventory that should be on hand at the end of each budget period. The calculation of the days of inventory on hand is:

$$\frac{\text{Inventory}}{\text{Annual cost of goods sold} \div 365 \text{ days}}$$

Or, if inventory levels vary by quarter, divide the quarterly cost of goods sold by the number of days in the quarter. The calculation is:

$$\frac{\text{Inventory}}{\text{Quarterly cost of goods sold} \div 91 \text{ days}}$$

The estimation concept is shown in the following example.

EXAMPLE

Quest Adventure Gear has a division that manufactures sleeping bags. It maintains a substantial amount of raw materials in the form of premium goose down, polyester fill, rip stop nylon, and zippers, as well as finished goods. The company calculates the days of inventory on hand for the preceding quarter as follows:

<u>$1,000,000 ending inventory</u>
$1,875,000 quarterly cost of goods sold ÷ 91 days

= 49 days of inventory on hand

Quest expects that the division will continue to have roughly the same proportion of inventory to sales throughout the budget period, so it uses the same days of inventory on hand calculation to derive the ending inventory for each budget period as follows:

	Quarter 1	Quarter 2	Quarter 3	Quarter 4
Cost of goods sold (quarterly)	$1,875,000	$2,000,000	$2,100,000	$1,900,000
Cost of goods sold (monthly)	625,000	667,000	700,000	633,000
Days of inventory assumption	49 days	49 days	49 days	49 days
Ending inventory*	$1,021,000	$1,089,000	$1,143,000	$1,034,000

* Calculated as monthly cost of goods sold × (49 days ÷ 30 days)

The calculation reduces the quarterly cost of goods sold to a monthly figure, so that it can more easily be compared to the days of inventory on hand.

The ending inventory calculation can be thrown off by a number of factors. Consider the following issues, and adjust the calculation as needed:

- *Distant sourcing.* If the company begins to purchase goods from more distant locations, it will likely need to maintain larger amounts of safety stock to guard against any disruptions in deliveries.
- *Distribution system.* If the company alters its warehousing system, this will likely impact the amount of inventory required to keep the distribution pipeline full.
- *Manufacturing system.* If the company plans to change to a material requirements planning or just-in-time system during the budget period, this will likely reduce the amount of inventory on hand.
- *Materials mix.* The mix of materials, labor, and overhead is assumed to remain the same in the cost of goods sold. A higher mix of materials would call for a higher days of inventory assumption, and vice versa.
- *Obsolescence.* If a company's products are subject to rapid obsolescence, this makes it more likely that the obsolete items will remain in stock, thereby increasing the number of inventory days on hand.
- *Production change.* If the duration of the production process increases, as may be caused by a reconfiguration of the shop floor, then the amount of inventory held in work-in-process will also increase, and vice versa.
- *Stockpiling.* If management believes that some materials will be in short supply during the budget period, it may authorize the stockpiling of those materials in greater than normal quantities.

Finally, it is possible that there is a history of seasonal changes in the days of inventory measurement. If these changes are significant, consider using a different days of inventory measurement for each budgeted accounting period, based on the historical days of inventory measurement for each period.

Fixed Assets

The amount and timing of expenditures for fixed assets come from the capital budgeting process, and are easily transferred into a fixed asset table that can be used as a source document for the budgeted balance sheet. Further, it may be useful to include in the schedule a standard amount of capital expenditures for each new employee hired; this typically includes the cost of office furniture and computer equipment. Finally, consider including a reserve in the schedule for as-yet unspecified fixed assets. There will always be unforeseen asset purchases, so be sure to reserve some funds for them.

In addition, you can add to the table a calculation of the depreciation associated with newly-acquired assets. Also include an estimate of the depreciation associated with *existing* assets, which you can easily derive either from the fixed asset tracking spreadsheet or software. This information is used in the budgeted income statement.

The following example illustrates the concepts of scheduling fixed assets and depreciation.

EXAMPLE

Quest Adventure Gear plans to hire 10 administrative staff into one of its divisions during the budget year, and also plans to buy a variety of fixed assets. The following schedule itemizes the major types of fixed assets and the timing of their acquisition. It also includes a summary of the depreciation for both the existing and to-be-acquired assets.

	Quarter 1	Quarter 2	Quarter 3	Quarter 4
Fixed asset purchases:				
Furniture and fixtures	$28,000	$0	$0	$32,000
Office equipment	0	40,000	0	0
Production equipment	100,000	25,000	80,000	0
Vehicles	32,000	0	32,000	0
Unspecified purchases	15,000	15,000	15,000	15,000
Subtotal	$175,000	$80,000	$127,000	$47,000
Purchases for new hires:				
Headcount additions	3	2	1	4
$6,000 × New hires	$18,000	$12,000	$6,000	$24,000
Total fixed asset purchases	$193,000	$92,000	$133,000	$71,000
Depreciation on new purchases:				
Furniture and fixtures (7 year)	$1,000	$1,000	$1,000	$2,142
Office equipment (5 year)	0	2,000	2,000	2,000
Production equipment (10 year)	2,500	3,125	5,125	5,125
Vehicles (5 year)	1,600	1,600	3,200	3,200
Unspecified purchases (5 year)	750	1,500	2,250	3,000
Subtotal	$5,850	$9,225	$13,575	$15,467
Depreciation on existing assets	108,000	107,500	105,000	99,500
Total depreciation	$113,850	$116,725	$118,575	$114,967

It is not usually necessary to budget for the derecognition of fixed assets from the accounting records, since these items typically have such a small remaining book value that their presence on the balance sheet is immaterial.

Accounts Payable

A significant short-term liability listed in the balance sheet is accounts payable. You can estimate it with a reasonable amount of precision, because there is usually a constant relationship between the level of credit purchases from suppliers and the amount of unpaid accounts payable. Thus, if you can calculate the days of accounts payable that are usually on hand, then you can relate it to the estimated amount of credit purchases per accounting period and derive the ending accounts payable balance. The formula for accounts payable days is:

$$\frac{\text{Accounts payable}}{\text{Annual credit purchases} \div 365}$$

Or, if the days of accounts payable changes by quarter, divide the quarterly credit purchases by the number of days in the quarter. The calculation is:

$$\frac{\text{Accounts payable}}{\text{Quarterly credit purchases} \div 91}$$

The estimation concept is illustrated in the following example.

EXAMPLE

Quest Adventure Gear has a division whose annual purchases on credit in the past year were $4,250,000. Its average accounts payable balance during that period was $410,000. The calculation of its accounts payable days is:

$$\frac{\$410{,}000 \text{ accounts payable}}{\$4{,}250{,}000 \text{ annual credit purchases} \div 365}$$

$$= 35 \text{ accounts payable days}$$

Quest expects that the division will continue to have roughly the same proportion of credit terms with its suppliers through the budget period, so it uses the same accounts payable days amount to derive the ending accounts payable for each budget period as follows:

	Quarter 1	Quarter 2	Quarter 3	Quarter 4
Purchases on credit (monthly)	$350,000	$380,000	$390,000	$400,000
Accounts payable days assumption	35 days	35 days	35 days	35 days
Ending accounts payable*	$408,000	$443,000	$455,000	$467,000

* Calculated as monthly purchases on credit × (35 days ÷ 30 days)

The problem with the calculation of accounts payable is where to find the information about credit purchases. To calculate the amount of credit purchases, start with the total expenses for the measurement period and subtract from it all payroll and payroll tax expenses, as well as depreciation and amortization. There are other adjusting factors, such as expense accruals and payments made in cash, but this simple calculation should approximate the amount of purchases on credit.

Additional Estimation Elements

There are a few other line items in the balance sheet that require estimation for the budget period. These items are usually adjusted manually, rather than through the use of any formulas. They are:

- *Prepaid expenses.* This line item includes expenses that were paid in advance, and which therefore may be charged to expense at some point during or after the budget period. Examples of prepaid expenses are prepaid rent and insurance. These items may not change in proportion to the level of general corporate activity, so it is best to track them on a separate spreadsheet and manually determine when there will be additions to and deletions from the account.
- *Other assets.* There are likely to be a smorgasbord of stray assets on a company's books that are aggregated into this account. Examples of other assets are rent deposits, payroll advances, and accounts receivable from

company officers. As was the case with prepaid expenses, these items may not change in proportion to the level of corporate activity, so track them separately and manually adjust the budget for any changes in them.

- *Income taxes payable.* If a company is earning a taxable profit, then it must make estimated tax payments on the 15th days of April, June, September, and December. You can either schedule these payments to equal the tax paid in the previous year, or a proportion of the actual tax liability in the budget year. Budgeting for this liability based on the tax paid in the previous year is quite simple. If you choose to instead budget for a liability equal to a proportion of the actual tax liability in the budget year, then use the effective tax rate expected for the entire year.

  If you are budgeting for this liability based on the net income in the budget year, it can be difficult to estimate. You may be using accelerated depreciation for the calculation of taxable income, as well as other deferred tax recognition strategies that cause a difference between taxable and actual net income. If such is the case, track these differences in a supporting budget schedule.

- *Accrued liabilities.* There may be a variety of accrued liabilities, such as unpaid vacation time, unpaid wages, and unpaid property taxes. In some cases, such as property taxes, the liability is unlikely to vary unless the company alters its property ownership, and so can be safely extended through the budget period with no alterations. In other cases, such as unpaid vacation time and unpaid wages, there is a direct correlation between the general level of corporate activity (such as headcount) and the amount of the liability. In these cases, use a formula to adjust the liability based on the appropriate underlying measure of activity.

- *Notes payable.* This can encompass loans and leases. Most of these items are on fixed repayment schedules, so a simple repayment table is usually sufficient for tracking the gradual reduction of notes payable. Also, the amount of each periodic debt repayment should be deducted from the amount of cash on hand. Additions to the notes payable line are addressed in the financing budget.

- *Equity.* The equity section of the balance sheet is composed of a beginning balance that is simply rolled forward from the previous period, a retained earnings balance into which you incorporate any gains and losses as the budget period progresses over time, and various equity-related financing issues that are addressed in the financing budget.

There are a number of line items shown here, so be prepared to maintain a number of supporting schedules to keep track of the ending balances for them.

The Cash Line Item

After filling in all other parts of the balance sheet, the cash line item becomes the "plug" entry to make the statement balance. Just because you enter an amount in the cash line item does not mean that the company will necessarily generate that amount of cash. An early iteration of a budgeted balance sheet has a strange way of revealing an astonishing surplus of cash! Instead, once you have created the initial version of the balance sheet, test it to see if all of the line items are reasonable. Use the following techniques to do so:

- *Growth impact.* If the company is planning on substantial growth, this means that the investment in accounts receivable and inventory should grow significantly, which will consume cash. Conversely, if the company plans to shrink in size, it should be converting these same items into cash. Thus, if the proposed balance sheet appears to be retaining a consistent amount of working capital through the budget period, irrespective of the sales level, you probably need to revise the working capital line items.
- *Historical comparison.* Compare all line items in the proposed balance sheet to the same line items in the balance sheet for various periods in the preceding year. Are the numbers about the same, or are they approximately in the same proportions to each other? If not, investigate why there are differences.
- *Turnover analysis.* Compare the amount of accounts receivable, inventory, and accounts payable turnover in the proposed budget to the actual turnover ratios for these items in the preceding year. Unless you are making significant structural changes in the business, it is likely that the same turnover ratios should apply to the budget period.

The following table shows the impact on cash of turnover changes in the balance sheet. In particular, note the changes in the "Caused By" column that are required to alter turnover levels. If management does not take any of these actions, then do not budget for a change in turnover – instead, the business will likely experience the same turnover as last year.

Turnover Table

Type of Turnover	Cash Impact	Caused By
Accounts receivable turnover - Increase	Cash increases	More aggressive collection activity, tighter credit policy
Accounts receivable turnover - Decrease	Cash decreases	Less collection activity, looser credit policy
Inventory turnover – Increase	Cash increases	Reduce safety stock levels, use just-in-time deliveries, reduce number of product options
Inventory turnover – Decrease	Cash decreases	Increase safety stock levels, engage in bulk purchases
Accounts payable turnover - Increase	Cash decreases	Pay suppliers quicker, take early payment discounts, use suppliers with shorter payment terms
Accounts payable turnover - Decrease	Cash increases	Pay suppliers more slowly, stop taking early payment discounts, use suppliers with longer payment terms

If you are satisfied that the budgeted balance sheet appears reasonable after these tests, then the cash line item may also be considered achievable.

The Financing Budget

Once a first draft of the budget has been prepared and a preliminary balance sheet constructed, you will get an idea of the cash requirements of the business, and can then construct a financing budget.

This budget addresses the need of a business for *more* cash. You can construct a financing budget that addresses this need in two ways:

- *Obtain a loan*. At a minimum, it is usually possible to obtain an asset-based loan (i.e., one that is backed by a company's accounts receivable and inventory). You will need to monitor the allowable amount of this debt by submitting a borrowing base certificate to the lender at regular intervals. However, these loans are also limited to a proportion of those assets, and so may not be overly large. Other loans that are not tied to assets usually carry a substantially higher interest rate.

- *Sell stock*. If the existing shareholders are amenable, consider selling stock in the company to current or new investors. Unlike a loan, there is no obligation to pay the money back, so this addition to equity reduces the financial risk of the company. However, investors expect a high return on their investment in stock through an increase in the value of the company.

In addition to these financing solutions, you might also consider going back into the main budget and making one or more of the following changes, thereby altering the amount of cash needed by the business:

- *Cost reduction.* There may be some parts of the business where expenses can be pruned in order to fund more activities elsewhere. Across-the-board reductions are usually a bad idea, since some parts of the business may already be running at a minimal expenditure level, and further reductions would cut into their performance.
- *Discretionary items.* If there are discretionary expenditures in the budget whose absence will not have an immediate impact on the business, consider reducing or eliminating them or changing the date on which you purchase them.
- *Dividends.* If there are dividends planned that have not yet been authorized by the board of directors, then consider either reducing them or delaying the payment date.
- *Sales growth.* If the budgeted level of sales is creating a significant requirement for more working capital and capital expenditures, consider reducing the amount of planned growth to meet the amount of financing that is available.
- *Sell assets.* If there is a strong need for cash that is driven by an excellent business opportunity, it may be time to sell off assets in lower-performance parts of the business and invest the funds in the new opportunity.

Once you have made all of the preceding adjustments, construct the financing budget. It should contain an itemization of the cash position as stated in the budgeted balance sheet, after which you itemize the various types of financing needed to ensure that the company maintains a positive cash balance at all times. In addition, there should be a section that derives from the balance sheet the total amount that the company can potentially borrow against its assets (the borrowing base); this establishes an upper limit on the amount of borrowing. The following example illustrates the concept of the financing budget.

EXAMPLE

Quest Adventure Gear has completed a first draft of its budget, and finds that there are several cash shortfalls during the budget period.

The controller constructs the following financing budget to address the problem.

	Quarter 1	Quarter 2	Quarter 3	Quarter 4
Available borrowing base:				
Ending inventory	$1,200,000	$1,280,000	$1,310,000	$1,350,000
Ending trade receivables	1,800,000	1,850,000	1,920,000	1,980,000
Allowable inventory (60%)	720,000	768,000	786,000	810,000
Allowable receivables (80%)	1,440,000	1,480,000	1,536,000	1,584,000
Total borrowing base	$2,160,000	$2,248,000	$2,322,000	$2,394,000
Preliminary ending cash balance	-$320,000	-$480,000	-$600,000	-$680,000
Debt Funding:				
Beginning loan balance	$2,000,000			
Available debt*	160,000	88,000	74,000	72,000
Adjusted ending cash balance	-$160,000	-$232,000	-$278,000	-$286,000
Equity Funding:				
Stock issuance	$400,000	0	0	0
Final ending cash balance	$240,000	$168,000	$122,000	$114,000

* Calculated as the total borrowing base minus existing debt

The financing budget reveals that Quest has already used most of the debt available under its loan agreement, and is only able to incrementally borrow in each quarter as the amount of underlying assets gradually increases. To fund the remaining cash shortfall, Quest plans to sell $400,000 of stock to investors in the first quarter. This not only provides enough cash to cover the projected shortfall, but also leaves a small residual cash buffer.

If the financing budget includes a provision for more debt, then also include a line item in the budgeted income statement to address the associated incremental increase in interest expense. This means that there is a feedback loop between the financing budget and the balance sheet from which it draws its beginning cash balance; your financing solutions may impact the beginning cash balance upon which the financing budget is based, which in turn may impact the amount of financing needed.

The Budgeted Balance Sheet

The budgeted balance sheet is derived from all of the preceding discussions in this chapter about the components of the balance sheet. The balance sheet should be compiled in two parts: a detailed compilation that contains a variety of calculations, and a summary-level version that is indistinguishable from a normal balance sheet. The following sample of a detailed balance sheet compilation includes a discussion of each line item. The numbers in the sample are irrelevant – we are only trying to show how the balance sheet is constructed.

Sample Detailed Balance Sheet Compilation

Line Item	Source	Amount
Assets		
Cash	The amount needed to equalize both sides of the balance sheet	$225,000
Accounts receivable	Based on sales by period and days receivables outstanding	450,000
Inventory	Based on cost of goods sold by period and days of inventory on hand	520,000
Prepaid expenses	Based on beginning balance and adjusted for specific changes	55,000
Fixed assets	Based on beginning balance and changes in the capital budget	1,490,000
Accumulated depreciation	Based on beginning balance and changes in the capital budget	-230,000
Other assets	Based on beginning balance and adjusted for specific changes	38,000
Total assets		$2,548,000
Liabilities		
Accounts payable	Based on credit purchases and days of accounts payable	$182,000
Accrued liabilities	Based on schedule of specific liabilities or based on corporate activity	99,000
Income taxes payable	Based on either the tax paid in the previous year or a proportion of the actual tax liability in the current year	75,000
Notes payable	Based on the beginning balance	720,000
- Debt repayments	Based on a schedule of required repayments	-120,000
+ New debt	From the financing budget	90,000
Total liabilities		$1,046,000
Equity		
Retained earnings	Based on the beginning balance	802,000
- Dividends	As per management instructions	-75,000
- Treasury stock purchases	As per management instructions	-50,000
+ Profit/loss	From the budgeted income statement	475,000
+ Stock sales	From the financing budget	350,000
Total equity		$1,502,000
Total liabilities and equity		$2,548,000

For the purposes of the budgeted balance sheet, we are not overly concerned with whether an asset or liability is classified as short-term or long-term. Given the inevitable inaccuracies inherent in a budgeted balance sheet, there is little point in making this designation. Further, the information is not useful from the perspective of constructing a budget, since it is not used by management for decision making.

Accompanying Documentation

An explanatory text may be included with the master budget, explaining the company's strategic direction, how the budget will assist in accomplishing specific goals, the key assumptions upon which the budget is based, and the management actions needed to achieve the budget. Examples of some key assumptions commonly found in a budget are:

- *Bottleneck.* State what the company's constrained resource is, and any expected changes to it during the budget period.
- *Capital purchases cost per new employee.* If you hire a new employee, there is an assumed start-up cost for each person, such as a desktop or laptop computer, telephone, and office furniture. These expenditures can automatically appear in the budget whenever there is a net increase in headcount.
- *Commodity costs.* State the cost at which you expect to pay for key commodities used by the company during the budget period.
- *Wage increase percentage.* Though there may be a variety of pay rate changes across the entire group of employees, there will likely be an average rate of wage increase that management does not want to exceed.

It is also useful to append to the master budget a set of key performance metrics that are calculated based on the information in the budget. For example, these metrics may include accounts receivable turnover, inventory turnover, sales per salesperson, and earnings per share. These metrics are useful for pointing out to management the areas in which improvement actions are needed to enhance the probability of achieving the financial goals in the budget.

Further, consider stating the time periods when specific step costs are to be incurred, the amount of those costs, and the triggering events that will cause the expenditures. For example, you could point out that sales in the third quarter will exceed the capacity of the existing production line by 15 percent, which will require an investment of $500,000 in a supplemental production line. Management needs to be aware of all major step costs, so that they can determine whether actual activity levels still require these investments as predicted in the budget.

When compiling this documentation, keep it as succinct as possible. Managers do not want to wade through hefty supporting documents for the information they need. If possible, try to keep all accompanying documentation down to just a few pages.

Summary

In a smaller business, the key component of the master budget is the budgeted income statement. It is easily compiled from the other budgets already addressed in this book, and does a good job of showing managers how their budget assumptions translate into corporate financial performance. However, this simple version of the master budget lacks a comparison to the financial position of the business during the budget period. This additional information is needed to ascertain whether the company has the financial resources to support the level of business activity shown in the budgeted income statement. Consequently, it is very useful to also construct a budgeted balance sheet; this document is more difficult to create, requiring a number of additional calculations. Despite these difficulties, the balance sheet can provide useful indicators of whether there are problems with the assumptions used to construct the budget.

Chapter 17
Nonprofit Budgeting

Introduction

A budget is a necessary financial control for a nonprofit organization, which typically operates with little room for financial shortfalls. In this chapter, we describe the unique aspects of revenue and expense budgeting that pertains to nonprofits.

The Revenue Budget

The amount of revenue that a nonprofit expects to receive during the next year drives the amount of expenditures that it can undertake during that period. This means that a reasonable method for predicting revenue is critical to a nonprofit. There are several ways to quantify predicted revenue. If an organization relies upon specific grants to generate most of its revenue, one budgeting method is to itemize expected receipts by grant, as noted in the following exhibit.

Budgeting can be especially difficult for a nonprofit when it is uncertain of the sources of support that it will need in the upcoming budget period. If so, one option is to create a Resource Development line item, which is used to budget for sources of support that are not yet apparent. This subcategory is shown in the following exhibit, where resource development comprises the bulk of all budgeted revenue.

Sample Revenue Budget by Grant

Contract	Quarter 1	Quarter 2	Quarter 3	Quarter 4
Existing Grants:				
HHS #01327	$175,000	$175,000	$25,000	$--
HHS #AC124	460,000	460,000	460,000	25,000
HHS #BG0047	260,000	280,000	280,000	260,000
Subtotal	$895,000	$915,000	$765,000	$285,000
Resource Development:				
DOA Farm Analysis	$--	$--	$150,000	$300,000
BLM Lease Analysis	--	210,000	600,000	550,000
NGS Survey Review	10,000	80,000	80,000	100,000
Subtotal	$10,000	$290,000	$830,000	$950,000
Totals	$905,000	$1,205,000	$1,595,000	$1,235,000

If a nonprofit runs one or more programs, an alternative is to itemize expected revenues by program, with additional detail located in a supporting schedule. An example for several programs follows.

Sample Program Revenue Budget

	Quarter 1	Quarter 2	Quarter 3	Quarter 4
Program A revenue	$905,000	$1,205,000	$1,595,000	$1,235,000
Program B revenue	880,000	920,000	1,115,000	970,000
Totals	$1,785,000	$2,125,000	$2,710,000	$2,205,000

Or, if a large amount of revenue comes from individual donors, it can make sense to itemize expected receipts from the largest donors, and then cluster all smaller expected donations into a single line item. Doing so focuses attention on contacting the largest existing donors to maintain high levels of contact, thereby improving the odds of receiving a continuing stream of donations from them. The following sample exhibit illustrates the layout of this format. Note that the individual donors listing is in order by size of expected donations, so the most attention is paid to those at the top of the list.

Sample Donor Revenue Budget

	Quarter 1	Quarter 2	Quarter 3	Quarter 4
Smith, Donald	$55,000	$-	$10,000	$45,000
Arbuckle, Mary	38,000	25,000	15,000	5,000
Davis, Eduardo	50,000	-	-	-
Emery, Francis	-	24,000	-	24,000
Bingo, Marco	-	-	40,000	-
McKenzie, Elwood	7,000	7,000	7,000	7,000
Druthers, Kinsey	-	25,000	-	-
All other donors	70,000	35,000	60,000	85,000
Totals	$220,000	$116,000	$132,000	$166,000

If a nonprofit earns revenues from several or all of the sources just described, it can make sense to derive a master revenue budget that aggregates all of the various revenue sources, with each source summarized in a single line item. For example, the following exhibit aggregates all of the revenue totals from the preceding sample exhibits.

Sample Master Revenue Budget

	Quarter 1	Quarter 2	Quarter 3	Quarter 4
Contract revenue	$905,000	$1,205,000	$1,595,000	$1,235,000
Program revenue	1,785,000	2,125,000	2,710,000	2,205,000
Donor revenue	220,000	116,000	132,000	166,000
Totals	$2,910,000	$3,446,000	$4,437,000	$3,606,000

There can be a considerable amount of uncertainty in the projected revenue figures. If so, consider conducting a periodic recasting of the budget to see if the projections have changed, and altering expenditures to be in proper alignment with expected revenues.

The Management and Administration Budget

Those activities not directly related to fundraising or programs are considered to fall within the management and administration classification. This classification provides operational support to the entire nonprofit organization, and ensures that other activities run as smoothly as possible. The main activity areas provided by it include:

- Accounting and finance services
- Facility maintenance
- Human resources services
- Information technology maintenance
- Risk management and legal services
- Strategic planning and budgeting

The proportion of expenditures assigned to this classification is of deep concern to donors, who do not want to see their contributions "squandered" on areas outside of the core programs offered by a nonprofit. For this reason, the executive directors of nonprofits pay considerable attention to paring back management and administration expenses. They also have a deep understanding of the extent to which management and administration expenses can be allocated to programs.

The following example illustrates the basic layout of a management and administration budget.

EXAMPLE

Newton Education compiles the following management and administration budget, which is organized by expense line item:

	Quarter 1	Quarter 2	Quarter 3	Quarter 4
Audit fees	$35,000	$0	$0	$0
Bank fees	500	500	500	500
Insurance	5,000	5,500	6,000	6,000
Payroll taxes	10,000	10,500	10,500	11,000
Property taxes	0	25,000	0	0
Rent	11,000	11,000	11,000	14,000
Salaries	140,000	142,000	144,000	146,000
Supplies	2,000	2,000	2,000	2,000
Travel and entertainment	4,500	8,000	4,000	4,000
Utilities	2,500	3,000	3,000	4,000
Other expenses	1,500	1,500	1,500	2,000
Total expenses	$212,000	$209,000	$182,500	$189,500

The preceding example reveals a common characteristic of most line items in the management and administration budget, which is that most costs are fixed over the short term, and so only vary slightly from period to period. The exceptions are pay increases and scheduled events, such as audits. Otherwise, the main reason for a sudden change in an expense is a step cost, such as increasing the headcount.

If you simply carry forward these costs into the budget from the previous year, you will not know if the organization is being efficient in its expenditures. To find out, consider separating the management and administration costs into their constituent parts, such as the cost of the accounting, treasury, and human resources departments, and calculate each of these costs as a percentage of total revenues. Then compare these percentages to the industry average or a best-in-class benchmark. The comparison may reveal that some parts of this budget are operating at excessively high cost levels.

The Fundraising Budget

Fundraising is the sales and marketing component of a nonprofit, tasked with raising funds via a variety of methods to support the expenditure level of the organization. The activities of this group can include:

- Grant proposals
- Direct solicitation of individuals and businesses for contributions
- E-mail solicitations through a mailing list of donors
- Passive solicitation via a nonprofit's website
- Seminars regarding estate planning
- Fundraising events, such as charity balls and art auctions
- Contacting employers regarding matching contributions

The fundraising budget contains somewhat different expense line items than are usually found in the management and administration budget. There is a greater emphasis on compensation, advertising, and travel expenditures. An example of this budget format follows:

Fundraising Budget by Expense Type

Expense Type	Quarter 1	Quarter 2	Quarter 3	Quarter 4
Salaries and wages	$270,000	$275,000	$320,000	$380,000
Payroll taxes	22,000	27,000	35,000	41,000
Promotions	0	50,000	85,000	42,000
Advertising	20,000	22,000	22,000	28,000
Grant research	0	0	35,000	0
Travel and entertainment	40,000	20,000	80,000	70,000
Office expenses	15,000	15,000	21,000	21,000
Other	5,000	5,000	5,000	5,000
Totals	$382,000	$484,000	$723,000	$727,000

When reviewing the fundraising budget, there are several that call for detailed analysis. The first is the relationship between the expenditures *for* the fundraising staff and corresponding revenues generated *by* that staff. Consider the following factors when deciding whether this expenditure is reasonable:

- *Historical trend.* If the fundraising staff has historically been able to generate a certain amount of contributions per person, it should be quite difficult for them to exceed this productivity level in the new budget year, so be wary of large presumed productivity increases.
- *Diminishing returns.* It is increasingly difficult to extract more donations from existing target groups, so question such revenue increases where the related expenses do not increase to an even greater extent.

The second area to investigate is the justification for promotional expenditures. The fundraising staff should provide an analysis of the estimated number of target contributors reached, and the conversion rate for those contributors. This is a difficult analysis area, since projections are difficult to verify.

Program and Grant Budgets

The reason why a nonprofit exists is to provide some kind of service, which is called a *program*. Examples of programs are providing meals to the elderly, offering free training classes, and distributing printed materials about safety hazards.

A program generates its own revenue and incurs its own expenses, so the budget for it looks just like the statement of activities; there are one or more revenue line items, which are offset by a set of expected expenses. We do not provide a sample budget for a program, since the types of revenues and expenses incurred will vary substantially by program. However, the general budget format already shown for the management and administration budget will serve for a program, with the addition of revenues.

When a government issues a grant to a nonprofit, there is usually an expectation that the nonprofit will formulate a budget for the funds to be spent. This budget is then loaded into the grants tracking module of the accounting software, and is used as a monitoring tool for funds expended against specific grants.

It is especially difficult to allocate expenses to grants, since some expenses (such as staff time) may involve several different grants or other activities. If there is not a consistent or logical basis of allocation for these expenditures, it is quite likely that, over time, the amounts charged against grant budgets will not be supportable. This can be a significant problem when grant expenditures are audited. Consequently, the accounting staff needs to spend an especially large amount of time examining budget-versus-actual reports for grants, to ensure that allocations were correctly assigned to each grant.

Summary

It is critical for a nonprofit to maintain and monitor a budget, since nonprofits rarely have sufficient cash reserves to soften the impact of excessively low revenues or high expenses. This means that the management team should build a review of the budget versus actual report into its monthly (if not weekly) management meetings. If this analysis indicates that there will be a funding shortfall, the team must take action at once to remedy the situation.

Chapter 18
Flexible Budgeting

Introduction

The traditional budget model is a static one – that is, it does not change even if the underlying activity level of the business differs during the budget period from the level assumed when the budget was constructed. This is a major problem when the actual activity level *does* change – which is extremely common. A possible solution to the static budget is the flexible budget. In this chapter, we describe how a flexible budget works, and its advantages and disadvantages.

The Flexible Budget

A flexible budget calculates different expenditure levels for variable costs, depending upon changes in the amount of actual revenue or other activity measures. You input the actual revenues or other activity measures into the flexible budget once an accounting period has been completed, and it generates a budget that is specific to the inputs. You then compare the budget versus actual information for control purposes. The steps needed to construct a flexible budget are:

1. Identify all fixed costs and segregate them in the budget model.
2. Determine the extent to which all variable costs change as activity measures change.
3. Create the budget model, where fixed costs are "hard coded" into the model, and variable costs are stated as a percentage of the relevant activity measures or as a cost per unit of activity measure.
4. Enter actual activity measures into the model after an accounting period has been completed. This updates the variable costs in the flexible budget.
5. Enter the resulting flexible budget for the completed period into the accounting system for comparison to actual expenses.

This approach varies from the more common static budget, which contains nothing but fixed amounts that do not vary with actual revenue levels. Budget versus actual reports under a flexible budget tend to yield variances that are much more relevant than those generated under a static budget, since both the budgeted and actual expenses are based on the same activity measure. This means that the variances will likely be smaller than under a static budget, and will also be highly actionable. The following two examples show a flexible budget in action.

EXAMPLE

Quest Adventure Gear has a budget of $10 million in revenues and a $4 million cost of goods sold. Of the $4 million in budgeted cost of goods sold, $1 million is fixed, and $3 million varies directly with revenue. Thus, the variable portion of the cost of goods sold is 30% of revenues. Once the budget period has been completed, Quest finds that sales were actually $9 million. If it used a flexible budget, the fixed portion of the cost of goods sold would still be $1 million, but the variable portion would drop to $2.7 million, since it is always 30% of revenues. The result is that a flexible budget yields a budgeted cost of goods sold of $3.7 million at a $9 million revenue level, rather than the $4 million that would be listed in a static budget.

EXAMPLE

Quest Adventure Gear has always budgeted for sales of its polycarbonate climbing helmets using a static budget, but sales have differed markedly from expectations, resulting in large variances in its production budget. For the new budget year, Quest is experimenting with a flexible budget. This budget is divided into variable cost and fixed cost components, with the variable costs being tied to the number of unit sales of the helmet. The resulting budget is shown in the following table, which notes both budgeted and actual results for the first month of the budget period.

Helmet Production Department	Budgeted Unit Costs	Budget January	Actual January	Variances
Revenue (at $90/unit)		$135,000	$135,000	$0
Units sold		1,500	1,500	
Variable costs:				
Helmet components	$21.50	32,250	33,100	-850
Fixed costs:				
Direct labor crewing		18,000	19,500	-1,500
Manufacturing overhead		41,500	40,750	750
Gross margin		$43,250	$41,650	-$1,600

The budget model multiplies the $21.50 budgeted unit cost of the helmet components by the 1,500 actual units sold to arrive at budgeted variable costs for the month of $32,250. All other costs shown in the budget are fixed.

You can create a flexible budget that ranges in level of sophistication. Here are several variations on the concept:
- *Basic flexible budget.* At its simplest, the flexible budget alters those expenses that vary directly with revenues. There is typically a percentage built into the model that is multiplied by actual revenues to arrive at what expenses should be at a stated revenue level. In the case of the cost of goods sold, a cost per unit may be used, rather than a percentage of sales.
- *Intermediate flexible budget.* Some expenditures vary with other activity measures than revenue. For example, telephone expenses may vary with

changes in headcount. If so, you can integrate these other activity measures into the flexible budget model.

- *Advanced flexible budget*. Expenditures may only vary within certain ranges of revenue or other activities; outside of those ranges, a different proportion of expenditures may apply. A sophisticated flexible budget will change the proportions for these expenditures if the measurements they are based on exceed their target ranges.

In short, a flexible budget gives a company a tool for comparing actual to budgeted performance at many levels of activity.

The Flexible Budget Variance

A flexible budget variance is any difference between the results generated by a flexible budget model and actual results. If actual revenues are inserted into a flexible budget model, this means that any variance will arise between budgeted and actual *expenses*, not revenues.

If the number of actual units sold is inserted into a flexible budget model, there can then be variances between the standard revenue per unit and the actual revenue per unit, as well as between the actual and budgeted expense levels.

For example, a flexible budget model is designed where the price per unit is expected to be $100. In the most recent month, 800 units are sold and the actual price per unit sold is $102. This means there is a favorable flexible budget variance related to revenue of $1,600 (calculated as 800 units × $2 per unit). In addition, the model contains an assumption that the cost of goods sold per unit will be $45. In the month, the actual cost per unit turns out to be $50. This means there is an unfavorable flexible budget variance related to the cost of goods sold of $4,000 (calculated as 800 units × $5 per unit). In aggregate, this works out to an unfavorable flexible budget variance of $2,400.

In general, the total flexible budget variance should be smaller than the total variance that would be generated if a fixed budget model were used, since the unit volume or revenue level in a flexible budget model is adjusted to match actual results (which is not the case in a fixed model).

Advantages of Flexible Budgeting

The flexible budget is an appealing concept. We note three particular advantages in this section.

- *Usage in variable cost environment*. The flexible budget is especially useful in businesses where costs are closely aligned with the level of business activity, such as a retail environment where overhead can be segregated and treated as a fixed cost, while the cost of merchandise is directly linked to revenues.
- *Performance measurement*. Since the flexible budget restructures itself based on activity levels, it is a good tool for evaluating the performance of

managers - the budget should closely align to expectations at any number of activity levels. It is also a useful planning tool for managers, who can use it to model the likely financial results at a variety of different activity levels.

- *Budgeting efficiency*. Flexible budgeting can be used to more easily update a budget for which revenue or other activity figures have not yet been finalized. Under this approach, managers give their approval for all fixed expenses, as well as variable expenses as a proportion of revenues or other activity measures. Then the budgeting staff completes the remainder of the budget, which flows through the formulas in the flexible budget and automatically alters expenditure levels. This approach can improve the efficiency of the budget formulation process, especially when the management team is working its way through a large number of iterations.

These points make the flexible budget an appealing model for the advanced budget user. However, before deciding to switch to the flexible budget, consider the countervailing issues in the following section.

Disadvantages of Flexible Budgeting

The flexible budget at first appears to be an excellent way to resolve many of the difficulties inherent in a static budget. However, there are also a number of serious issues with it, which we address in the following points:

- *Formulation*. Though the flex budget is a good tool, it can be difficult to formulate and administer. One problem with its formulation is that many costs are not fully variable, instead having a fixed cost component that must be calculated and included in the budget formula. Also, a great deal of time can be spent developing cost formulas, which is more time than the typical budgeting staff has available in the midst of the budget process. Consequently, the flexible budget tends to include only a small number of variable cost formulas.

- *Closing delay*. You cannot pre-load a flexible budget into the accounting software for comparison to the financial statements. Instead, you must wait until a financial reporting period has been completed, then input revenue and other activity measures into the budget model, extract the results from the model, and load them into the accounting software. Only then can you issue financial statements that contain budget versus actual information, with variances between the two. These extra steps will delay the issuance of financial statements.

- *Revenue comparison*. In a flexible budget, there is no comparison of budgeted to actual revenues, since the two numbers are the same. The model is designed to match actual expenses to expected expenses, not to compare revenue levels. There is no way to highlight whether actual revenues are above or below expectations.

- *Applicability*. Some companies have so few variable costs of any kind that there is little point in constructing a flexible budget. Instead, they have a massive amount of fixed overhead that does not vary in response to any type of activity. For example, consider a web store that downloads software to its customers; a certain amount of expenditure is required to maintain the store, and there is essentially no cost of goods sold, other than credit card fees. In this situation, there is no point in constructing a flexible budget, since it will not vary from a static budget.

In short, a flexible budget requires extra time to construct, delays the issuance of financial statements, does not measure revenue variances, and may not be applicable under certain budget models. These are serious issues that tend to restrict its usage.

Summary

The concepts introduced in this chapter revolve around the ability of a company to identify which costs are fixed, which are variable, and which are a mix of the two. You need to be able to differentiate between these types of costs and apply them properly within the flexible budget. To assist in this examination of costs, please review the following Cost Variability chapter. It discusses how costs can vary with such factors as purchase quantities, production batch sizes, and experience. After reviewing the chapter, you will likely find that few costs are purely variable – they may vary somewhat, but not entirely, with an activity measure. This makes it more difficult to construct a flexible budget that truly flexes in a realistic manner as activity levels change.

Chapter 19
Cost Variability

Introduction

Some costs may appear to be fixed, but *all* costs are variable outside of certain limits. Since all costs vary, you need to understand their behavior in order to construct a proper budget. This chapter explores the variety of situations in which costs vary, with particular attention to whether labor costs are really variable, how purchased component costs vary with volume, whether costs actually vary at the batch level, and how costs vary over time.

Mixed Costs

A mixed cost is a cost that contains both a fixed component and a variable component. As the level of usage of a mixed cost item increases, the fixed component of the cost will not change, while the variable component will increase. The formula for this relationship is:

$$Y = a + bx$$

The components of the formula are:
    Y = Total cost
    a = Total fixed cost
    b = Variable cost per unit of activity
    x = Number of units of activity

For example, if a company owns a building, the total cost of that building in a year is a mixed cost. The depreciation associated with the asset is a fixed cost, since it does not vary from year to year, while the utilities expense will vary depending upon the company's usage of the building. The fixed cost of the building is $100,000 per year, while the variable cost of utilities is $250 per occupant. If the building contains 100 occupants, then the mixed cost calculation is:

$125,000 Total cost = $100,000 Fixed cost + ($250/occupant × 100 occupants)

EXAMPLE

Blitz Communications has a broadband contract with the local cable company, which it pays $500 per month for the first 500 megabytes of usage per month, after which the price increases by $1 per megabyte used. The following table shows the mixed cost nature of the

156

situation, where there is a baseline fixed cost, above which the cost increases at the same pace as usage:

Megabyte Usage	Variable Cost	Fixed Cost	Total Cost
500	$0	$500	$500
600	100	500	600
700	200	500	700
800	300	500	800
900	400	500	900

Mixed costs are common in a corporation, since many departments have a certain amount of baseline fixed costs in order to support any activities at all, and also incur variable costs to provide varying quantities of service above the baseline level of support. Thus, the cost structure of an entire department can be said to be a mixed cost.

A common question to deal with is how much a product costs. The quickest route to an answer is to extract the cost from a product's bill of materials. Here is an example of a typical bill of materials (for a desk phone):

Component	Quantity	Cost/Each	Total Cost
Base	1	$2.50	$2.50
Keypad	1	0.45	0.45
Microphone	1	0.65	0.65
Cord	1	0.80	0.80
Shell	1	3.75	3.75
Speaker	1	1.15	1.15
Overhead	--	4.20	4.20
			$13.50

The sample bill of materials has a total cost of $13.50, and you may be tempted to answer any inquiries with that number. However, the bill is essentially a mixed cost, because the first six components are completely variable, while the seventh item (overhead) is fixed.

How fixed is the overhead cost listed in the bill of materials? Let us suppose that the overhead is comprised of costs related to the production line on which the phone is built, the costs traceable to the production line are $42,000 per month, and the line manufactures 1,000 phones per month. If the production line manufactures one less unit per month, it will still incur $42,000 of costs. Thus, over the indicated time span, the overhead cost assigned to the phone is entirely fixed.

Because of the mixed nature of the costs ascribed to the phone, it would be better to inform users that the totally variable cost of the phone is $9.30, and that there is an additional fixed overhead cost of $4.20 per unit. If the user of this information needs it to develop a price for a one-time pricing situation, it is much more valuable to know about the variable cost component, and develop a price based on it, rather than on the full cost of the product.

Separating out mixed costs is only one of the issues we should consider when addressing cost variability. In particular, the cost of overhead shown in the preceding example can broken down further, as we will see in the next section.

Labor-Based Fixed Costs

The cost of labor used to manufacture goods is described as "direct labor," but in fact it behaves less like a variable cost and more like a fixed cost. The true test of a variable cost is whether it changes in direct proportion to the underlying activity (such as the production of one incremental unit). Direct labor rarely behaves in this fashion, and usually only to the extent of any piece rate bonus payments made, which is a relatively rare form of payment.

In a normal production environment, approximately the same number of direct labor employees are working every day, even if the amount of production varies somewhat. The number of workers will certainty shift over time as the production manager adjusts to the vagaries of the production schedule, but these changes are usually over a longer period than the cycle time needed to manufacture a product. Thus, there is no direct link between the production of a single unit and the labor used to create it.

Managers strongly prefer to avoid laying off production employees, even in the face of declining production. Here are several reasons why they prefer to avoid layoffs:

1. *Legal restrictions.* Some countries impose restrictions on large layoffs, requiring a notification period and sometimes large severance payments.
2. *Skills.* Employees usually have significant skill sets, and a company would have to train new employees later, when production ramps up again.
3. *Unemployment taxes.* The unemployment tax that companies pay will increase if they lay off a large number of employees.
4. *Unions.* There may be a collective bargaining agreement that restricts the company's ability to lay off workers, and which may also make it reluctant to hire more employees.

Thus, direct labor is really a fixed cost when considered in relation to the cost of a single unit of production.

Let's return to the bill of materials for the desk phone. A bill usually includes a line item for the cost of direct labor, so we will show it again with that item added:

Component	Unit Type	Quantity	Cost/Each	Total Cost
Base	Each	1	$2.50	$2.50
Keypad	Each	1	0.45	0.45
Microphone	Each	1	0.65	0.65
Cord	Each	1	0.80	0.80
Shell	Each	1	3.75	3.75
Speaker	Each	1	1.15	1.15
Direct labor	Hour	0.25	15.00	3.75
Overhead	--	--	4.20	4.20
				$17.25

The bill of material now contains two fixed costs, which are direct labor and overhead. These two costs together comprise 46% of the total cost of the product in the example, which is quite substantial. Given this cost structure, it would be best to respond to any inquires about the cost of the phone with a clear differentiation of the two types of costs. For short-term pricing decisions in particular, management needs to know that the variable cost of the phone is only $9.30 and not the full cost of $17.25.

Costs Based on Purchase Quantities

The costs of many purchased components vary considerably, based on the quantities in which they are purchased. For example, if you buy a widget in a standard supplier's economy pack of 100 units, the supplier charges $5.00 per unit. However, if you need a smaller quantity, which requires the supplier to break its normal packaging and ship the widget to you in a custom-sized shipping container, the price increases to $15.00. Further, if you need to buy in massive quantities, such as a truckload, the supplier can reduce the price further, to $3.50 per unit. Thus, the cost of a purchased component can vary substantially, depending upon the quantities in which it is purchased.

EXAMPLE

Blitz Communications is considering developing a new desktop phone. The marketing department estimates that there is a 25% chance that the phone will sell 20,000 units or less, a 60% chance that it will sell between 20,000 and 50,000 units, and a 15% chance that it will sell more than 50,000 units. The phone is to be constructed almost entirely from purchased parts, with final assembly at the Blitz factory.

The controller's cost analysis is:

Component	(25% Probability) 20,000 Units or Less	(60% Probability) 20,001 – 50,000 Units	(15% Probability) 50,000+ Units
Price/Unit	$25.00	$25.00	$25.00
Base	3.00	2.50	2.00
Keypad	0.54	0.45	0.36
Microphone	0.78	0.65	0.52
Cord	0.96	0.80	0.64
Shell	4.50	3.75	3.00
Speaker	1.38	1.15	0.92
Direct labor	3.75	3.75	3.75
Overhead	8.00	4.20	2.00
Cost Total	$22.91	$17.25	$13.19
Profit	$2.09	$7.75	$11.81
Profit %	8%	31%	47%

The analysis uses the 20,001 to 50,000 unit range as the baseline. If product sales fall below the 20,001 unit level, the analysis shows that purchased component costs will increase by 20%, and that costs will decrease by 20% if the product sells more than 50,000 units. Further, the amount of fixed overhead costs must be spread over fewer units if the product sells 20,000 units or less, with the reverse effect if it sells more than 50,000 units.

The analysis reveals the problem that management faces; there is a one in four chance that the profit of the product will severely underperform, with a lower probability of outsized profits. Consequently, management needs to decide if it should take the risk of releasing the product into the market, or of setting a lower price to attract more sales, or of reengineering the product to reduce its cost.

Costs Based on Production Batch Sizing

If a company manufactures its products primarily in-house, then it needs to be aware of how costs vary with the size of production batches.

The historical view of the cost of a production batch is that there is a very significant cost associated with setting up a new production run, and that this cost must be allocated to the components or products created during that production run. For example, it takes $10,000 of staff time to re-set several machines to produce a different product, as well as $2,000 of spoilage from initial test runs of the production line; 2,000 units are run through the production line. Therefore, the $12,000 of setup costs should be allocated to the 2,000 units at an allocation rate of $6 per unit.

But is this allocation warranted? The $10,000 of staff time used in the example was probably for salaried positions that would not have been laid off if the batch setup never occurred – they would just work on something else or be underutilized. Employees experienced in machine setups are a valuable resource, and are rarely laid off. Therefore, is there really a direct link between the efforts expended to set up

160

machines for a production batch? No. The only situation where a cost allocation would be warranted is when the setup team is paid a bonus when it completes a setup; in this situation, you could allocate the cost of the bonus to the batch, because the bonus would not have been incurred if the setup had not been completed.

However, the cost of spoilage *is* associated with a specific batch, because that cost would not have been incurred if the batch had not been set up. To continue with the same example, we should allocate the $2,000 of spoilage over the 2,000 units produced, which results in an allocation rate of $1 per unit.

Thus, costs can be linked to the presence of a production batch, but only to the extent that the costs would not have occurred if the batch had never been produced.

Cost Based on Step Costs

Costs can vary whenever they reach a step cost boundary. For example, a production manager finds that his facility can produce a maximum of 3,000 widgets per week if he uses one shift, but that he needs to start a second shift in order to meet any additional demand. When he adds on the shift, the company will have to incur certain additional fixed costs, such as the salary of a supervisor for that shift.

When a company exceeds a step cost boundary and incurs a new step cost, how does this impact the cost of an individual unit of production? For incremental costing decisions, it does nothing at all, since the variable cost of producing a single unit has not changed. It has, however, increased the total overhead cost of the production system, as well as (presumably) the ability of the system to produce more units.

For the purposes of the cost variability topic of this chapter, the main consideration is the existence of any impending step costs, their amount, and how they impact the production system. When management becomes aware of an impending step cost, it needs to decide if it has a long-term need for the additional production capacity that the step cost represents, or whether it makes more sense to avoid the step cost by either turning away additional business or outsourcing it.

Time-Based Costs

All costs are variable over the long term. If a company is leasing a warehouse for ten years, then the cost of that warehouse is fixed for ten years, but is variable over a period of ten years and one day, when you can elect to not renew the lease. Further, the company could possibly sub-lease the warehouse, which makes it a variable expense within a few days. It is useful to keep in mind that there are ways to modify or eliminate supposedly immovable costs, either through the passage of time or more innovative solutions.

Some fixed costs are more immovable than others, or at least a company may have more incentive to retain some fixed costs than others. Here is a subdivision of costs that provide a different perspective on the situation, presented in order from the easiest to the most difficult to avoid:

- *Sunk costs.* A sunk cost is a cost that a company has incurred, and which it can no longer recover by any means. Do not consider a sunk cost when making the decision to continue investing in an ongoing project, since you cannot recover the cost. However, many managers continue investing in projects because of the sheer size of the amounts already invested in the past. They do not want to "lose the investment" by curtailing a project that is proving to not be profitable, so they continue pouring more cash into it. Thus, these costs have already been incurred, but there is a tendency to build upon them with more expenditures in the future.
- *Discretionary costs.* A discretionary cost is a cost or capital expenditure that can be curtailed or even eliminated in the short term without having an immediate impact on short-term profitability. However, a prolonged period of reduction in these costs can have such impacts as reducing the quality of a company's product pipeline, reducing awareness by customers, and increasing machine downtime. Examples of discretionary costs are advertising, equipment maintenance, and research and development.
- *Committed costs.* A committed cost is an investment that a company has already made and cannot recover by any means, as well as obligations already made that the business cannot get out of. For example, if a company buys a machine for $40,000 and also issues a purchase order to pay for a maintenance contract for $2,000 in each of the next three years, all $46,000 is a committed cost, because the company has already bought the machine, and has a legal obligation to pay for the maintenance.

Of the costs noted here, sunk costs have already been incurred and do not need to be incurred again, so you can make a (relatively) easy decision to not let them impact future expenditure decisions. Discretionary costs can be avoided, but the negative impact of doing so tends to build up over time. Finally, committed costs are the most difficult to avoid prior to their normal termination dates.

Most fixed costs that are considered to be fixed in the short term fall into one of these categories. All three are related in some way to the passage of time – sunk costs have already occurred, discretionary costs tend to become more important over time, and committed costs can be avoided once a certain period of time has passed. It is important to realize which category a fixed cost falls into, so that you can more easily determine its true level of variability over time.

Experience-Based Costs

If a company is in a situation where it may ramp up to much larger production volumes, the experience curve will likely take effect. The experience curve is the concept that an organization requires less time or cost to produce a product as the production volume increases. The concept is usually stated as a percentage improvement for every doubling of production volume.

The experience curve works because organizations become more efficient at very high production volumes, partially because the company continually develops new production techniques and procedures, and partially because it can afford to install more expensive automation. Even if the experience curve percentage holds through increasing volumes of production, the cost reductions gradually decline as a percentage of total costs, simply because the total amount of costs from which the percentage is derived also decline.

EXAMPLE

Blitz Communications has begun selling a new office phone model, and initial indications are that it is being received well in the marketplace. Corporate management is wondering if they should reduce the price to spur sales, and asks the controller to create an experience curve analysis of its likely cost at certain volume levels, based on the company's prior experience with other models.

The controller conducts a review of the issue over the past few years, and concludes that the company has a 6% experience curve. He develops the following table of how the experience curve will alter the cost of the product:

Production Volume	Learning Curve %	Cost Per Unit	Incremental Cost Reduction
5,000	6%	$25.00	--
10,000	6%	23.50	$1.50
20,000	6%	22.09	1.41
40,000	6%	20.76	1.33
80,000	6%	19.52	1.24
160,000	6%	18.35	1.17

Management examines the table and concludes that the telephone has the potential to sell in annual volumes of 80,000 units. The product is currently priced at $40, which yields a profit of 37.5%. Management lowers the price to $31, which yields almost the same profit at the $19.52 cost level predicted at an annual unit volume of 80,000.

The example shows that cost reductions caused by the experience curve can be substantial. Consequently, if you believe that the subject of a cost analysis may be impacted by the experience curve, be sure to include it in your analysis over the anticipated range of production volumes.

The experience curve effect tends to be less substantial if the production of the item in question is sporadic, since employees need to relearn production processes. The effect is more dramatic if a company continually manufactures a product, since employees can lock in and build upon their prior experience with the product.

The experience curve may be a particularly important cost accounting concept if you work for a company that intends to capture large amounts of market share through low pricing. These organizations use the experience curve to make assumptions about how their costs will be lower at higher volume levels, and set their prices based on having production volumes that they have not yet achieved.

This results in short-term losses at the initially lower production volumes, and then gradually improving profits as the company ramps up its production volume.

EXAMPLE

Blitz Communications decides to adopt the $31 price point that was described in the preceding example. It is selling 5,000 units of the telephone model when it adopts this price point, and gradually increases its sales over two years until it reaches the target volume of 80,000 units per year. The experience curve estimates derived in the last example prove to be correct, with resulting profits shown in the following table.

Sales Volume	Price Per Unit	Cost Per Unit	Profit Per Unit	Profit Percentage
5,000	$31.00	$25.00	$6.00	19.4%
10,000	31.00	23.50	7.50	24.2%
20,000	31.00	22.09	8.91	28.7%
40,000	31.00	20.76	10.24	33.0%
80,000	31.00	19.52	11.48	37.0%

The table reveals that, because of the cost reductions brought about by the experience curve, Blitz approximately doubles its profit percentage on the new telephone by increasing its production volumes by 16x over the two-year period.

The experience curve can be a powerful tool for an aggressive management team, but you must also factor in competitive responses. Other companies do not take a loss of market share lightly, and so will either lower their product prices as well, or roll out new products that compete more closely with your offerings. Consequently, it can be quite difficult to achieve the sales volumes and associated profit improvements shown in the last example. In reality, a company would have to drop its prices further to fend off competitors, and it would also be less likely to reach its targeted sales levels.

Incorporating Cost Variability into Reports

This chapter has shown that precise costs can be difficult to pin down, since they are only fixed within certain ranges. Outside of those ranges, costs can vary wildly. Consequently, when you issue a budget, it is very helpful to include a supplement showing the ranges within which the cost information is valid. Better yet, show the costs that would arise in the adjacent ranges, especially if you suspect that actual results may fall outside of the target range.

EXAMPLE

Blitz Communications is interested in selling one of its telephones in several other countries through distributor agreements. By doing so, it can increase the production volume of the phone from 25,000 units per year to 100,000. There is a risk that sales will not be that high, since the telephone must pass certification requirements in all of the target countries. Blitz is also exploring further distributor agreements for sales in additional countries. Blitz management assigns a probability of 25% to sales being approximately 50,000 units per year, 50% for sales being 100,000 units, and 25% that sales will reach 200,000 units. The production at the 50,000 through 100,000 unit levels can be accommodated by an existing production line, which will produce this telephone exclusively. Ramping up to 200,000 units will require construction of a new production line. The wholesale price of the product will be $50. The company estimates that the benefits from its experience curve are 6%.

Management asks the controller for an analysis of what the telephone costs will be. He constructs an analysis for all three scenarios, as follows:

	(25% Probability) 50,000 Units	(50% Probability) 100,000 Units	(25% Probability) 200,000 Units
Price per unit	$50.00	$50.00	$50.00
Components	28.00	25.00	22.00
Labor and overhead	8.00	6.00	8.00
Experience factor*	-0.48	-0.70	-1.35
Cost subtotal	35.52	30.30	28.65
Profit	$14.48	$19.70	$21.35
Profit %	29%	39%	43%

* Applied only to the labor and overhead cost.

The component cost of the phone is by far its largest cost component, and this cost declines as production volumes increase, due to volume purchase discounts. The entire overhead and labor cost of the production line is applicable to this analysis, since the line is reserved for production of this specific telephone. The cost of labor and overhead per unit declines to $6.00 at the 100,000 unit level, since these costs are being spread across the maximum number of units that the line can support. The labor and overhead cost increases to $8.00 per unit at the 200,000 unit level, because the cost of a new production line has been added.

In addition, Blitz needs to add sales, administrative, and legal staff to handle the distributors in the other countries. The costs are directly related to this telephone product, since Blitz is setting up the distributors solely to handle it. These additional costs start at $400,000 for the initial 50,000 units of production, double at the 100,000 unit level, and double again at the 200,000 unit level. These additional costs are shown in the following table, along with an analysis of the profits that can be generated at the various volume levels.

	(25% Probability) 50,000 Units	(50% Probability) 100,000 Units	(25% Probability) 200,000 Units
Gross margin per unit	$14.48	$19.70	$21.35
Units sold	50,000	100,000	200,000
Total gross margin	$724,000	$1,970,000	$4,270,000
Administration costs	400,000	800,000	1,600,000
Profit	$324,000	$1,170,000	$2,670,000

The analysis reveals that this is an extremely worthwhile endeavor, where the projected reduction in the purchase prices of components drive considerable profit improvements at the highest volume levels. Based on this information, management decides on an all-out effort to increase international sales of the product.

Giving management the extra information noted in the preceding exhibit is extremely helpful, but it also requires a great deal of extra accounting time to complete. Consequently, you do not need to include the extra range of information if the cost analysis is a routine one where actual results are likely to fall within the specified range. You can save the effort of constructing a more comprehensive analysis for those situations where there is a broad range of possible outcomes, and the monetary effects on the company from those outcomes can be severe.

The accounting staff cannot be expected to know about the uses to which a cost analysis will be put, so it helps to ask a few probing questions about analysis requests, such as:

Questions	Comments
How do you plan to use this information?	General question to get an overview of the topic.
What production volumes are expected?	Determine the probability that the most likely and high/low volumes will be reached.
What time period does this cover?	If the project covers a short time period, you can probably use direct costs, but will need to include full costs for a longer-term situation. If the time period is lengthy, then this may also trigger contractually-mandated changes in cost as of specific future dates.
Will this change throughput?	If the project impacts the bottleneck operation, be sure to note the impact on throughput in your report.
Will this change operating expenses?	See if there will be any specific cost reductions or increases. In particular, inquire about any step costs that may be triggered.

The answers to these questions will help determine the scope of the topic, so that you can build any cost variability into the report.

Summary

This chapter has presented a variety of issues to be aware of when determining the cost of a product, service or activity. In short, costs will vary outside of a limited range, so be sure of your assumptions before completing a budget. There may be a reasonable chance that the actual result will fall outside of the range for which you state costs; if so, include estimates of what might happen to costs in the less probable areas, so that management will have a comprehensive understanding of the most likely range of outcomes.

A related subject is constraint analysis, which holds that a company is a single production system, and that the only issue that matters is maximizing the throughput (sales minus totally variable costs) passing through the bottleneck operation. This concept is addressed in the author's *Constraint Management* book. If you are aware of the two concepts of cost variability and constraint analysis, you will have an excellent understanding of how a company creates a profit, and how to structure a budget to show which actions or events will change that profit.

Chapter 20
The Zero-Base Budget

Introduction

Zero-base budgeting is the process of conducting a thorough, top-to-bottom analysis of the need for expenditures in a budget period. It is the reverse of a more traditional technique called incremental budgeting, which involves carrying forward the budgeted or actual results from the previous period with minor adjustments. In this chapter, we present both incremental budgeting and zero-base budgeting, so that you can see the extremes of how rigorously (or not) a budget should be examined.

Incremental Budgeting

Incremental budgeting is budgeting based on slight changes from the preceding period's budgeted or actual results. This is a common approach in businesses where management does not intend to spend a great deal of time formulating budgets, or where it does not perceive any great need to conduct a thorough evaluation of the business.

The primary advantage of incremental budgeting is that it is simple to use, being based on either recent financial results or a recent budget that can be readily verified. Also, if a project requires funding for multiple years in order to achieve a certain outcome, incremental budgeting is structured to ensure that funds will keep flowing to the project.

There are several downsides of incremental budgeting that make it a less than ideal choice. The issues are:

- *Budgetary slack.* Managers tend to build too little revenue growth and excessive expenses into incremental budgets, so they will always have favorable variances. This is called *budgetary slack*.
- *Budget review.* When a budget is carried forward with minor changes, there is little incentive to conduct a comprehensive review of the budget, so that inefficiencies and budgetary slack are automatically rolled into new budgets.
- *Fosters overspending.* It fosters an attitude of "use it or lose it" in regard to budgeted expenditures, since a drop in expenditures in one period will be reflected in future periods, too.
- *Incremental in nature.* It assumes only minor changes from the preceding period, when in fact there may be major structural changes in the business or its environment that call for much more significant budget alterations.
- *Perpetuates resource allocations.* If a certain amount of funds were allocated to a specific business area in a prior budget, then the incremental budget assures that funding will be allocated there in the future, too - even if it no longer needs as much funding, or if other areas require more funding.

168

- *Risk taking.* Since an incremental budget allocates most funds to the same uses every year, it is difficult to obtain a large funding allocation for a new activity. Thus, incremental budgeting tends to foster a conservative maintenance of the status quo, and does not encourage risk taking.
- *Variance from actual.* When the incremental budget is based on a prior budget, there tends to be a growing disconnect between budgeted and actual results.

In short, incremental budgeting results in such a conservative mindset in a business that it may help destroy a company over the long term. Instead, engage in a thorough strategic re-assessment of a business when constructing a budget, as well as a detailed investigation of expenditures. The result should be significant changes in the allocation of funds from period to period, as well as targeted operational changes that are intended to improve the competitive position of the business. One process for conducting this review is called zero-base budgeting; it is explained in the next section.

Overview of Zero-Base Budgeting

A zero-base budget requires managers to justify *all* of their budgeted expenditures, rather than the more common approach of only requiring justification for incremental changes to the budget or the actual results from the preceding year. Thus, a manager is theoretically assumed to have an expenditure base line of zero (hence the name of the budgeting method). In reality, a manager is assumed to have a minimum amount of funding for basic departmental operations, above which additional funding must be justified. The intent of the process is to continually refocus funding on key business objectives, and terminate or scale back any activities no longer related to those objectives.

The basic process flow under zero-base budgeting is:
1. Identify business objectives
2. Create and evaluate alternative methods for accomplishing each objective
3. Evaluate alternative funding levels, depending on planned performance levels
4. Set priorities

The concept of paring back expenses in layers can also be used in reverse, where you delineate the specific costs and capital investment that will be incurred if you add an additional service or function. Thus, management can make discrete determinations of the exact combination of incremental cost and service for their business. This process will typically result in at least a minimum service level, which establishes a cost baseline below which it is impossible for a business to go, along with various gradations of service above the minimum.

One cost area that falls outside of the rigorous examination imposed by zero-base budgeting is the direct costs associated with providing a product or service. The zero-base concept addresses levels of service provided, whereas direct costs (such as the direct materials used in a product) *must* be incurred in order to generate a sale – there is no management decision involved.

Conversely, zero-base budgeting can be applied everywhere else in a business; such as corporate functions, research and development, engineering, maintenance, sales and marketing, procurement, and so forth. The concept is particularly applicable where costs must be expended in order to achieve a goal. For example, if a manager is assigned a budget of $1 million in the marketing area and only spends $980,000, was this good or bad? There was a cost savings, but did the manager achieve whatever goal was intended when the budget was assigned? Since zero-base budgeting establishes a link between a goal and an expenditure, you can tell if the amount spent was worthwhile. Examples of the actions that can be taken under a zero-base budget include:

Activity Area	Reduced Funding	Increased Funding
Accounting	Reduce collections and increase bad debt write-offs	Add collections staff to reduce bad debts
Information Systems	Eliminate desktop computer support	Roll out a work-from-home solution
Maintenance	Reduce to minimum maintenance level	Install preventive maintenance program
Marketing	Drop general awareness campaign	Add product survey program
Procurement	Eliminate competitive bidding	Implement supplier certification
Warehouse	Eliminate cycle counting program	Install wireless bar code scanners

The Zero-Base Budgeting Process

The key steps in zero-base budgeting are to develop *decision packages* and then rank the decision packages. The first step involves examining each discrete activity that a company engages in and associating funding with them in a document called a decision package, while the second step uses either cost/benefit or subjective analysis to rank the decision packages in order of importance. You then assemble all of the decision packages that have been approved for funding, assign them to a section of the budget (usually the responsibility area of a manager), and assign related costs to those budget sections. This results in the final budget. We will now expand upon the steps in this process.

Step 1 - Develop Decision Packages

A decision package is a document that provides management with sufficient information about a business activity to decide how to rank it against other activities, ultimately resulting in a decision to approve or reject it. The package should include the following information:

- Purpose of the activity
- Consequences to the business of not performing it
- Alternatives to performing it
- Costs and benefits associated with it
- Performance metrics related to it

You may create a different decision package for a great many business activities. Here is a sample list of business activities that may have decision packages built around them:

Functional Area	Business Activities
Accounting	Accounts payable, budgeting, collections, credit granting, financial analysis, fixed asset tracking, internal auditing, management reporting, payroll, record keeping, tax reporting, tax planning
Administration	Board of directors, building maintenance, grounds maintenance, janitorial, mail delivery, reception, safety, security, travel management
Engineering	Equipment procurement, operations analysis, plant design, process development, safety analysis, tool design, work measurement
Human resources	Benefits analysis, compensation analysis, job evaluations, labor relations, recruiting, training
Information technology	Backup management, equipment maintenance, program maintenance, system design and development
Legal	Contract reviews, contract negotiations, litigation, patent analysis, patent licensing, trademark analysis
Logistics	Inventory counting, materials transportation, putaways, picking, receiving, shipping
Procurement	Bid management, contract negotiation, purchase order processing
Production	Equipment planning, parts control, preventive maintenance, production planning, routine maintenance

Functional Area	Business Activities
Quality assurance	Finished goods testing, inbound testing, in-process testing, supplier certification
Research and development	Administrative support, equipment maintenance, research by project
Risk management	Claims management, loss prevention, insurance management, warranty claims analysis
Sales and marketing	Advertising, brochure management, catalog management, order processing, promotions, sales force management, sales forecasting, test marketing

Senior management should issue to the department managers an overview of the general level of activity that it expects the business to handle during the upcoming budget period. The department managers use this information as a guideline in the development of their decision packages. These guidelines could include such factors as:

- The estimated number of units of each product to be sold
- The identity of any new geographical regions to be served
- The number of new stores to be opened
- Changes in the size or location of company facilities
- Expected company headcount
- Planned changes to centralize or decentralize operations

When managers develop decision packages, the key item in the decision package is the discussion of activity alternatives. This can involve alternative ways to perform an activity, or different levels of effort to perform the activity. In the first case, you would describe the best way to perform the activity in detail, and then state other alternatives and why they were discarded. In the second case, you would state the minimum level of effort, and then address the result of different levels of effort in one or more additional decision packages. The minimum level of effort is considered to be at roughly 50% - 75% of the current level of operation. The alternatives presented under the level of effort classification should address the following levels of expenditure:

- Eliminate the activity entirely.
- Minimum level. This is the cost required to operate the activity at the minimum level; the company's objectives may not be achieved. This is the level below which any activity is no longer effective, and would likely be terminated.
- Current level. This is the cost required in the budget period to maintain the current level of activity. This may not be the historical cost level, since planned efficiency improvements may reduce costs, or inflation may increase costs.

172

- Increased level. This is the amount required to operate the activity at a higher level of performance.

When constructing a zero-base budget, it may be difficult to allocate overhead expenses to the various funding packages, because you cannot predict with certainty which cost packages management will select, and the levels of overhead arbitrarily allocated to the various packages may not reflect the amount of overhead that the business will actually incur. The best solution is to sidestep the problem by including all overhead expenditures in a baseline cost package that represents the minimum cost structure of the company. Any other overhead that would be incurred above this level should be associated with a higher-level cost package.

EXAMPLE

The controller of Quest Adventure Gear is developing a decision package for the accounts receivable collections activity. He describes the best way to perform the activity as follows:

Recommended decision package. Maintain the current method of using four dedicated collection personnel, at a cost of $40,000 each. This level of effort is needed to minimize bad debts and avoid shipping holds for orders currently in process.

Alternatives not recommended.

- *Shift collections to sales staff.* The sales staff has the best hands-on knowledge of customers, but engaging in collections research and contacts would reduce the time they could otherwise spend on sales activities.
- *Outsource collections.* An outside collections firm would apply aggressive pressure on customers and may therefore obtain payment sooner than usual, but might also exacerbate relations with customers, and would also be very expensive.

Level of effort.

1. **Minimum expenditure level.** Reduce the collections staff to two full-time employees. This ensures at least one contact with all customers having receivable balances over $25,000 in each month. There would be no contact with customers under this receivable balance level until receivables are at least 60 days old. **Cost = $80,000.**
2. **Current staffing level.** Retain four full-time collection employees. This ensures contact with all customers having receivable balances over $10,000, once receivables are at least 40 days old. **Cost = $160,000.**
3. **Expanded staffing.** Add an in-house attorney to the collections staff. Doing so allows us to file claims in small claims court as well as larger cases, and collect on judgments. This approach eliminates the need to outsource collections. The elimination of outsourcing fees will offset half of the incremental cost of this option. **Cost = $240,000.**

In the example, the controller could provide additional explanatory information associated with each option. For example, if he were explaining the third option under the level of effort, he might itemize the additional incremental cost associated with the third option for the next few quarters or years. By doing so, senior management would be apprised of any sudden changes in costs in later periods. The example shows that the cost of hiring the attorney in the third option was $80,000. But what if the controller expected to increase the attorney's pay by $20,000 in the following year in order provide a competitive wage? That knowledge might lead senior management to not select the third option. In the following sample format, note that we do not present this information as a single line item, but rather at its gross cost, followed by any offsetting cost savings; we then provide the net cost to the company after both issues have been combined. This gives senior management more complete information about the decision package. Also, the gross cost is certain, while the projected cost savings are an estimate, and so may be worth discussing. Thus, it makes sense to separate the two items for examination.

Sample Cost Estimate Format for Decision Package

Level of Effort Option 3 – Add Attorney

	Quarter 1	Quarter 2	Quarter 3	Quarter 4	Quarter 5	Quarter 6
Gross cost	$20,000	$20,000	$20,000	$20,000	$25,000	$25,000
Related cost savings	-5,000	-9,000	-17,000	-22,000	-24,000	-25,000
Net cost	$15,000	$11,000	$3,000	-$2,000	$1,000	$0

The sample cost estimate format shows that the attorney will gradually ramp up his or her productivity to the point where there is no net cost by the fourth quarter, but that a projected annualized pay boost of $20,000 in the fifth quarter will make this an essentially breakeven proposition.

It may also be useful to include in the decision package an itemization of the metrics that will change as the result of making a decision. Only include this information if it may have an impact on the decision of the reviewer. Also, if you include it, be sure to include historical comparisons, so that a trend line of changes is shown. The following sample shows the impact on days sales outstanding (DSO) if senior management were to select the minimum expenditure level for the collections function. Note that two-year historical comparative information is included.

Sample Metrics Format for Decision Package

	Historical 2 Years Ago	Historical 1 Year Ago	Budget Period Year 1	Budget Period Year 2
Days sales outstanding	50	49	55	62

It is also possible that, depending on the circumstances, there is only one option available. If so, state the reason(s) for the lack of alternatives. It is more likely that there are a variety of sub-optimal solutions; if so, state those solutions and the reasons why they yield inadequate results, so that senior management gains a better picture of the situation.

> **Tip:** When the manager of a functional area prepares a variety of cost packages for consideration by senior management and suspects that they may select the minimum service level, watch for cases where the manager *increases* the amount of expense at the minimum service level. Doing so allows him to actually provide the higher service level that he wants, rather than the true minimum service level that senior management wants.

The preceding example should make it clear that a vastly greater amount of work is required to prepare decision packages than would normally be the case under a traditional budgeting environment. A truly comprehensive and well thought-out set of decision packages will likely require the input of multiple people, so this approach tends to involve the opinions of more employees than just the department managers.

A manager who is directly responsible for an activity should prepare all decision packages associated with it. Senior management should evaluate all decision packages submitted and select which packages to use. That evaluation occurs in the next step.

Step 2 - Rank Decision Packages

Once the senior management team has received all decision packages from around the company, it must rank them in order of decreasing benefit or importance. This includes an analysis of the consequences associated with reducing funding from the current level for each decision package. The managers forwarding the decision packages should provide a preliminary ranking of the packages, based on their knowledge of the company's objectives. These opinions are quite valuable, since lower-level managers have the best operational knowledge of the company, and therefore of where changes in funding will have the greatest impact. In most cases, the senior management team will likely accept the recommendations of their subordinates. Only in cases where a clear change of direction or resource allocation is indicated will senior managers find it necessary to alter these recommendations.

In a large company, it may be necessary to consolidate sets of decision packages together, each describing a different scenario, and then make a decision for the entire set of decision packages. For example, the lowest level of a business may be its retail stores, for which there are separate distribution and sales systems by geographic region. Mid-level managers could select the best options for decision packages at the level of the geographic region in order to meet a company-wide goal of reducing costs. This may involve shuttering some stores and centralizing warehouses. At the executive level of the company, managers could decide among these consolidated decision packages, perhaps to pursue cost reduction in one region in order to fund more extensive growth through store expansions in a different region. This means that senior-level managers may not find it necessary to wade through each individual decision package; instead, they can select from a small number of pre-selected groupings, based on general company objectives.

> **Tip:** Be sure to include expenditures for fixed assets in the decision packages, so that managers can see the complete set of cash flows associated with a decision. This may also involve the disposition of existing fixed assets if management decides to scale back on or eliminate existing activities. You can also include in the decision packages different ways to acquire fixed assets, such as through outright purchases, leases, or short-term rentals.

In most cases, a company is constrained in its selection of decision packages by the amount of available funding. In this environment, senior management will likely only have a modest amount of discretionary funds available, and so will need to rank the decision packages to determine where to allocate funds. This is not necessarily a case of assigning funds to the decision package that has the largest monetary payback. Instead, the ranking system should highlight those areas in which additional or reduced expenditures have the greatest and least impact on company objectives, respectively. Based on both a quantitative and subjective analysis of the rankings, senior management then decides where to allocate funds.

The following table illustrates the incremental cost levels associated with a variety of decision packages. It does not include a discussion of which objectives will be met (or not) at each funding level, but does show the aggregate levels of funding included in the decision packages. This information is useful for determining the range of potential funding requirements, as well as the minimum level of funding at which a company can operate.

Summary of Decision Package Funding Levels

Decision Unit	Last Year Actual Cost	Minimum Package	Current Level	Increased Level
Accounts payable	$230,000	$170,000	$55,000	$25,000
Budgeting	60,000	0	62,000	78,000
Collections	120,000	60,000	65,000	25,000
Credit granting	50,000	0	52,000	23,000
Financial analysis	38,000	15,000	25,000	30,000
Fixed asset tracking	25,000	5,000	20,000	0
Internal auditing	48,000	24,000	25,000	15,000
Management reporting	35,000	10,000	27,000	20,000
Payroll	92,000	80,000	14,000	11,000
Record keeping	39,000	20,000	19,000	3,000
Tax reporting	65,000	50,000	15,000	7,000
Tax planning	35,000	0	40,000	30,000
Totals	$837,000	$434,000	$419,000	$267,000
Cumulative total		434,000	853,000	1,120,000
Cumulative % of last year actual		52%	102%	134%

Once the management team selects the various funding levels it wants in all functional areas, it assembles its selections into a budgeted income statement. This income statement includes the usual revenue and direct costs normally found in any income statement, but then the remainder of the document is comprised of the various decision packages. The following sample is an extremely simplified version of what this income statement might look like, using just a few decision packages.

Sample Budgeted Income Statement

	Package Type	Amount	Totals
Revenue		$8,000,000	$8,000,000
Direct materials		2,500,000	
Direct labor		1,000,000	
Fixed overhead		2,200,000	
Cost of goods sold			5,700,000
Accounting:			
Accounts payable	Current	60,000	
Collections	Minimum	40,000	
Payroll	Increased	93,000	
			193,000
Logistics:			
Putaways	Current	80,000	
Picking	Increased	45,000	
Receiving	Minimum	64,000	189,000
Production:			
Production planning	Current	155,000	
Routine maintenance	Current	109,000	
			264,000
Sales and marketing:			
Advertising	Increased	300,000	
Order processing	Minimum	100,000	
Sales force management	Current	550,000	
			950,000
Total expenses			7,296,000
Net income before taxes			$704,000

Advantages of Zero-Base Budgeting

There are a number of advantages to zero-base budgeting, which include:

- *Alternatives analysis.* Zero-base budgeting requires that managers identify alternative ways to perform each activity (such as keeping it in-house or outsourcing it), as well as the effects of different levels of spending. By forcing the development of these alternatives, the process makes managers consider other ways to run the business.
- *Budget inflation.* Since managers must tie expenditures to activities, it becomes less likely that they can artificially inflate their budgets – the change is too easy to spot.
- *Communication.* The zero-base budget should spark a significant debate among the management team about the corporate mission and how it is to be achieved.

- *Eliminate non-key activities.* A zero-base budget review forces managers to decide which activities are most critical to the company. By doing so, they can target non-key activities for elimination or outsourcing.
- *Mission focus.* Since the zero-base budgeting concept requires managers to link expenditures to activities, they are forced to define the various missions of their departments – which might otherwise be poorly defined.
- *Redundancy identification.* The review may reveal that the same activities are being conducted by multiple departments, leading to the elimination of the activity outside of the area where management wants it to be centered.
- *Required review.* Using zero-base budgeting on a regular basis makes it more likely that all aspects of a company will be examined periodically.
- *Resource allocation.* If the process is conducted with the overall corporate mission and objectives in mind, an organization should end up with strong targeting of funds in those areas where they are most needed.

In short, many of the advantages of zero-base budgeting focus on a strong, introspective look at the mission of a business and exactly how the business is allocating its resources in order to achieve that mission.

Problems with Zero-Base Budgeting

The main downside of zero-base budgeting is the exceptionally high level of effort required to investigate and document department activities; this is a difficult task even once a year, which causes some entities to only use the procedure once every few years, or when there are significant changes within the organization. Another alternative is to require the use of zero-base budgeting on a rolling basis through different parts of a company over several years, so that management can deal with fewer such reviews per year. Other drawbacks are:
- *Bureaucracy.* Creating a zero-base budget from the ground up on a continuing basis calls for an enormous amount of analysis, meetings, and reports, all of which requires additional staff to manage the process.
- *Gamesmanship.* Some managers may attempt to skew their budget reports to concentrate expenditures under the most vital activities, thereby ensuring that their budgets will not be reduced.
- *Intangible justifications.* It can be difficult to determine or justify expenditure levels for areas of a business that do not produce "concrete," tangible results. For example, what is the correct amount of marketing expense, and how much should be invested in research and development activities?
- *Managerial time.* The operational review mandated by zero-base budgeting requires a significant amount of management time.
- *Training.* Managers require significant training in the zero-base budgeting process, which further increases the time required each year.
- *Update speed.* The extra effort required to create a zero-base budget makes it even less likely that the management team will revise the budget on a continuous basis to make it more relevant to the competitive situation.

A further consideration is that, once you have created a zero-base budget, it is *still* a budget – with all of the problems related to the stifling of initiative that have already been enumerated in other chapters.

Conditional Budgeting

A variation on zero-base budgeting is the concept of *conditional budgeting*. Under conditional budgeting, you do not authorize spending the full amount of a budget for a budget period. Instead, you associate a certain amount of specific expenditures with a certain level of revenue, gross profit, or net income. Because of the structure of this type of budgeting, it is very important to segregate the various types of revenue by probability of occurrence. These levels can include:

- *Secure revenue.* This revenue is very likely, even under the most pessimistic projections. The sources of this information are likely to be the current order backlog and an analysis of historical sales that are very likely to occur again.
- *Event-driven sales.* This revenue is based on very specific events, such as a promotional campaign, opening a new store, or creating a new sales region.
- *Incremental revenue.* This category is where you place the less-likely items that arise from such factors as an estimate of increased same-store sales, increased market share, or sales to new customers who are currently serviced by competitors.

When creating the various levels of expenditure that are associated with revenue levels, there will be a minimum revenue level below which it is difficult to go, because the company's fixed costs must be incurred at the baseline cost level, and there will be substantial losses if revenues cannot offset the fixed costs.

Different types of costs are more likely to appear in the various expense tranches. You might see the following cost layers:

- *Minimum cost layer.* Contains all fixed costs, plus the bare minimum expenditures required to keep the company operational over the short-term. This level pares equipment maintenance, does not advocate new fixed asset acquisitions, and may reduce pay levels.
- *Long-term existence cost layer.* Contains those costs required to keep the company in operation over the long term. This includes adequate levels of equipment maintenance, moderate capital expenditures, and market rates of compensation.
- *Robust growth.* Contains those costs required to attain a leading position in the industry. This level includes enhanced training, funds for acquisitions, and a strong research and development department.
- *Incidental items.* Contains those items useful for "rounding out" a company's expenditures, but which are not needed to be a long-term competitive business. This level includes significant donations, improved corporate facilities, enhanced employee benefits above the level needed to normally retain employees, and so forth.

If you were to use the conditional budgeting approach to release a large amount of expenditures as soon as a specific revenue target was reached, the result would appear to be a massive step cost that may cause a considerable profit decline. Instead, it may be more prudent to set up a ranking system within each cost tranche, and then gradually authorize expenses based on this ranking as revenues increase through a predetermined range.

In summary, conditional budgeting reacts to the revenue levels being experienced by a business, releasing funds as revenues reach certain predetermined target levels. Zero-base budgeting, on the other hand, involves the specific targeting of certain expenditure levels in advance of the beginning of the budget period, so that expenditure levels are locked in during the budget period.

Summary

Zero-base budgeting is more of a management technique than strictly a budgeting system, since it calls for a periodic re-examination of the way in which a company does business. As such, it is extremely time-consuming, and may be considered a threat by those managers whose areas of responsibility could be reduced by it. Even if you do not choose to use it for these reasons, or are trying to avoid budgeting in general, it may be worthwhile to use the concept occasionally, for these reasons:

- To review the priorities of the business and how expenditures address those priorities
- To delve into the cost structure of the company's service and support activities
- To avoid across-the-board cost cutting, in favor of highly targeted and well thought-out reductions in less-critical areas
- To have plans in place for differing expenditure levels, which can be quite useful in the event of a sudden change in revenues

In short, the work required for zero-base budgeting is significant, but it may still make sense to engage in this process from time to time, just to ensure that the business is appropriately spending funds in support of its objectives.

Chapter 21
Operating without a Budget

Introduction

It can be quite time-consuming to create a budget, and you may then find that it is not especially useful, especially if the company does not take well to the command and control style of management that typically accompanies a budget. If you would prefer to avoid a budget, consider the alternative outlined in this chapter. If you are willing to modify the reporting system, decision making, and organizational structure of the business, it is entirely possible to not only operate without a budget, but to thrive while doing so. Operating without a budget is particularly useful in the following environments:

- *Rapid change.* When the business environment is rapidly changing, a business may need to reposition itself and head off in new directions within a short period of time. In this case, long-term planning is useless, and the emphasis is instead on rapidly testing new business models.
- *Rapid innovation.* When the rate of innovation in an industry is high, a business must constantly fund a portfolio of experiments. If an experiment succeeds, the company must pursue it with great vigor, which would result in the scrapping of any existing budget on short notice.

This chapter discusses the reporting systems, goal setting, management roles, compensation issues, and other changes needed to operate without a budget.

> **Related Podcast Episode:** Episode 131 of the Accounting Best Practices Podcast discusses how to operate without a budget. You can listen to it at: **accounting-tools.com/podcasts** or **iTunes**

Alternatives to the Budget

We have spent most of this book describing how to construct a budget. However, as noted in the first chapter, there are so many downsides to the entire concept of a budget that you may not want to have one at all. If so, how do you operate without one? It is quite possible to do so if you are willing to change several systems and the corporate approach to managing employees. We will briefly address both issues in this section, and then expand on the concepts in the following sections.

In order to have a properly functioning organization that operates without a budget, it is necessary to alter three systems. They are:

- *Forecast.* The forecast is a rolling forecast that is updated at frequent intervals, and especially when there is a significant event that changes the competitive environment of the business. The forecast is simply the expected outcome of the business in the near term, and is intended to be an early warning indicator of both threats and opportunities. It is completely detached from any compensation plans. The rolling forecast is covered in the next chapter.

- *Capital budgeting*. Requests for funds to buy fixed assets are accepted at all times of the year. Funding allocations are based on expected results and the needs of the requesting business unit. There is no longer a formal once-a-year capital budgeting review.
- *Goal setting*. Employees jointly set targets that are relative to the performance of other business units within the company, and against other benchmark organizations. If there is a bonus plan, it is based on these relative results.

A key point is that the forecast and capital budget are not related to targets. By separating these processes from any corporate targets, there is no incentive for employees to fudge their forecasts or fixed asset funding applications in order to earn bonuses.

From the management perspective, it is critical that senior managers step away from the traditional budget based command and control system and replace it with a great deal of local autonomy. This means that local managers can make their own decisions as long as they stay within general guidelines imposed by senior management. The focus of the organization changes from short-term budgets to medium-term to long-term financial results. There is no emphasis on budget variances, since there is no budget.

Also, senior management must trust its employees to spend money wisely. The expectation is that an employee is more likely to question the need for any expenditure, instead of automatically spending all funds granted under a budget allocation.

From a more general perspective, if a company abandons budgeting, how does it maintain any sort of direction? The answer depends upon the structure of the business and the environment within which it operates. Here are several examples of how to maintain a sense of direction:

- *Margin focus*. If a business has a relatively consistent market share, but its product mix fluctuates over time, it may be easier to focus the attention of managers on the margins generated by the business, rather than on how they achieve those margins. This eliminates the structural rigidity of a budget, instead allowing managers to obtain revenues and incur expenses as they see fit, as long as they earn the net profit margin mandated by senior management.
- *Key value drivers*. If senior management believes that the company will succeed if it closely adheres to specific value drivers, then it should have the company focus its attention on those specific items, and not hold managers to overly-precise revenue or profit goals. For example, the key to success in

an industry may be an overwhelming amount of customer support; if so, focus the entire company on maximizing that one competitive advantage.

- *Few products and very competitive environment.* If a business relies upon only a small number of products and is under constant competitive pressure, then decisions to change direction must be made quickly, and the organization must be capable of reorienting its direction in short order. This calls for a centralized management environment where a small team uses the latest information to reach decisions and rapidly drive change through the organization. In this case, a budget is not only unnecessary, but would interfere with making rapid changes. Thus, keeping employees focused on the operational direction given by senior management is vastly more important than meeting revenue or expense targets; taken to an extreme, employees may never even see the financial results of their areas of responsibility, because the focus is on operations, not financial results.

We have described in general terms how to operate without a budget. In the following sections, we will address various aspects of the no-budget environment in more detail.

Forecasting without a Budget

A good replacement for a budget is the rolling forecast. This is a simple forecast that contains information only at an aggregate level, such as:

- Revenues by product line
- Expenses aggregated into a few line items
- Customer order backlog
- Cash flow

The intent is to create a system that is easily updated, and which gives the organization a reasonable view of what the future looks like for at least the next few months. A key reason for having a rolling forecast is to bring up issues as soon as possible, so that a company can initiate corrective actions to deal with them. Thus, the goal of a rolling forecast is not to attain a specific target, but rather to provide early notice of problems and opportunities.

Employees should update their parts of the rolling forecast about once a month, and should only spend a short time doing so – a fine level of detail is not expected. Since the forecast is updated regularly, it does not have a great deal of impact on the organization if the forecast proves to be incorrect – after all, a new version will replace it shortly, so there is very little time during which a bad forecast can impact the business.

While it is customary to update a forecast at fixed periodic intervals, an alternative approach is to update it whenever there is a significant event that impacts the business. There may be events that trigger a forecast update only for a local business unit, and not for the entire company, while other events may be so significant that they warrant a complete review of the forecast. Such events should be rare, but should trigger an immediate response from the company, so that employees know what to expect.

Given the extremely short time line and minimal time allocated to updating a forecast, it rarely makes sense to derive multiple forecasts that also address best case and worst case scenarios. Instead, since the time period covered is so short, there should be minimal divergence from the best case scenario, so you can avoid creating extra forecasts.

The time period covered by the rolling forecast depends upon the ability of a company to project its activities into the future. If there are many long-term contracts, it may be entirely reasonable to compile a rolling forecast that extends more than a year into the future. However, if the company has a bad history of projecting results, then do not waste time doing so excessively far into the future. Instead, only forecast for the period where you have a reasonable expectation of achieving a prediction. If this means that the forecast period is only a few months, then that is sufficient – generating a longer-term forecast is a waste of time.

Another way of formulating the correct period for a rolling forecast is to estimate the amount of warning that employees need to trigger ongoing business activities, such as altering product prices, and launching new products and related promotions.

Tip: There may be situations where it is of some importance to make the best possible guess concerning a forecast. If so, consider setting up an internal prediction market, where large numbers of employees are encouraged to submit a best guess. Since many people may have access to information that can contribute to the forecast, the result can be unusually prescient.

The rolling forecast is accompanied by a rough work plan that is adjusted as frequently as the forecast. No one has to submit the work plan to a higher authority for approval. Instead, employees formulate their direction, document it in the work plan, and adjust it to compensate for both current and expected future events.

The rolling forecast is covered in more detail in the Rolling Forecast chapter.

Capital Budgeting

As noted in the Capital Budgeting chapter, the process of reviewing and approving capital expenditures can be lengthy and complex. How does this mesh with an environment in which there is no formal budget? Even if there is no budget, there should still be a rolling forecast. Given the presence of a rolling forecast, three prospects for dealing with capital expenditures suggest themselves:

- *Fast track approvals.* Many capital budgeting proposals are positioned at the lower end of the range of possible dollar amounts, and so require both fewer funds and less analysis. For these items, senior management should maintain a pool of funds at all times, and fast track the review process for any capital budget proposals submitted. This process is designed to support the bulk of all capital expenditures needed by front-line teams.

- *Near-term projections.* The treasury staff should maintain a short-term forecast of available cash flow, so that managers can see if cash will be available for capital budget requests. If the forecast indicates a cash flow problem, then projects can be delayed until more funds are available.
- *Long-term projections.* Senior management should maintain a rolling five-year forecast. This can be quite a brief document, showing general estimates of where the market will be, and the company's position within it. Based on this forecast, the company can determine its long-term capital expenditure plans for high-cost items.

Those capital expenditures designated as fast track approvals require no attention from senior management, since the funds involved are not large. However, the largest expenditures should be labeled as strategic commitments, and therefore fall within the responsibility of senior management.

If a business has cash constraints that do not allow it to give appropriate funding to all capital projects, then senior management will likely have to become involved in more approvals. If so, they should use the following criteria when making funding choices:

1. *Legal requirements.* If the company is required to make a capital investment in order to comply with a legal or regulatory requirement, then fund it.
2. *Strategic direction.* If a lack of funding will prevent a profit center from completing a key activity that meshes with the corporate strategic direction, then fund it.
3. *Throughput.* If the overall throughput of a system can be increased by making a capital investment, and there is sufficient demand to use the extra capacity, then fund it.
4. *Return on investment.* Once all projects falling under the preceding categories have been funded, allocate funding to the remaining projects based on their returns on investment.

A good way to limit profit centers from demanding an excessive amount of funds for capital projects is to designate them as investment centers and charge them the corporate cost of capital for all invested funds. This arrangement should keep them from requesting funds for projects whose returns are below the cost of capital. If the availability of funds to the company as a whole becomes restricted, you can increase the cost of capital, which should reduce the flow of capital budgeting requests.

When you eliminate the annual budget, this also means that the annual review of existing projects is eliminated. Instead, it is far better to engage in more frequent reviews of project status. Doing so will reveal problem areas where it makes sense to terminate a project entirely, thereby making more funds available for use in other capital projects. These more frequent reviews should not be excessively detailed, or else they will consume too much time. Instead, there should be a brief review of the time to completion in comparison to the original estimate, as well as of the funds expended to date in comparison to the original projection. If either of these metrics reveals a significant negative variance, then more analysis is called for.

Goal Setting without a Budget

The senior management team typically integrates its corporate goals into the budget – so what happens to the goals when the budget is terminated? As we pointed out in the first chapter, creating fixed targets can cause a variety of behavioral problems that are highly counterproductive. But if there are no goals, how do employees know what to do?

The answer is to use continual improvement goals that will place the company in the top quartile of those companies or internal profit centers against which it measures itself. For example, a retail chain can measure the profitability of its stores, and have the lowest-performing stores attempt to match the performance already reported by the top 25 percent of stores. Further, the same company can benchmark the performance of other "best in class" companies and have its top-ranking stores attempt to attain benchmarked performance levels.

For large companies having many similar profit centers, tracking performance against peers within the company can be the best basis for such goal setting, for several reasons:

- *Internal support.* Everyone works for the same company, so employees of the top-performing profit centers should be willing to assist other profit centers to improve their performance.
- *Similar environment.* The various profit centers presumably work within the same industry, and deal with similar customers and suppliers, so their results should not only be quite comparable with each other, but their business practices should be readily transferable to other profit centers.
- *Been done.* Employees may baulk at the idea of being measured against the performance of another company that may not even operate in the same industry; but this objection does not apply if the benchmark originates within the company – the benchmark has already "been done," and within the same industry.

The tracking of internal peer performance can result in an extensive reporting system where employees can readily access the results of profit centers by geographical region, or store size, or product line, or customer. The result can be an exceptional internal database that reveals who conducts business the best, and how to contact them for advice.

EXAMPLE

Mr. Dennis Houlihan has just opened a new branch of the Second Base sports bar in Boston. As a new branch, the results of the Boston branch will likely initially rank among the worst of the 150 sports bars operated by the company. Mr. Houlihan consults the company's internal database of profit centers to find comparable locations, and finds that the New York and Atlanta branches perform exceptionally well. He contacts their managers for advice regarding how to improve the performance of his operations.

The trick to goal setting in this environment is to not make such goals appear to be fixed targets that are agreed upon in advance, but rather goals to aspire to achieve, with compensation being paid on the extent to which they *are* achieved.

Strategy without a Budget

The traditional approach to budgeting is that strategy is finalized before the beginning of the budget year, and is not revised until the same period in the following year. Also, strategy is debated and settled among the top management team, perhaps allowing for some input from others lower in the corporate hierarchy. This approach may be suitable in a monopolistic industry, such as electrical power generation. However, most industries experience a vastly more robust amount of competition, and so would benefit from two key changes in the formulation of strategy, which are:

- *Timing.* When the competitive environment changes constantly, then corporate strategy needs to change at the same pace. This may require minor tweaks to the strategy every few months, and possibly a major change as soon as a structural shift in the industry becomes apparent. Thus, strategy development must change from an annual event to an ongoing process.
- *Formulation authority.* Senior management still needs to ultimately manage the overall direction of the company. However, this must truly be at a strategic level, not tactical. Lower-level managers and teams must focus on how the strategy is to be implemented at a tactical level and on a continuous basis, and give feedback to senior management regarding the practicality of the plan. There should also be a clear set of decision authorizations that allow profit centers to make most decisions with no further interference from senior management; however, clear divergences from the corporate strategy should require the approval of senior management.

EXAMPLE

Latham Lumber has lumber yards in 30 states, all under local management. Latham's senior management team has adopted a decentralized management structure, under which local managers are allowed to make all operational decisions as long as they follow these guidelines:

- Annual cash flow is above the median for a peer group of competitors
- Capital purchases are pre-authorized up to $3 million per year
- The business is focused on serving the needs of independent contractors

The staff of the Albuquerque branch of Latham Lumber sees an opportunity to open a new location near a vast subdivision that has just sold out. The investment will be under $3 million, but the focus of the location would be on homeowners, rather than independent contractors, so this decision is bumped up to senior management for resolution.

Both of the proposed changes in strategy development are necessary offshoots from the concept of shifting responsibility as far down in the organization as possible. Thus, if you shift expenditure authority down to employees, then you need to shift some elements of strategy down as well.

In short, when there is no budget, it does not mean that there is no strategy. On the contrary, senior management must still formulate it, and lower levels of the organization must interpret their key objectives and performance indicators based on that strategy. Ultimately, a company must have a system where everyone is clear about the overall direction of the business, as well as their roles in it.

Management Guidelines

Managers throughout a no-budget business must have a clear understanding of the company's overall strategy, and how they are expected to implement it within their areas of responsibility. Further, they must understand how decisions are made within the company, including:

- Which decisions they are expected to make
- Which decisions must be shifted to senior management
- The extent to which they can re-direct the activities of their areas of responsibility without the approval of senior management
- When they should give feedback to management regarding how local conditions are impacting the corporate strategy

When decisions are being forcefully shifted down into the corporate hierarchy, employees must know the answers to these questions in order to succeed in their jobs.

The Role of Senior Management

If decision making is being pushed deep into the ranks of an organization, what role remains for the members of senior management? They no longer have a budget to control, so what is their role?

First, there will be fewer senior managers, simply because there is almost no "command" work left. The elimination of the budget will likely thin the ranks of management considerably, especially those positioned in the middle of the corporate hierarchy who were most involved in monitoring performance. For those that remain, the role will encompass the following responsibilities:

- *Monitor performance*. It is still necessary to monitor the performance of the company, though senior managers should only interfere in an operation when its results are clearly falling well below expectations.
- *Exception detection*. An offshoot of the preceding point is that senior management should review all types of information to see if there are any changes in trends or other unusual patterns that could signal a need for a change in strategic direction. These changes may be too subtle to be noticed by a front-line employee, and can only be seen when viewed at a more ag-

188

gregate level. Spotting these issues early can be critical to the long-term health of a business, and so is an appropriate task for senior managers.

- *Strategy*. The high-level strategy of the company remains under the control of the senior management team. They set the general direction of the company, and then let the rest of the company work on the tactical aspects of implementing it.
- *Financial analysis*. Senior managers, or at least the corporate staff, can assist profit center employees with a variety of issues to help them obtain better performance. The people providing this assistance essentially become in-house consultants. Examples of some analyses that they might be engaged in are:
  - o Which products and services create the largest and smallest profit?
  - o Should we drop a product or product line?
  - o Should we drop a customer?
  - o Can we increase prices?
  - o Should any functional areas be outsourced?

- *Acquisitions*. The purchase of another company or its assets is a highly specialized activity that is best handled by a core team of experts. Even if an acquisition is requested from lower down in the corporate hierarchy, the actual transaction will likely be handled by corporate management.
- *Acquisition integration*. The senior management team can be involved in some coordination of the acquisition integration process, but most of the integration team will be drawn from the more high-performing profit centers. These people are best able to transfer knowledge to the employees of the acquiree. Still, there may be a need for a coordinator from senior management to ensure that adequate resources are allocated to the acquiree.
- *Coaching*. Especially during the early years of a conversion to a no-budget environment, senior managers must be deeply involved in training the rest of the organization to take on the roles and responsibilities once held by senior managers. This is a gradual process, as senior managers provide training, hand off selected functions, evaluate the results, and decide when to push more responsibility down into the organization.
- *Rapid response*. The reduced number of senior managers will likely create an extremely broad span of control (if any). This means that in the rare cases where a decision must be escalated to senior management, it can reach the apex of the company almost immediately and be sent back with a decision within a very short period of time.

Since senior managers are accustomed to much more direct action than the preceding list of activities implies, it will be necessary to completely restructure not only their job descriptions, but also the job descriptions of everyone else in the company to formally shift responsibilities downward in the organization.

Further, it is entirely possible that senior managers accustomed to the command style will not be able to switch to the mode of management needed for a "no budget" environment. They will continually attempt to interfere in the affairs of local profit centers with an ongoing stream of directives. If so, the chief executive officer should initiate the departure of these managers, with their replacements being more comfortable with enabling employees to run the business.

A further issue is that the "no budget" system is a rare one that might be derailed by the arrival of a new CEO from outside the organization. Consequently, this type of organization should be especially careful to promote from within when hiring for senior positions.

Corporate Staff Roles

The corporate staff is usually deeply involved in the development and subsequent monitoring of the budget, as well as associated performance plans and bonus payments. So what happens to them when the command and control structure goes away? There are several possible changes:

- *Consulting.* Quite a few of the corporate staff will change roles, from focusing on controlling the business to assisting businesses with whatever problems they may have. For example, the corporate staff can provide lease or buy analyses to profit centers, or investigate possible market opportunities, or explore the tax impact of opening a storefront in a new location. This is a fundamental role shift, where a person essentially becomes an in-house consultant. This can be a rewarding change, but may be difficult for some people to handle.
- *Perception.* Because of the just-noted switch to consulting activities, the rest of the company should experience a substantial improvement in its reckoning of the value of the corporate staff. They are now sought-after assets who can provide valuable assistance. This is a substantial improvement over the command and control environment, where most employees try to avoid contact with the corporate staff.
- *Headcount.* A decentralized environment requires far fewer corporate staff. Thus, though some people will become effective in-house consultants, there will be no need for many others. These people may shift into the company's new profit centers, or find work with other companies.

Board Approvals

It is customary in many organizations for the board of directors to formally approve the annual budget. If there is no budget, then the board can (and should) approve a statement of the overall strategic direction of the company, and may become involved in the larger capital budget purchasing decisions. Further, it is customary for the board to review the financial statements of the firm at many of its meetings. Thus, the absence of a budget does not prevent the board of directors from reviewing the direction of the company; it merely focuses on other aspects of operations.

Compensation without a Budget

If you eliminate a company's budget and along with it the traditional bonus contract, then how do you compensate employees? Here are the key issues to consider when designing a new method of compensation:

- *Baseline.* The foundation for the traditional bonus contract is the baseline from which performance during the measurement period is to be tracked. This number is usually a negotiated figure, which means that it is subject to a great deal of politicking. An excellent alternative is to use one of the following options as a replacement baseline:
    - o *Historical trend line.* If the actual performance from the last year is used as the baseline for future performance, there is no way to create a less-effective negotiated baseline. However, if earlier performance was substandard, employees may be overly compensated for achievements that are better than the prior year, but not necessarily at the level of the competition. Also, if the company needs to reorient its business, focusing on improvements from the last year may not be sufficient.
    - o *Peer group performance.* The company can benchmark its performance against other "best in class" companies, and compensate employees based on their performance against this "gold standard." Another option is to divide the company into a multitude of profit centers, and use the performance of the best profit centers as the baseline. This latter approach may work best, since performance is derived from the company's specific competitive situation, rather than from the performance of another company that may operate in a different market.
- *Unit of measure.* The unit of measure for a traditional bonus plan is probably profitability, but that does not have to apply to a situation where you want to focus the attention of employees on other key success factors. For example, in a rapidly-expanding market, the most important issue may be revenue growth, even if there are no profits. Or, if a company has gone through a leveraged buyout, debt reduction (and therefore cash flow) may be the most important concern. Or, a niche strategy may mandate a high level of customer support. The central point in the selection of the unit of measure is that it provides a measure of progress toward the company's strategic objectives.
- *Team basis.* The traditional model favors bonuses for individuals. However, when longer-term goals are paramount, it requires the ongoing efforts of a large team to achieve above-average performance. Thus, it makes more sense to eliminate individual bonus plans in favor of group-based bonuses. Ideally, there should be one bonus plan, and it should include *every* person in the company. With one bonus plan, every employee has an incentive to help everyone else to optimize their performance. Conversely, if there were to be localized bonus plans, it is more likely that employees in different

bonus plans would not assist each other, since they would have no economic reason for doing so. The worst situation is to only have individual bonuses for a small number of managers, since the rest of the company has no reason to work hard so that someone else can earn a large bonus.

- *Bonus calculation.* The calculation of a bonus can be a nefariously difficult and arcane formula under a traditional budget plan which sometimes results in no bonus at all, despite the best efforts of an employee, or an inordinately large bonus because the circumstances were just right. In a no-budget situation, it makes more sense to not establish a detailed compensation plan in advance. Instead, use one of the options just noted to create a baseline for measurement, and pay out an appropriate amount based on changes from that baseline. In general, this approach means limiting bonus payments to a certain percentage of profits or cash flow, so that the company is not crippled by inordinately large payments. Also, paying all bonuses from existing profits or cash flow means that compensation will always be supportable, since the company has already earned the money.

- *Nature of the bonus.* A company that wants to *really* focus the attention of its employees on long-term performance should consider *not* immediately paying out the bonuses that it grants to employees. A better alternative is to pay all or a portion of the bonus into a fund, which in turn invests at least some of the money in the company's shares. The fund then pays out both the accumulated bonuses and any earnings to employees when they retire. By taking this approach, a company is ensuring that employees have a significant interest in the performance of the company's stock, which in turn is driven by their ability to improve its earnings and cash flow over time.

- *Comprehensive evaluation.* A traditional bonus contract focuses on the achievement of very few targets – perhaps just profits – in order to trigger a bonus. This can lead to considerable "gaming" to twist the system to achieve only the specified targets, perhaps to the long-term detriment of the business. A better approach is to establish a large group of performance factors that an evaluation committee can use to ascertain the improvement (or decline) of the business during the measurement period. Such a comprehensive system may start with profitability, but then go on to measure (for example) backlog, customer turnover, employee turnover, absentee levels, average accounts receivable outstanding, the debt level, and new product launches to obtain a more well-rounded view of how the organization has changed.

EXAMPLE

Mr. Jones is a traditional manager who is accustomed to moving heaven and earth to meet his profit target and earn a bonus. For the past year, he made the designated profit bonus, but ignored the company's move to a more comprehensive evaluation system. The committee discovered that he only achieved the budget by eliminating training and maintenance expenditures, which seriously impact staff knowledge and machine downtime. The committee therefore awarded Mr. Jones a minimal bonus for the year.

Compensation under this system should be based on *relative* improvement, rather than performance against a fixed target. This is a key concept, for it does not tie employees to a number or other metric that may be increasingly irrelevant over time. Thus, if there is a steep economic decline, it may still be quite reasonable to issue a bonus to the members of a profit center even if their profits dropped, because the profit decline was less than the median rate of decline for other parts of the company. Conversely, if the market is expanding rapidly, it may not make sense to issue bonuses to the members of a profit center that earned fewer profits than the median rate of profit increase for the company.

It is extremely useful to base all bonus compensation on a single company-wide profit sharing pool. By doing so, the members of the various profit centers will have a strong incentive to work together to create more profits. If the employees in profit centers were to instead be paid just on their own performance, then they would be far less likely to assist other parts of the company. Another effect of this arrangement is that a poorly-performing profit center may even receive unsolicited offers of help from other profit centers, because its poor performance is adversely affecting the compensation of other employees.

One type of compensation that has no place in a no-budget company is the stock option. A stock option generates a return for its holder if the price of the underlying stock increases. However, there is not necessarily a relationship between the price of the stock and the actual performance of the company. A stock price may go up due to general price volatility, speculation regarding a takeover, or simply because the valuation of the entire stock market is increasing due to an improvement in general economic conditions. None of these scenarios are impacted by the performance of the person to whom a stock option is granted. Indeed, the reverse can be the case – a person could engender phenomenal company performance, while a variety of factors *decrease* the value of his or her stock options. Consequently, it is better to use compensation devices that only provide increased pay if the company performs better than its peer group.

Controls without a Budget

The budget and the command and control system are both considered to be robust types of controls, since they ensure that someone is examining actual results against a standard, and tracking down variances. However, is this really the case?

The budget and the command and control system are both designed to be *detective* controls, which mean that they find control breaches after they have already occurred and funds have already been lost. While useful, this type of control is not especially robust. A better type of control is the *preventive* control, which keeps control breaches from ever occurring in the first place.

In a "no budget" scenario where responsibility is pushed down in the organization, there are more people involved in running the business, more people whose compensation is tied to its success, and therefore more people who are interested in having stronger controls. Thus, even in the absence of a budget, it is entirely likely that employees will demand a strong control system simply to ensure their own success. The system of controls may develop in a decentralized manner, as the corporate staff assists the profit centers with the controls most applicable to them, but this does not mean that the system will not be a robust one.

Further, a decentralized system calls for an extremely broad-based sharing of financial and operational information. Such a transparent environment can be a very effective control, for there is nowhere for someone to hide inappropriate expenditures of any size.

Behavioral Norms

Senior managers may point to specific individuals within a company who might take advantage of the situation if a tight budgeting system were not imposed; however, this justification is based on the concept of imposing a command and control system on an entire company in order to prevent possible deleterious activities by just a few people. It would certainly be easier to only restrict the behavior of those few people, or even encourage them to work elsewhere, rather than impose a repressive level of control on the entire company. Thus, a reasonable alternative to the command and control system is to imbue the organization with a strong sense of ethics and limits to acceptable behavior, and then act decisively when one of the few miscreants in the company breaks those boundaries.

Another argument by senior management in favor of strong controls over expenditures is that there are always a few employees who add improper expenditures to their expense reports, which only detailed cost reviews will find. This certainly does happen from time to time, but only few employees engage in this sort of behavior. In most cases, it seems odd that a company will entrust its employees with expensive assets, design products, and deal with important customers, and yet assume that they will run a few unwarranted expenses through their expense reports. In reality, nearly all employees can be trusted within a framework of a modest number of controls. Instead, it is certainly worth considering the use of well-defined behavioral norms, and coming down hard on any employees who step outside of those norms. Doing so means that the company is acting forcefully against a small number of employees, while not punishing all other employees with an oppressive set of controls.

Profit Knowledge

If there is to be no budget, then the entire organization requires more knowledge of how the company makes money, so that they can contribute to making more of it. This calls for company-wide education by the accounting staff of how the company earns money, where it loses money, and the profit that the company earns from specific transactions. Thus, the sales and marketing staff should know how much profit the company makes on each product, so that it can increase sales of those items. Similarly, the engineering staff must be encouraged to use target costing to create products that generate acceptable returns. Target costing is the process of projecting the costs expected to be incurred to create a new product and how this will impact product profitability levels. Further, the customer service department must know which customers generate the most profit for the company, so they will pay particular attention to them.

Ultimately, the amount of information transparency should be so great that it is nearly impossible for someone to hide an inappropriate expenditure.

Information Exchange

A great deal of responsibility is shifted down to the front lines of a business when there is no budget. In this situation, employees need to discuss alternatives with each other for how to run their profit centers, as well as where to find solutions to their problems, and cast around for ideas regarding how to improve their operations. None of these requirements can be met in the work silos that are part of a traditional organization. Instead, employees need new ways to communicate with each other. This may involve company-sponsored blogs, newsletters, more formal gatherings, and so forth, with the goal of creating a massive number of connections amongst employees. This approach is completely at odds with the traditional view of restricting information to a select few within each department, and so can be a wrenching change for those employees who used to control all of the corporate information.

Hiring, Promotions, and Continuity

As has been noted in this chapter, operating without a budget calls for an entirely different way of doing business – and one that is not widely practiced. Thus, a company that wants to follow this path must do so by training employees internally in how the system operates, and providing them with ongoing coaching for many years. This scenario has the following impacts on hiring, promotions and employee continuity:

- *Hiring*. The hiring process requires even more interviews than usual to pick out those candidates who seem most able to take on responsibility and operate well in a profit center environment.
- *Promotions*. There should be a system for locating those employees most comfortable with the new system, who are willing to coach others in how the system works, and who have the potential to become part of the management team. Conversely, no one should be promoted who might want to convert back to the command and control system, or even adopt some elements of that system.
- *Continuity*. Given the rarity of people trained in the no-budget system, it is imperative that a company using this system retain its employees for the maximum amount of time. Otherwise, it will spend inordinate amounts to train replacement employees. Long continuity calls for the creation of an unusually employee-friendly environment, but only for those who are clearly willing to work with the system. Those employees who resist the system

should be encouraged to work elsewhere in firms that are managed in a more traditional manner.

The worst mistake that a no-budget company can make is to hire a senior executive team from the outside, since these people are quite capable of rooting out the entire system and reverting to a command and control environment. Instead, it is much better to promote people from within the company to the executive ranks, for they understand the system and are committed to continuing it.

Customer Ownership

Under the no-budget system, it makes considerable sense to drive responsibility as far down into the organization as possible, which in turn suggests that there should be many profit centers. However, if there are many profit centers servicing the same customer, who "owns" each customer? Generally, each customer should be assigned to a single profit center, even though a customer may deal with multiple profit centers. The reasons for doing so are:

- *Responsibility*. There must be one profit center that is ultimately responsible for each customer. Otherwise, there is a risk that a customer with a problem will be shunted among multiple profit centers before a resolution is achieved; this delay does not constitute good customer service.
- *Poaching*. If the various profit centers are allowed to poach customers from each other, this will likely be achieved through price reductions, which reduces the profitability of the company as a whole.

It may appear that a profit center that is established earlier than another profit center will have captured a larger group of customers, and so will always own the financial results associated with those customers. However, senior management can become involved in the matter from time to time and transfer ownership to a new profit center if it becomes apparent that the new profit center is generating most of the products and services for the customer.

Service Center Pricing

Under a traditional accounting system, such internal service centers as the maintenance department or trucking department are allocated operational funds. Under a more decentralized system, there is no central budgeting authority to assign funds to these service centers. Instead, each service center must negotiate the prices it can charge to the other departments for its services, and those other departments can go outside the company if they can achieve a better deal by doing so. This approach effectively creates a budget for each service center which is based upon the market price for similar services. Taking this approach ensures that the service centers have lean operations.

Service centers should charge their costs to users. This does not mean that they should have a zero expenditure level by the end of the year, with all costs incurred having been passed along to users. Such a condition would only arise if a service center were 100% utilized throughout the year. In reality, a service center only charges for actual usage, and its services will probably not be completely utilized throughout the period. This is the same condition that a freestanding business would experience – it is rarely in a situation where its services are totally consumed.

These service center issues do not necessarily mean that all support services be handled locally by each profit center. On the contrary, it may be quite cost-effective to handle a number of issues from a central location, such as information systems, tax planning, and financing. Thus, it is possible to have a decentralized decision-making system while still providing the entire business with centralized services.

Accounting Reports

When responsibility is shifted into the depths of an organization, information needs to flow along with it. This means that the accounting staff must create and issue reports at great speed to the entire organization, thereby creating a rapid feedback loop from which the company can take corrective action.

The information provided by the accounting staff may encompass more than financial information. Indeed, such information may be downplayed if senior management wants to encourage employees to focus on other key performance indicators.

EXAMPLE

The management information systems manager of Quest Adventure Gear is creating feedback reports for various people within the company. His reports include the following:

Title	Information Provided
Customer service manager	Customers gained; customers lost
Engineering manager	Engineering change orders; warranty claims
Maintenance manager	Downtime at bottleneck operation
Sales manager	Sales discounts granted; Days sales outstanding

A more balanced approach is to issue a complete package of financial and operating information throughout the company, which usually includes the following:

- *Rolling forecast.* This is a general-level forecast that requires little time to update, and may cover a period of as little as three months. See the Rolling Forecast chapter for more information.
- *Leading indicators.* This is a very limited set of leading indicators that strongly indicate the direction of the market in which the company operates.
- *Performance comparisons.* This is the operational and financial performance of the various profit centers, and is presented only for the key information that the company is most interested in. The various profit centers use this information to compare their results. It is intended to be both a spur for more

action and the source document for the eventual payment of performance-based bonuses.

- *Benchmark comparisons.* If the company chooses to benchmark performance against that of one or more outside companies, it can compare the recent performance of the company against that of the benchmark. This information can be used to calculate performance-based bonuses.
- *Financial results.* This information should be issued at the level of responsibility of the recipient, and should be formatted to show the results for each of the last 12 months in order to present a trend line, and preferably aggregated so that readers are not overwhelmed with detail. There are several ways to present financial information. A general format follows.

Sample Presentation of Financial Results

Cost Center	Current Month	Same Month Last Year	Current Y-T-D	12-Month Average/Month	Quarterly % Change
Accounting department	$50,000	$58,000	$163,000	$52,500	-4%
Engineering department	125,000	137,000	490,000	131,000	-3%
Maintenance department	72,000	55,000	160,000	60,000	+11%
Power plant	150,000	147,000	440,000	153,000	+1%

The preceding report shows that the accounting and engineering departments appear to be successfully pruning their costs, while the maintenance department has experienced a significant expense surge that is worthy of further investigation.

A variation on the trend line report is to include a percentage change line, which may be more useful to report users. Whether you use this feature is entirely up to recipients. Some people find that a percentage change number provides better information than the raw numbers upon which it is based.

There are a few reports that may still be needed by senior management, and which the rest of the company does not need to see. For example, there may be cash flow forecasts needed by the treasurer to anticipate cash borrowing and investments. There may also be transfer pricing reports needed by the tax manager to predict future tax payments. Generally, these are reports intended for specialists, and so are of no interest to the rest of the company.

Transfer Pricing

A transfer price is the price at which one part of an entity sells a product or service to another part of the same entity. There are a number of transfer pricing methods, such as using the market price, or a negotiated price, or cost plus a margin. Transfer pricing is used to avoid paying income taxes in high-tax regions, and so is a significant focus of government auditing activities.

When there is no budget, the flow of costs through a company must be as transparent as possible, which means that there can be no transfer prices built into the reports seen by employees. Instead, only the actual cost of a product that is transferred between departments should be shown.

If transfer prices must be used for tax recognition purposes, then they should be included in a separate set of reports that are only used for tax reporting purposes.

Investor Relations

When the investment community is accustomed to receiving budget information from a publicly-held company, withdrawing the budget is essentially reducing the amount of information that they receive. In the absence of this information, investors and analysts may be somewhat more inclined to take their business elsewhere, or at least will be increasingly uncertain of the future direction of the company.

You can alleviate this problem by replacing budget information with other types of more relevant information. For example, the investor relations officer could issue a rolling three-month forecast once every three months. This gives recipients a fairly accurate portrayal of what the next quarterly financial statements will contain. In addition, there may be a general projection covering the next year, but which does not contain quarterly targets. The company can also release information about key performance indicators, such as backlog, market share, and customer retention; this information can provide a solid foundation for the analysis work of an outside analyst.

Releasing this different mix of information to the investment community may even limit the impact of short sellers, since there will be so much information in the marketplace that the current stock price will likely be very realistically valued, with minimal price volatility. This leaves little room in which a short seller can earn a profit.

Implementation of the No-Budget Environment

The changes noted in this chapter make it clear that operating effectively without a budget essentially requires a retooling of the entire system of running a company. Employees are accustomed to the command and control environment (even if they do not like it), and so will require substantial re-education into a decidedly different system that they have never seen or heard of before.

The implementation process for this change is a slow one. Even if senior management is willing to adopt the new concept at once, the rest of the company will require time to become accustomed to it. The new approach calls for the development of entirely new systems of governance, new reports, and new policies and procedures. Further, employees must believe that senior management is really turning over a broad range of responsibilities to them, and will not interfere in their decisions – and it takes time for this belief to grow in response to the actions of senior managers.

For these reasons, the best approach to a no-budget environment is a gradual one, where senior management and employees jointly develop the new system over time, perhaps through pilot projects in some parts of the company, or through a broader rollout. The correct implementation requires a company to keep the business running properly despite any problems arising during the transition, so expect a number of years to pass before the transition has been completed.

Summary

Once a company commits to the "no budget" environment and spends several years transitioning to it, what does the environment look like? The following can be expected:

- *Use it or lose it.* There is no longer a mentality of "use it or lose it" in the company. Instead, actual costs incurred are tracked on a historical trend line, with ongoing peer pressure to reduce costs. Thus, the negotiation of a cost budget and subsequent use of it near the end of the year are gone.
- *Forecast integration.* Instead of creating a full-year budget and then forgetting about it until the next year, the company updates a forecast every month. Given the immediate relevance of this information, managers are more likely to use it to plan their profit center activities over the near term.
- *Profit knowledge.* Every employee who deals with customers knows the profit associated with each transaction, which they can use to influence sales to customers.
- *Compensation based on relative performance.* There is no longer a negotiated fixed target to reach each year. Instead, employees do their best to improve their performance against that of an internal peer group or an external benchmarked organization, and they are paid based on their relative performance. This means that there is no false amplification or reduction of revenue forecasts, since forecasts are now divorced from the calculation of compensation.
- *Feedback loop.* In order for the entire organization to operate without a budget, there is an extraordinarily fast feedback loop for all types of information, so that employees see the results of all key financial and operating information as soon as possible. Further, the reports are "sliced and diced" so that only the information relevant to an individual is reported to him.
- *Customer service.* The attentiveness of employees to the needs of customers will have increased noticeably, since nearly all decisions relating to customers can be made at once, rather than being sent up to a higher level for approval.
- *Training.* Since it is impossible to shift responsibility down in an organization without giving employees sufficient knowledge to handle it, there is an ongoing training program, coupled with a regularly-scheduled needs assessment for every employee. The funds allocated to training are substantial.
- *Employee turnover.* There has been an initial spike in employee turnover, as those not accustomed to the new system leave for other companies who still use a traditional command and control system. After this one-time surge, employee turnover has plunged, since the quality of work has substantially increased.

In general, the no-budget environment is a simpler one than the more traditional command and control system. This may not be immediately apparent, given the large effort needed to transition to the no-budget environment. However, consider the situation from a cost perspective – there are fewer people involved in a no-budget company, since many of the corporate staff and mid-level managers who used to maintain the command and control environment are gone. Certainly, there is a higher degree of information sharing and interaction among profit centers, but the *complexity* of the system has declined. Further, those people still with the company who used to monitor expenditures and demand explanations for variances are now employed more usefully, providing information to more employees and assisting them with a variety of internal consulting projects.

Chapter 22
The Rolling Forecast

Introduction

Reality diverges from your budget extremely quickly, especially if the sales backlog is only large enough to support operations for the next few months. If so, sales could change so fast that the budget will look like science fiction by the second quarter of the year, and not even bear a slight resemblance to actual results by the end of the year. The solution may be a rolling forecast. In this chapter, we discuss how to create a rolling forecast, and a variation on the concept, called continuous budgeting.

The Rolling Forecast Process

A rolling forecast is a recasting of a company's financial prospects on a frequent basis. The frequency of forecasting means that the forecast could potentially occupy a central role in a company's planning activities. In this and the following section we address several aspects of that role – the timing of updates, the updating method, the time period covered, and the format of the forecast.

Ideally, a rolling forecast could be created as soon as a company issues its financial statements for the most recent reporting period. By doing so, management can update the existing forecast based in part on the information contained in the most recent financial statements. You may want to update the forecast on a monthly basis, but do so only if the resulting information is useful to management – which is usually only the case in a volatile market. In most situations, a quarterly update to the forecast is sufficient, and is not looked upon as quite so much of a chore by the management team. An alternative view of when to update a forecast is whenever there is a significant triggering event. This may be a change in the business environment, the release of a new product, the loss of a key employee, and so forth. If you are updating only after a triggering event, the revision of a rolling forecast may be quite sporadic.

The rolling forecast is usually considered to be a much more frequent creation than the annual budget, so you need a revision process that minimizes the amount of updating effort. Here are several ways to construct a rolling forecast, beginning with the simplest approach:

1. *Adjust recent results.* Copy forward the company's most recent actual financial results, and then adjust revenues and expenses based on any changed expectations for the forecasting period. This method is essentially based on historical results. It requires the input of very few people, and can be created very quickly.
2. *Block revision.* Only forecast at a very high level, where there is essentially a single line item block for the expenses of an entire department. There may

be somewhat more detail for the revenue portion of the forecast, since this is the most critical area. This information will likely be extracted from the most recent historical results, but may be subject to more revision than the method just discussed. This approach can also be constructed quickly, with input from just a few people.

3. *Detailed revision.* Forecast every line item in the financial statements "from scratch." This approach takes substantially more time and requires broad-based input. Few companies are willing to expend the time needed for this level of forecasting.

Of the preceding methods, either the first or second should work well, because they require little time to create. When forecasting requires little time, it is more likely to be accepted on a long-term basis by employees. Ideally, it should take no more than one day to update a rolling forecast.

Another issue with the rolling forecast is the time period to be covered by it. There is no universally correct period. Instead, the time period covered depends on the nature of the business. Here are several examples of situations calling for different forecast periods:

- *Software development.* A business creates software and launches it through the Internet. Its investment in fixed assets is low. Competing products can appear at any time, and the market can pivot in a new direction at a moment's notice. In this case, management probably does not need a forecast that extends more than three months into the future.

- *Market leading manufacturer.* A business is the dominant low-cost provider of industrial goods in its market niche, thanks to its heavy investment in fixed assets and production technology. The market is probably steady and changes little, so management can get by with a quarterly forecast update that extends over a two-year period.

- *Government contractor.* A company has a backlog of long-term contracts with the federal government. Its cost structure is easily predicted, and revenues are based largely on contracts that are already in hand. Management probably only needs a quarterly forecast update, with particular emphasis on the revenues generated by specific contracts. The forecast duration should match the duration of key contracts.

- *Retail business.* A company sells highly fashion-oriented retail goods from multiple stores. Sales levels are highly variable, so management probably needs a monthly forecast that has a particular emphasis on sales by product line and by store.

Another way to view the duration of the forecast period is whether extending it further into the future will alter any management decision making. If not, there is no point in creating the extended forecast. A good way to determine the correct duration is to start with a rolling 12-month forecast and adjust the duration after a few months to more closely fit the needs of management. It is quite common to have a forecast duration of at least one year, and rarely more than two years.

In summary, you generally want to update a rolling forecast on a fairly frequent basis, do so at an aggregated level, and for a period that can be as little as a few months and extending up to two years.

The Rolling Forecast Format

What should a rolling forecast look like? As just noted, keep it relatively short in order to make the updating task as easy as possible. However, this does not mean that the entire forecast should be encompassed within just a few lines. Instead, consider structuring the forecast to address the key variables in the business, so that managers focus on changes in just those areas that will make a difference to the business.

The following sample format is designed for a manufacturing business that produces roughly the same items every year and in predictable quantities. There is a focus on the cost of commodities and managing the bottleneck operation, which leads to more detail on those specific items.

Sample Rolling Forecast for Manufacturing Operation

	Quarter 1	Quarter 2	Quarter 3	Quarter 4
Sales	$8,200,000	$8,225,000	$8,290,000	$8,320,000
Cost of goods sold	5,330,000	5,593,000	5,720,000	5,741,000
Gross margin	$2,870,000	$2,632,000	$2,570,000	$2,579,000
Gross margin percentage	35%	32%	31%	31%
Other expenses	2,510,000	2,535,000	2,550,000	2,565,000
Net profit or loss	$360,000	$97,000	$20,000	$14,000
Bottleneck utilization	92%	98%	105%	108%
Platinum cost/pound	$1,700	$1,750	$1,775	$1,775
Palladium cost/pound	$700	$705	$710	$715

The rolling forecast for the manufacturing operation reveals a decline in gross margins and net profits over time, which appears to be caused by an increase in the cost of platinum, which is listed on the report as a key commodity. Also, note that the forecast is in quarters, not months – the company has a sufficiently stable product line and marketplace that it does not need to update its forecast every month. Finally, the forecast reveals that there is a growing problem with the overutilization of the company's bottleneck operation, which management needs to address.

What about if a company has minimal fixed costs and is located in a highly volatile marketplace – such as software development for smart phone apps? In this environment, a product may have a short life span or highly variable revenues, so the focus tends to be more on detailed revenue information and the rollout dates for new products. The following sample format could be applied to such a situation:

Sample Rolling Forecast for a Software Developer

	January	February	March	April
Revenue:				
App – Geolocator	$80,000	$75,000	$60,000	$45,000
App – Find my car	55,000	65,000	65,000	40,000
App – Family tracker	160,000	160,000	100,000	80,000
Total revenue	$295,000	$300,000	$225,000	$165,000
Expenses	165,000	175,000	175,000	180,000
Net profit or loss	$130,000	$125,000	$50,000	-$15,000
Product release dates:				
App – Backcountry locator	1/21/xx			
App – Wildlife tagger			3/5/xx	
App – Urban locator				4/4/xx

The rolling forecast for the software developer makes it clear that revenues decline rapidly, so revenues must be the key focus of the organization. There is also considerable emphasis on the release dates of new products, which will hopefully drive renewed revenue growth. Note that the preceding example format is expressed in months, rather than quarters. In a volatile marketplace, a quarterly update may be far too long an interval to show the rapid changes in sales that will likely occur.

What about a situation where a company relies upon a number of large contracts with its customers? In this case, the key focus must be on the revenue stream associated with each contract, as well as on the dates when contracts will terminate. The following sample format could be applied to such a situation:

Sample Rolling Forecast for a Contractor

	Quarter 1	Quarter 2	Quarter 3	Quarter 4
Revenue:				
Air Force contract	$1,700,000	$1,720,000	$1,690,000	$850,000
Marine Corp contract	2,400,000	2,350,000	130,000	0
USGS contract	850,000	875,000	430,000	0
Total revenue	$4,950,000	$4,945,000	$2,250,000	$850,000
Expenses	4,300,000	4,290,000	1,950,000	830,000
Net profit or loss	$650,000	$655,000	$300,000	$20,000
Contract terminations:				
Air Force contract				11/20/xx
Marine Corps contract			7/11/xx	
USGS contract			8/15/xx	

The rolling forecast for the contractor is driven entirely by revenues. The company can easily cut back on staffing when there is no work, so its expenses are not a concern. The non-financial information in the forecast keeps management aware of the truly critical item – when customer contracts are scheduled to expire.

What about a situation where certain elements of the forecast are more volatile than other elements? If so, construct an update table that specifies how frequently information should be reviewed, and adjust the model as indicated by the table. The following table shows how updating frequencies might be specified for a clothing retailer:

Sample Forecasting Frequency for a Retailer

Line Item	Volatility	Update Frequency	Comments
Revenue	High	Daily	Shifts in fashion occur at lightning speed, so management must be aware of sales by stock keeping unit on a daily basis
Labor costs	Medium	Monthly	Shifts in the local labor market may require that the company boost its pay at regular intervals
Merchandise costs	Medium	Monthly	The company exercises reasonable control over its purchases of merchandise through bulk purchasing arrangements, so costs do not change that frequently
Facility rent	Low	Quarterly	Facility rentals are long term and not subject to change
Other expenses	Low	Quarterly	There is little volatility in all other costs

Continuous Budgeting

A variation on the rolling forecast is continuous budgeting. Continuous budgeting is the process of continually adding one more month to the end of a multi-period budget as each month goes by. This approach has the advantage of having someone constantly attend to the budget model and revise budget assumptions for the last incremental period of the budget. The downside of this approach is that it may not yield a budget that is more achievable than the traditional annual budget, since the budget periods prior to the incremental month just added are not revised. We do not revise these budget periods for two reasons:

- *Accounting software updates.* The budget is loaded into the accounting software for budget-versus-actual reporting analysis, and would be time-consuming to change if the budget were to be continually revised.
- *Budgeting labor.* It is much less labor intensive to only add one budget period than it is to revise the entire remaining portion of a budget.

The continuous budgeting concept is usually applied to a twelve-month budget, so there is always a full-year budget in place. However, the period of this budget may not correspond to a company's fiscal year. For example, a company uses the period January through December as its fiscal year. After it completes January, the company adds January of the following year to its continuous budget, and drops the January just completed.

Continuous budgeting calls for considerably more management attention than is the case when a company produces a one-year static budget, since some budgeting activities must now be repeated every month. In addition, if a company obtains the input of many employees to create its budgets on a continuous basis, then the total employee time used over the course of a year is substantial. Consequently, it is best to adopt a leaner approach to continuous budgeting, with fewer people involved in the process.

It is generally easier to use a rolling forecast than a continuous budget, since a continuous budget requires the review of all of the revenue and expense line items that are usually included in a full-year budget. A rolling forecast concentrates attention on only a few of the more crucial elements of a full budget, and so is easier to update.

Summary

The rolling forecast is an ideal way to give employees the best possible estimate of what will probably occur in the near future. The forecasting process is specifically designed not to be elaborate, on the grounds that a simple update is more likely to be accepted by a company than a lengthy, bureaucratic budgeting production. And by keeping the model simple, you can focus on the key drivers of success, rather than being bogged down in the details.

It is possible to run a rolling forecast in conjunction with an annual budgeting process, but many companies find that the higher accuracy level of a rolling forecast makes it sufficient for their needs, and so dispense with the annual budget entirely.

Chapter 23
Budgeting Procedures

Introduction

The creation of an annual budget can be an extremely convoluted affair that may span many months, and which involves a variety of restarts and iterations. It is quite likely that the budget will not even be complete until partway into the new budget year. You can add a great deal of structure to the budgeting process with a set of procedures that assign responsibilities and due dates to all phases of the budgeting project, and thereby increase the odds of having the budget completed on time. In this chapter, we discuss the basic steps of these budgeting procedures, as well as related tasks.

Procedure – Formulation of the Budget

The process of preparing a budget should be highly regimented and follow a set schedule, so that the completed budget is ready for use by the beginning of the next fiscal year. Here are the basic steps to follow:

1. *Update budget assumptions.* Review the assumptions about the company's business environment that were used as the basis for the last budget, and update as necessary.
2. *Review bottlenecks.* Determine the capacity level of the primary bottleneck that is constraining the company from generating further sales, and define how this will impact any additional company revenue growth.
3. *Available funding.* Determine the most likely amount of funding that will be available during the budget period, which may limit growth plans.
4. *Step costing points.* Determine whether any step costs will be incurred during the likely range of business activity in the upcoming budget period, and define the amount of these costs and at what activity levels they will be incurred.
5. *Create budget package.* Copy forward the basic budgeting instructions from the instruction packet used in the preceding year. Update it by including the year-to-date actual expenses incurred in the current year, and also annualize this information for the full current year. Add a commentary to the packet, stating step costing information, bottlenecks, and expected funding limitations for the upcoming budget year. Also state any guidelines for capital budgeting requests.
6. *Issue budget package.* Issue the budget package personally, where possible, and answer any questions from recipients. Also state the due date for the first draft of the budget package.

7. *Obtain revenue forecast.* Obtain the revenue forecast from the sales manager, validate it with the CEO, and then distribute it to the other department managers. They use the revenue information at least partially as the basis for developing their own budgets.

8. *Obtain department budgets.* Obtain the budgets from all departments, check for errors, and compare to the bottleneck, funding, and step costing constraints. Adjust the budgets as necessary.

9. *Validate compensation.* Send the compensation requests contained within the department budgets to the human resources manager for validation. This should include matching against pay ranges and ascertaining whether payroll taxes are being correctly calculated.

10. *Validate bonus plans.* Have the senior management team validate the terms under which bonus plans have been arranged, and whether the conditions of those agreements are reasonable. If bonus payments are more likely than not to occur, include them in the budget, along with applicable payroll taxes.

11. *Obtain fixed asset disposal information.* Obtain an itemization from the departments of fixed assets to be disposed of, and the prices likely to be obtained for them. Include this information in the financing budget.

12. *Obtain capital budget requests.* Validate all capital budget requests and forward them to the senior management team with comments and recommendations. Match to the fixed asset disposal report to ensure that assets are being replaced.

13. *Update the budget model.* Input all budget information into the master budget model. Verify that payroll tax rates in the model are updated for the budget year. Update the depreciation expense in the model, based on the fixed asset disposal and capital budget request information already received.

14. *Review the budget.* Meet with the senior management team to review the budget. Highlight possible constraint issues, and any limitations caused by funding restrictions. Also test for the validity of the turnover ratios for accounts receivable, inventory, and accounts payable in relation to historical metrics, as well as sales per salesperson. Note all comments made by the management team, and forward this information back to the budget originators, with requests to modify their budgets.

15. *Process budget iterations.* Track outstanding budget change requests, and update the budget model with new iterations as they arrive. Be sure to update estimated interest expense and income, as the financing portion of the budget is clarified.

16. *Obtain approval.* Forward the budget to the board of directors for approval.

17. *Issue the budget.* Create a bound version of the budget and distribute it to all authorized recipients.

18. *Adjust chart of accounts.* Eliminate accounts in the chart of accounts too small to not have an associated budget, where applicable. Also add accounts where a new budget line item has been created.

19. *Load the budget.* Load the budget information into the financial software, so that you can generate budget versus actual reports.

20. *Verify loaded budget.* Compare the budget loaded into the accounting software to the approved budget version, and adjust for any errors.
21. *Lock down budget.* Initiate password protection of the budget model. Also, create a copy of the model and archive the copy.
22. *Document process issues.* Once all other steps have been completed, review the entire budgeting process with the budget staff, and prepare a memo regarding how the process can be improved in the following year.

It is quite likely that some deliverables required under this budget will be delivered late, which will throw off the timing of the entire procedure. You can minimize the amount of budget slippage by including a reasonable amount of buffer time at several spots in the schedule. These buffer times should gradually be used up over the course of the budget process, so that the final product is issued near the planned completion date.

Consider issuing a calendar of activities to anyone receiving the budget packet, so they know when information is to be returned to the budget team. This should be an abbreviated version of the complete schedule of activities used by the budget team. Consider a format similar to the following for a budget packet recipient:

Sample Calendar of Activities

Receipt Date	Actions to be Completed	Return Date
September 1	Receive list of budget assumptions for review.	September 5
September 10	Receive request for revenue forecast [sales manager only].	September 20
September 23	Receive budget package. Return with completed expenditure line items, step costing points, compensation levels, headcount requests, and bottleneck capacity levels (if any).	October 15
October 1	Receive capital budget disposal and request forms.	October 20
October 24	Receive first iteration of budget [senior management only]. Respond with comments.	October 28
November 5	Receive first iteration of budget (all managers) with commentary.	November 12
November 15	Receive second budget iteration with financing budget [senior management only]. Respond with comments.	November 19
November 23	Receive third iteration of budget (all managers) with commentary.	December 2

Receipt Date	Actions to be Completed	Return Date
December 5	Receive final budget iteration for review [CEO only]. Respond with comments.	December 8
December 10	Issue to board of directors for approval.	December 20
December 22	Receive final printed version of budget.	--

Procedure – Issue Budget Variance Reports

If the management team chooses to have budget variance reports, consider using the following procedure to manage the process:

1. Verify that the list of report recipients is still valid since the last report issuance date.
2. Verify that all budget-versus-actual reports have been properly parsed so that recipients will only receive report information for the areas for which they are responsible.
3. Set the reporting package to only issue reports where the budget variance is at least $___.
4. Print and issue the reports to the report recipients.
5. Schedule meetings with the report recipients to discuss the reasons for the budget variances.
6. Record comments regarding the variances, and issue the combined report to the chief operating officer.

This procedure is designed to minimize the number of variances to be investigated by setting a high variance threshold for review. Otherwise, managers will spend an inordinate amount of time investigating inconsequential variances.

Procedure – Subsequent Account Changes

Whenever you add an account to the chart of accounts, you may need to allocate some budget funds to it. Or, if you are deleting an account, you may need to shift associated budget funds to another account. The following procedure notes the steps to follow:

1. *Obtain approval.* Obtain the approval of the controller to add or delete an account from the chart of accounts.
2. *Delete account.* If deleting an account, follow these steps:
    a. Note the budget amount assigned to the account in each accounting period.
    b. Verify with the controller where these budget amounts are to be assigned.
    c. If the budget is being shifted to a new responsibility area, obtain the approval of the person who was responsible for the budget, and notify the newly-responsible person of the change.

    d. Move the budget amounts and verify the accuracy of the move.
3. *Add account.* If adding an account, follow these steps:
    a. Inquire whether an existing budgeted amount will be assigned to it, and which account will be reduced to fund this budget.
    b. If the budget is being shifted to a new responsibility area, obtain the approval of the person who was responsible for the budget, and notify the newly-responsible person of the change.
    c. Move the budget amounts and verify the accuracy of the move.

Summary

It is not sufficient to merely issue the procedures noted in this chapter and assume that the budget model will miraculously create itself. Instead, it requires continual follow-up for each step in the process, as well as cajoling employees into submitting required documents on a timely basis. Nonetheless, procedures are an invaluable guideline, not only for the company at large, but more specifically for the team that is responsible for shepherding the budget through to completion.

Chapter 24
Budgeting Efficiencies

Introduction

Depending upon the level of detail, a budget is one of the most complex documents that a business will create, while the budgeting process needed to create it is equally difficult to manage. Consider using some or all of the error reduction, data verification, and both model and process simplification suggestions in this chapter to increase the level of efficiency in the budgeting process.

> **Related Podcast Episode:** Episode 71 of the Accounting Best Practices Podcast discusses budget model improvements. You can listen to it at: **accounting-tools.com/podcasts** or **iTunes**

Budget Model Efficiencies

There are three ways to improve a budget model. First, you can use a variety of techniques to eliminate the errors in an electronic spreadsheet that is being used to compile a budget. Second, you can adopt several methods for verifying the information in a budget model. Finally, you can simplify the model, thereby reducing the chance of there being errors to correct. We explore all three options in this section.

Spreadsheet Error Checking

One of the fundamental sources of flaws in a budget is that nearly everyone creates it using an electronic spreadsheet. The electronic spreadsheet is a magnificent tool, but it is all too easy to inadvertently introduce an error with an incorrect formula or cell reference. If you have created a spreadsheet, have someone else review it in detail. This person should verify that the ranges for each subtotal and total are correct, that the totals across the bottom of each spreadsheet (for individual months or quarters) correctly sum to the total down the right side (the line item totals), that any information being automatically pulled from a different spreadsheet page is linked to the correct cell, and that formulas are correct.

This error review work should absolutely *not* be done by the person who created or currently maintains the spreadsheet, since they are so familiar with it that they are unlikely to spot what might be considered a glaring error. Instead, use someone who is familiar with spreadsheets, but who does not interact with the budget on a regular basis. This task could even be handed off to an auditor, who likely has the necessary skills and no vested interest in covering up an error.

It is also useful to summarize the budget model in two ways, to see if the totals of the two methods are the same. If there is a difference in the two summarizations, there is probably a summarization error somewhere in the model. One summarization should be by department, and the other by expense line item, as follows:

- *Department totals.* This takes the grand total expense for each budget period from the individual department budgets and aggregates them on a single page. Thus, the summarization could include totals for such departments as administration, engineering, and production.
- *Expense totals.* This takes the line item expense for each period from the individual department budgets and aggregates them on a single page. Thus, the summarization could include totals for such expenses as office supplies, payroll taxes, and salaries.

The problem you are trying to locate is a summarization error at the department level. Since the summarization by expense line item does not use these department-level summarizations, any disparity between the two methods should be caused by a departmental summarization error. The following example illustrates the problem.

EXAMPLE

The controller of Quest Adventure Gear wants to know if there is a summarization error somewhere in the company's budget. To find it, he summarizes the budget results of all five company departments in a separate section of the budget, along with a separate summarization of all expenses by individual expense line item. The result appears in the following two tables:

Summarization by Department

	Quarter 1	Quarter 2	Quarter 3	Quarter 4
Accounting department	$83,000	$86,500	$79,250	$84,500
Engineering department	320,000	324,000	317,500	321,750
Production department	840,000	901,000	894,000	903,000
Purchasing department	95,000	103,000	98,000	105,750
Sales department	210,000	215,000	203,000	217,000
Total expenses	$1,548,000	$1,629,500	$1,581,750	$1,632,000

Summarization by Expense

	Quarter 1	Quarter 2	Quarter 3	Quarter 4
Depreciation	$95,000	$98,000	$102,000	$105,000
Office expenses	42,000	40,500	43,000	46,000
Payroll taxes	97,500	104,000	99,750	103,500
Salaries	1,133,500	1,192,000	1,147,000	1,190,500
Travel and entertainment	180,000	195,000	200,000	187,000
Total expenses	$1,548,000	$1,629,500	$1,591,750	$1,632,000

There is a disparity of $10,000 between the totals of the two tables. The problem appears to originate in the third quarter, where the summarization by department is lower by $10,000.

Upon further investigation, the controller finds that the expense budget for the engineering department contains an error in the summarization total in the third quarter, as shown in the following table.

Engineering Department Budget Containing Error

	Quarter 1	Quarter 2	Quarter 3	Quarter 4
Depreciation	$15,000	$15,000	$16,000	$16,000
Office expenses	7,000	7,500	8,000	8,500
Payroll taxes	24,000	24,500	21,000	20,250
Salaries	274,000	277,000	272,500	277,000
Travel and entertainment	0	0	10,000	0
Total expenses	$320,000	$324,000	$317,500	$321,750

The total expenses line for the engineering department contains a summarization formula that does not include the final row of expenses, which is the travel and entertainment line. Since only the third quarter contained a budgeted expenditure for this line, the error was not apparent in the other quarters.

Upon correction of the summarization total, the controller finds that the summarizations by department and expense match. It is unlikely that any other summarization errors exist in the budget model.

Another way to locate errors in the model is to compare the preceding year's budget model (from which the current model was presumably copied) to actual results for that year. The differences between budget and actual results *should* be based on simple differences in expectations versus actual results. However, it is also possible that a really glaring difference was caused by an error in the budget model. Consider using the following techniques to spot these errors:

- *Set revenue to actual.* If the budget model was designed to be a flex budget, where expenses automatically change to match revenue levels, enter the actual revenue figures for the budget period in the model. This should alter the results of the model to be close to actual results. If this is not the case, investigate the larger variances. There may be errors in the model or at least assumptions that should be modified.

- *Match compensation and payroll taxes.* The compensation calculations in a budget are among the most complicated in the entire budget, because they incorporate pay rate changes, overtime, and payroll taxes that may include a wage base limit (which is the maximum amount of wages to which the social security tax applies). This level of complexity nearly ensures the presence of a calculation error. To locate these errors, compare actual employee gross pay for a prior period (found in the payroll register) to the gross pay listed in the budget for the same time period. If there is a difference, the budget model may be in error.

In short, you can conduct spreadsheet error checking either by having a second person examine the model, summarizing the budget material in different ways to spot anomalies, or analyzing the budget-to-actual information from the preceding year.

Verification Opportunities

How do you review an entire budget? For a larger corporation, there may be masses of line items on dozens or even hundreds of pages, so how is it possible to ascertain which items are either not correct or at least in need of serious additional review? Here are several ways to address the issue:

- *80/20 rule*. Only do an in-depth review of the 20 percent of all line items that comprise 80 percent of the revenues and expenditures in a budget. Any other items are so insignificant that even an egregious error is unlikely to cause much of an impact on the total amount of a budget.
- *Broad view*. Rather than delving into the minutest details of a budget, step back from the budget (figuratively speaking) and ask if the numbers make sense. In particular:
  o Does the company have sufficient capacity to achieve the budget?
  o Does the company have enough cash, or access to cash, to achieve the budget?
  o Where are the pitfalls that are most likely to keep the budget from being achieved?
  o If this is a stretch budget, has the company ever succeeded with such significant changes in the past? If not, what kept the company from achieving them?
  o How will competitors react to any newly budgeted activities?
- *Fixed cost continuance*. A fixed cost may not continue at the same historical expenditure level through the entire budget period. Such costs are sometimes subject to cost escalation clauses (especially multi-year rent agreements), so consider creating a separate list of all contractually-mandated cost changes, and compare it to the budget.
- *Contract expirations*. Does a long-term agreement expire during the budget period? If so, it is entirely possible that the cost will change significantly, so obtain the best possible estimate of the new cost from the purchasing manager or legal counsel.
- *Compare spending to events*. There may be a number of events during the budget period for which major expenditures are required, such as a trade show or a company Christmas party. If so, verify that expenditures in the budget are aligned with these events, and that sufficient funds have been allocated for them.

In short, you can verify the information in a budget by focusing only on the largest expenditures, inquiring into the company's general ability to achieve the budget, and searching for points at which costs change significantly.

Simplification Opportunities

The budget model is a complex document that requires a substantial amount of effort to maintain. You can mitigate this issue by periodically simplifying the model, using block budgeting, eliminating accounts, and aggregating compensation information. We will discuss these issues below.

A key problem with a spreadsheet-based budget model is that it tends to become more complex over time as more departments, assumptions, revenue and expense types, and so forth are added to it. This increased level of complexity makes it easier for errors to find their way into the model. To avoid this problem, include a step at the beginning of the annual budgeting procedure to examine the structure of the budget model from the preceding year and simplify it where possible.

In some companies, there is a budgeted amount for every line item in the chart of accounts. The accounting staff likes this level of budgeting, since it can insert a budgeted amount in the financial statements next to each line item and show variances between actual and budgeted expenditure levels. If senior management insists that department managers only spend the funds specifically authorized for each line item, this is called *line item budgeting*.

Line item budgeting is a very restrictive format and is not recommended, for it forces managers to monitor expenditures at an oppressively detailed level, as well as document any requests to shift budgeted funds between accounts.

A much better approach is the *block budget*, where funds are allocated to an entire department or other functional area, and managers are given authority to expend the funds as they see fit. This approach is much less restrictive and easier to manage. Also, it accommodates the natural variability in expenses that will arise from year to year, where some line item expenses will inevitably vary from expectations due to factors outside of the control of management.

The main reason why there are so many expense line items in a budget is because the budget is designed to mimic the structure of the chart of accounts. Therefore, if you want to simplify the budget, a good way to do so is to reduce the number of accounts in the chart of accounts. This can be a lengthy process, because you need to verify which accounts are no longer needed, move the balances (and perhaps the underlying detail) out of those accounts and into other accounts, and then modify company reports to reflect the change. This is a slow and tedious process, so you might consider eliminating just a few accounts per year, thereby gradually simplifying both the chart of accounts and the budget model over time.

An alternative to eliminating accounts is to simply remove them from the budget model. This means that there will be no budget associated with some financial statement line items. This may be acceptable for minor or rarely used types of expenses.

Another area in which budgets tend to be overly complex is in the calculation of compensation for every employee on the payroll. If your company has a large number of employees, this can result in a massive amount of data entry to ensure that the correct pay rates and annual pay review dates are included in the budget. In such cases, consider aggregating compensation by title, job function, work group, or department. By doing so, you can reduce the amount of information in the budget by several orders of magnitude. However, this requires the use of averages for the amount of budgeted compensation, as well as estimates for the timing of changes in compensation (though you can institute a policy for altering pay levels so that it always occurs on the same date of every year). The use of estimates always results in less accuracy, but this may be a worthwhile tradeoff if you can eliminate a large part of the budget model.

In short, you can achieve a certain amount of budget model simplification by requiring a periodic simplification review of the budget model, switching to block budgeting, reducing the number of accounts, and aggregating the calculation of employee compensation.

Simplification over Time

A comparison of historical to budgeted results may reveal that a company is not very good at predicting future revenues and expenses. If so, it may make sense to only include deep budget detail in the first few time periods covered by a budget. Beyond these periods, a simplified version of the budget can be substituted for the full-scale version. An alternative is to simply use a revenue forecast after the first few budget periods.

Budgeting Process Efficiencies

The preceding discussion of efficiencies only addressed the inner workings of the budget model – it did not cover the process leading up to the creation of the model. There are several possible areas of improvement in this process, which we discuss in this section.

One of the problems with the annual budget is that the budgeting staff only uses it during a specific time period, once a year. Because of the long intervals between usage, employees may forget how to use the system, and so will have to re-learn it the following year. To reduce this level of inefficiency, consider having the budgeting staff create a short procedure that touches upon the key points of operating the model, which they can use to refresh their memories when they begin using the model again at the start of the next budgeting cycle.

In addition, create an extensive budgeting procedure and calendar for the entire annual budgeting process, to be distributed to all participants in the process. This procedure should specify the due dates for all budget-related deliverables, who is responsible for each deliverable, and what the deliverable should look like. There should also be a qualified manager who can drive the budgeting process through to its completion as of a targeted date. Further, continually review and update the procedure every year to adjust it to match changes in the business and the requirements of the budget model. Only after multiple iterations and refinements of the procedure over several years can you expect to attain a process that generates a high-quality budget with the least amount of company-wide effort. The budgeting procedure is covered extensively in the Budgeting Procedures chapter.

It takes a considerable amount of time for a department manager to fill out a blank budget form that outlines his estimates of expected costs during an upcoming budget period. Completing the form takes managers away from their usual operational responsibilities, so it may be quite some time before they can attend to it. You can reduce this delay by issuing a pre-loaded budget form to the department managers. This form contains the budgeting staff's best estimate of what a department will expend, based on its historical results and as adjusted for expected changes in activity levels and the inflation rate. This approach works well in most situations, since the bulk of expense line items are essentially fixed or at least do not vary much over time.

When a department manager receives a pre-loaded budget, all that he has to do is make a few adjustments and return the completed document. The adjustment will likely involve step costs, such as the hiring of new staff or the acquisition of new equipment, which the budgeting staff might not have been aware of. The only problem with the pre-loaded budget concept is that department managers might try to avoid responsibility for their budgets on the grounds that they were following the dictates of the budgeting staff.

You can also consider restricting the number of budget iterations to a relatively small amount, such as two or three iterations. You can collect the bulk of the information you need with the first iteration of the budget, and then correct for gross errors and assumption changes in the second iteration. At that point, further refinement of the model will be pointless, since actual results are bound to vary enough over time that the company will be unable to achieve results that meet the level of precision built into a multi-iteration budget.

In short, you can improve the efficiency of the budgeting process with a tight budgeting procedure and timetable, filling in as much of the budgeting information on budget forms as possible for department managers, and restricting the number of budget iterations.

Participative Budgeting

Thus far, we have discussed how to increase the *efficiency* of budgeting. Also consider the *effectiveness* of budgeting, which means that you obtain the best possible results from the process. One tool for doing so is called participative budgeting. It is a budgeting process under which those people impacted by a budget are involved in the budget creation process.

This bottom-up approach to budgeting tends to create budgets that are more achievable than are top-down budgets that are imposed on a company by senior management with less participation by employees. Participative budgeting is also better for morale, and tends to result in greater efforts by employees to achieve what they predicted in the budget. However, a purely participative budget does not take high-level strategic considerations into account, so management needs to provide employees with guidelines regarding the overall direction of the company, and how their individual departments fit into that direction.

When participative budgeting is used throughout an organization, the preliminary budgets work their way up through the corporate hierarchy, being reviewed and possibly modified by mid-level managers along the way. Once assembled into a single master budget, it may become apparent that the submitted budgets will not work together, in which case they are sent back down to the originators for another iteration, usually with guidelines noting what senior management is looking for.

Because of the larger number of employees involved in participatory budgeting, it tends to take longer to create a budget than is the case with a top-down budget that may be created by a much smaller number of people.

Another problem with participative budgeting is that, since the people originating the budget are also the ones whose performance will be compared to it, there is a tendency for participants to adopt a conservative budget with extra expense padding, so that they are reasonably assured of achieving what they predict in the budget. This tendency is more pronounced when employees are paid bonuses based on their performance against the budget.

This problem of budgetary slack can be mitigated by imposing a review of the budget by those members of management who are most likely to know when budgets are being padded, and who are allowed to adjust the budget for this issue.

Summary

In this chapter, we discussed a variety of ways to increase the efficiency of the budgeting process, concentrating in particular on streamlining and correcting errors in the budget spreadsheet. You can avoid the spreadsheet issues entirely by purchasing budgeting software, which is designed to be relatively error-free. However, this software is expensive, and so is not usually a cost-effective option for a smaller business.

Another way to improve the efficiency of the budgeting process is, of course, to eliminate the budget entirely and instead use a rolling forecast, as was already discussed elsewhere in this book. Under that approach, the amount of information collected is quite small, and the forecasting procedure is so abbreviated that a discussion of budgeting efficiency is essentially irrelevant.

Chapter 25
Budget Reporting

Introduction

After creating a budget, compare it to actual results so that management can see how well the business is performing in comparison to their expectations. You can do so at a general level, merely reporting differences between budget and actual revenues and expenses. However, this does not show the reasons why variances have arisen. In this chapter, we address the various reporting formats that give management the actionable information they need to address unfavorable budget variances.

General Reporting Format

If you load a completed budget into the accounting software, there will almost always be a budget versus actual reporting format for the income statement and the various departmental income statements. This report reveals any variances between the budgeted and actual amounts. A budget variance is the difference between the budgeted amount of expense or revenue and the actual amount. The budget variance is favorable when the actual revenue is higher than the budget or when the actual expense is less than the budget. The format of such a report is similar to the one in the following sample.

Sample Budget versus Actual Income Statement

	Actual Results	Budget Results	Variance ($)	Variance (%)
Revenue	$1,000,000	$1,100,000	-$100,000	-9%
Cost of goods sold:				
Direct materials	300,000	330,000	30,000	9%
Direct labor	100,000	90,000	-10,000	-11%
Manufacturing overhead	150,000	155,000	5,000	3%
Total cost of goods sold	550,000	575,000	25,000	4%
Gross margin	$450,000	$525,000	-$75,000	-14%
Administration expenses	175,000	160,000	-15,000	-9%
Sales and marketing expenses	225,000	205,000	-20,000	-10%
Net profit or loss	$50,000	$160,000	-$110,000	-69%

This report format does not reveal a great deal of information by itself, since it only notifies management of the presence *of* a variance, not the reason *for* the variance.

Further, the budget upon which the variance is calculated may be so far out of line with actual results that the variance is essentially meaningless.

A subtle variation on this report format is to position the largest-dollar items at the top of the report, so that the areas in which variances are likely to be largest are where management can more easily see them. The following example illustrates the concept.

Sample Sales and Marketing Department Monthly Report

Expense Item	Actual	Budget	$ Variance	% Variance
Wages	$85,000	$82,000	-$3,000	-4%
Commissions	18,000	19,500	1,500	8%
Payroll taxes	8,000	7,500	-500	-7%
Trade shows	25,000	28,000	3,000	11%
Travel and entertainment	11,000	7,000	-4,000	-57%
Office expenses	6,500	3,500	-3,000	-86%
Promotional materials	5,000	5,000	0	0%
Other	1,200	500	-700	-58%
Totals	$159,700	$153,000	-$6,700	-4%

Note how the preceding report is structured to place wages and related expenses at the top of the report; this is because compensation costs are the largest expenditure for many departments, and so should be a center of attention.

An alternative format is one that presents a historical trend line of revenues and expenses for each line item in the income statement. Doing so eliminates the risk of comparing a completely inaccurate budget to your actual results. A sample report format follows.

Sample Trend Line Report Format

	Jan.	Feb	Mar.	Apr.	May
Accounting fees	$1,000	$1,100	$1,050	$1,900	$1,150
Legal	0	0	5,000	0	250
Maintenance	550	575	400	600	3,250
Office expenses	925	2,800	890	790	850
Travel and entertainment	6,500	1,200	1,350	1,400	995
Utilities	500	310	420	1,600	375
Totals	$9,475	$5,985	$9,110	$6,290	$6,870

The key assumption behind a trend line report is that most expenses do not vary much from period to period. If that assumption is true, then the report is excellent for highlighting anomalies over time.

No matter which of the preceding report formats you use, it is rarely sufficient to simply issue financial information to managers without at least some explanation of the larger variances. Instead, investigate the larger variances and issue a separate report that delves into the reasons for them. The following sample report states the amount of each expense or revenue item that requires explanation, and then spends a fair amount of time describing the situation.

Sample Variance Discussion Report

Line Item	Discussion
Product Alpha revenue	Revenues were $100,000 lower than expected, due to a product recall and free replacement. The problem was a design flaw that is being investigated by Engineering. Recommend stopping sales until an engineering change order is released.
Direct materials expense	Freight expense was $40,000 higher than expected, due to air freight of late delivery from overseas supplier. Recommend sourcing the part locally.
Rent expense	Expense was $20,000 lower than expected, due to renegotiation of building lease. Note that the lease now runs an additional three years.
Travel and entertainment expense	Expense was $25,000 higher than expected, due to damage to rental party room during company Christmas party.
Utilities expense	Electricity cost was $15,000 higher than expected, due to unusually cold December temperatures. Recommend additional building insulation.

Note that the best reports of this type very clearly quantify the issue and state the exact cause of the problem, possibly with an accompanying recommendation. The report needs to be sufficiently detailed that management can use it to resolve the underlying problem.

Revenue Reporting

If you want to report on specific types of variance issues related to revenues, the key variance calculations are for the selling price variance and the selling volume variance. We describe the calculation and usage of both variances in this section.

Selling Price Variance

The selling price variance is the difference between the actual and expected revenue that is caused by a change in the price of a product or service. The formula is:

(Actual price - Budgeted price) × Actual unit sales = Selling price variance

An unfavorable variance means that the actual price was lower than the budgeted price.

The budgeted price for each unit of product or sales is developed by the sales and marketing managers, and is based on their estimation of future demand for these products and services, which in turn is affected by general economic conditions and the actions of competitors. If the actual price is lower than the budgeted price, the result may actually be favorable to the company, as long as the price decline spurs demand to such an extent that the company generates an incremental profit as a result of the price decline.

EXAMPLE

The marketing manager of Quest Adventure Gear estimates that the company can sell a green widget for $80 per unit during the upcoming year. This estimate is based on the historical demand for green widgets.

During the first half of the new year, the price of the green widget comes under extreme pressure as a new supplier in Ireland floods the market with a lower-priced green widget. Quest must drop its price to $70 in order to compete, and sells 20,000 units during that period. Its selling price variance during the first half of the year is:

($70 Actual price - $80 Budgeted price) × 20,000 units = $(200,000) Selling price variance

---

There are a number of possible causes of a selling price variance. For example:
- *Discounts*. The company has granted various discounts to customers to induce them to buy products.
- *Marketing allowances*. The company is allowing customers to deduct marketing allowances from their payments to reimburse them for marketing activities involving the company's products.
- *Price points*. The price points at which the company is selling are different from the price points stated in its budget.
- *Product options*. Customers are buying different product options than expected, resulting in an average price that differs from the price points stated in the company's budget.

Sales Volume Variance

The sales volume variance is the difference between the actual and expected number of units sold, multiplied by the budgeted price per unit. The formula is:

(Actual units sold - Budgeted units sold) × Budgeted price per unit
= Sales volume variance

An unfavorable variance means that the actual number of units sold was lower than the budgeted number sold.

The budgeted number of units sold is derived by the sales and marketing managers, and is based on their estimation of how the company's product market share, features, price points, expected marketing activities, distribution channels, and sales in new regions will impact future sales. If the product's selling price is lower than the budgeted amount, this may spur sales to such an extent that the sales volume variance is favorable, even though the selling price variance is unfavorable.

EXAMPLE

The marketing manager of Quest Adventure Gear estimates that the company can sell 25,000 blue widgets for $65 per unit during the upcoming year. This estimate is based on the historical demand for blue widgets, as supported by new advertising campaigns in the first and third quarters of the year.

During the new year, Quest does not have a first quarter advertising campaign, since it was changing advertising agencies at that time. This results in sales of just 21,000 blue widgets during the year. Its sales volume variance is:

(21,000 Units sold - 25,000 Budgeted units) × $65 Budgeted price per unit
= $260,000 Unfavorable sales volume variance

There are a number of possible causes of a sales volume variance. For example:
- *Cannibalization.* The company may have released another product that competes with the product in question. Thus, sales of one product cannibalize sales of the other product.
- *Competition.* Competitors may have released new products that are more attractive to customers.
- *Price.* The company may have altered the product price, which in turn drives a change in unit sales volume.
- *Trade restrictions.* A foreign country may have altered its barriers to competition.

Overview of Cost of Goods Sold Variance Reporting

A number of variances have been developed for expenses categorized within the cost of goods sold. When you create a budget, you are creating a standard cost against which actual costs and usage can be compared. There are two basic types of variances from a standard that can arise, which are the rate variance and the volume variance. They are:
- *Rate variance.* A rate variance is the difference between the actual price paid for something and the expected price, multiplied by the actual quantity purchased. The "rate" variance designation is most commonly applied to the labor rate variance, which involves the actual cost of direct labor in comparison to the standard cost of direct labor. The rate variance uses a different designation when applied to the purchase of materials, and may be called the *purchase price variance* or the *material price variance*.
- *Volume variance.* A volume variance is the difference between the actual quantity sold or consumed and the budgeted amount, multiplied by the

standard price or cost per unit. If the variance relates to the sale of goods, it is called the *sales volume variance*. If it relates to the use of direct materials, it is called the *material yield variance*. If the variance relates to the use of direct labor, it is called the *labor efficiency variance*. Finally, if the variance relates to the application of overhead, it is called the *overhead efficiency variance*.

Thus, variances are based on either changes in cost from the expected amount, or changes in the quantity from the expected amount. The most common variances to report on are subdivided within the rate and volume variance categories for direct materials, direct labor, and overhead. Thus, the primary variances are:

	Rate Variance	Volume Variance
Materials	Purchase price variance	Material yield variance
Direct labor	Labor rate variance	Labor efficiency variance
Fixed overhead	Fixed overhead spending variance	Not applicable
Variable overhead	Variable overhead spending variance	Variable overhead efficiency variance

All of the variances noted in the preceding table are explained in the following sections, including examples to demonstrate how the variances are applied.

The Purchase Price Variance

The purchase price variance is the difference between the actual price paid to buy an item and its standard price, multiplied by the actual number of units purchased. The formula is:

(Actual price - Standard price) × Actual quantity = Purchase price variance

A positive variance means that actual costs have increased, and a negative variance means that actual costs have declined.

The standard price is the price that your engineers believe the company should pay for an item, given a certain quality level, purchasing quantity, and speed of delivery. Thus, the variance is really based on a standard price that was the collective opinion of several employees based on a number of assumptions that may no longer match a company's current purchasing situation.

EXAMPLE

During the development of its annual budget, the engineers and purchasing staff of Quest Adventure Gear decide that the standard cost of a green widget should be set at $5.00, which is based on a purchasing volume of 10,000 for the upcoming year. During the subsequent year, Quest only buys 8,000 units, and so cannot take advantage of purchasing discounts, and ends up paying $5.50 per widget. This creates a purchase price variance of $0.50 per widget, and a variance of $4,000 for all of the 8,000 widgets that Quest purchased.

There are a number of possible causes of a purchase price variance. For example:

- *Layering issue.* The actual cost may have been taken from an inventory layering system, such as a first-in first-out system, where the actual cost may vary from the current market price by a substantial margin.
- *Materials shortage.* There is an industry shortage of a commodity item, which is driving up the cost.
- *New supplier.* The company has changed suppliers for any number of reasons, resulting in a new cost structure that is not reflected in the budget.
- *Rush basis.* The company incurred excessive shipping charges to obtain materials on short notice from suppliers.
- *Volume assumption.* The budgeted cost of an item was derived based on a different purchasing volume than the amount at which the company now buys.

In what level of detail should you investigate a purchase price variance? The key issue is not to waste time on variances so small that managers are not going to take action. Instead, report on the 20 percent of issues that usually cause about 80 percent of the variance.

The following sample report format should contain sufficient information for a manager to engage in corrective action:

Sample Purchase Price Variance Report

Item No.	Item Description	Purchase Price	Standard Price	Variance	Reason
123A	Widget trim	$8.00	$7.00	-$1.00	Ordered below standard quantity
234B	Widget blue color	4.25	3.00	-1.25	Ordered odd size lot
567Q	Widget arm	20.00	16.50	-3.50	Incorrect specifications
891D	Widget case	15.00	12.00	-3.00	Ordered on short notice
112R	Widget housing	130.00	115.00	-15.00	Ordered below standard quantity
150F	Widget lens port	82.15	78.00	-4.15	Supplier price increase
115G	Widget trigger	4.25	3.75	-0.50	Ordered on short notice
227V	Widget base	37.50	32.00	-5.50	Supplier price increase
772J	Widget packing crate	24.00	21.50	-2.50	Ordered odd lot size

Material Yield Variance

The material yield variance is the difference between the actual amount of material used and the standard amount expected to be used, multiplied by the standard cost of the materials. The formula is:

$$\text{(Actual unit usage - Standard unit usage)} \times \text{Standard cost per unit}$$
$$= \text{Material yield variance}$$

An unfavorable variance means that the unit usage was greater than anticipated.

The standard unit usage is developed by the engineering staff, and is based on expected scrap rates in a production process, the quality of raw materials, losses during equipment setup, and related factors.

EXAMPLE

The engineering staff of Quest Adventure Gear estimates that eight ounces of rubber will be required to produce a green widget. During the most recent month, the production process used 315,000 ounces of rubber to create 35,000 green widgets, which is 9 ounces per product. Each ounce of rubber has a standard cost of $0.50. Its material yield variance for the month is:

$$\text{(315,000 Actual unit usage - 280,000 Standard unit usage)} \times \$0.50 \text{ Standard cost/unit}$$
$$= \$17,500 \text{ Material yield variance}$$

There are a number of possible causes of a material yield variance. For example:

- *Scrap.* Unusual amounts of scrap may be generated by changes in machine setups, or because changes in acceptable tolerance levels are altering the amount of scrap produced. A change in the pattern of quality inspections can also alter the amount of scrap.
- *Material quality.* If the material quality level changes, this can alter the amount of quality rejections. If an entirely different material is substituted, this can also alter the amount of rejections.
- *Spoilage.* The amount of spoilage may change in concert with alterations in inventory handling and storage.

It can be extremely difficult to ascertain the reasons for a material yield variance, since it is caused by operational issues in the production area, rather than something easily searchable in the accounting database. Consequently, it rarely makes sense to investigate anything but the largest variances. If you choose to do so, the report format is similar to the purchase price variance report just described, except that it is in units, rather than dollars. A sample report follows:

Sample Material Yield Variance Report

Item No.	Item Description	Actual Usage	Standard Usage	Variance	Reason
123A	Widget trim	540	500	-40	Incorrect standard
234B	Widget blue color	200	150	-50	Materials too old; disposed of
567Q	Widget arm	1,500	1,100	-400	Supplier shipped short
891D	Widget case	800	-720	-80	Incorrect machine setup
112R	Widget housing	150	0	-150	Item declared obsolete
150F	Widget lens port	300	100	-200	Receipt counting error
115G	Widget trigger	280	225	-55	Scrap due to machinist error
227V	Widget base	460	300	-160	Item declared obsolete
772J	Widget packing crate	950	800	-150	Damaged in transit

Labor Rate Variance

The labor rate variance is the difference between the actual labor rate paid and the standard rate, multiplied by the number of actual hours worked. The formula is:

(Actual rate - Standard rate) × Actual hours worked = Labor rate variance

An unfavorable variance means that the cost of labor was more expensive than anticipated.

The standard labor rate is developed by the human resources and industrial engineering employees, and is based on such factors as the expected mix of pay levels among the production staff, the amount of overtime likely to be incurred, the amount of new hiring at different pay rates, the number of promotions into higher pay levels, and the outcome of contract negotiations with any unions representing the production staff.

EXAMPLE

The human resources manager of Quest Adventure Gear estimates that the average labor rate for the coming year for Quest's production staff will be $25/hour. This estimate is based on a standard mix of personnel at different pay rates, as well as a reasonable proportion of overtime hours worked.

During the first month of the new year, Quest has difficulty hiring a sufficient number of new employees, and so must have its higher-paid existing staff work overtime to complete a number of jobs. The result is an actual labor rate of $30/hour. Quest's production staff worked 10,000 hours during the month. Its labor rate variance for the month is:

($30/hr Actual rate - $25/hour Standard rate) × 10,000 hours = $50,000 Labor rate variance

---

There are a number of possible causes of a labor rate variance. For example:

- *Incorrect standards.* The labor standard may not reflect recent changes in the rates paid to employees (which tend to occur in bulk for all staff).
- *Pay premiums.* The actual amounts paid may include extra payments for shift differentials or overtime.
- *Staffing variances.* A labor standard may assume that a certain job classification will perform a designated task, when in fact a different position with a different pay rate may be performing the work.

Labor Efficiency Variance

The labor efficiency variance is the difference between the actual labor hours used to produce an item and the standard amount that should have been used, multiplied by the standard labor rate. The formula is:

(Actual hours - Standard hours) × Standard rate = Labor efficiency variance

An unfavorable variance means that labor efficiency has worsened, and a favorable variance means that labor efficiency has increased.

The standard number of hours represents the best estimate of the industrial engineers regarding the optimal speed at which the production staff can manufacture goods. This figure can vary considerably, based on assumptions regarding the setup time of a production run, the availability of materials and machine capacity, employee skill levels, the duration of a production run, and other factors. Thus, the multitude of variables involved makes it especially difficult to create a budget that you can meaningfully compare to actual results.

EXAMPLE

During the development of its annual budget, the industrial engineers of Quest Adventure Gear decide that the standard amount of time required to produce a green widget should be 30 minutes, which is based on certain assumptions about the efficiency of Quest's production staff, the availability of materials, capacity availability, and so forth. During the month, widget materials were in short supply, so Quest had to pay production staff even when there was no material to work on, resulting in an average production time per unit of 45 minutes. The company produced 1,000 widgets during the month. The standard cost per labor hour is $20, so the calculation of its labor efficiency variance is:

$$\text{(750 Actual hours - 500 Standard hours)} \times \$20 \text{ Standard rate}$$
$$= \$5,000 \text{ Labor efficiency variance}$$

There are a number of possible causes of a labor efficiency variance. For example:

- *Instructions*. The employees may not have received written work instructions.
- *Mix*. The standard assumes a certain mix of employees involving different skill levels, which does not match the actual staffing.
- *Training*. The standard may be based on an assumption of a minimum amount of training that employees have not received.
- *Work station configuration*. A work center may have been reconfigured since the standard was created, so the budget is now incorrect.

Variable Overhead Spending Variance

The variable overhead spending variance is the difference between the actual and budgeted rates of spending on variable overhead. The formula is:

$$\text{Actual hours worked} \times \text{(Actual overhead rate - Standard overhead rate)}$$
$$= \text{Variable overhead spending variance}$$

A favorable variance means that the actual variable overhead expenses incurred per labor hour were less than expected.

The variable overhead spending variance is a compilation of production expense information submitted by the production department, and the projected labor hours to be worked, as estimated by the industrial engineering and production scheduling staffs, based on historical and projected efficiency and equipment capacity levels.

EXAMPLE

The cost accounting staff of Quest Adventure Gear calculates, based on historical and projected cost patterns, that the company should experience a variable overhead rate of $20 per labor hour worked, and builds this figure into the budget. In April, the actual variable overhead rate turns out to be $22 per labor hour. During that month, production employees work 18,000 hours. The variable overhead spending variance is:

18,000 Actual hours worked × ($22 Actual variable overhead rate
- $20 Standard overhead rate)
= $36,000 Variable overhead spending variance

There are a number of possible causes of a variable overhead spending variance. For example:

- *Account misclassification.* The variable overhead category includes a number of accounts, some of which may have been incorrectly classified and so do not appear as part of variable overhead (or vice versa).
- *Outsourcing.* Some activities that had been sourced in-house have now been shifted to a supplier, or vice versa.
- *Supplier pricing.* Suppliers have changed their prices, which have not been reflected in the budget.

Variable Overhead Efficiency Variance

The variable overhead efficiency variance is the difference between the actual and budgeted hours worked, which are then applied to the standard variable overhead rate per hour. The formula is:

Standard overhead rate × (Actual hours - Standard hours)
= Variable overhead efficiency variance

A favorable variance means that the actual hours worked were less than the budgeted hours, resulting in the application of the standard overhead rate across fewer hours, resulting in less expense incurred.

The variable overhead efficiency variance is a compilation of production expense information submitted by the production department, and the projected labor hours to be worked, as estimated by the industrial engineering and production scheduling staffs, based on historical and projected efficiency and equipment capacity levels.

EXAMPLE

The cost accounting staff of Quest Adventure Gear calculates, based on historical and projected labor patterns, that the company's production staff should work 20,000 hours per month and incur $400,000 of variable overhead costs per month, so it establishes a variable overhead rate of $20 per hour. In May, Quest installs a new materials handling system that significantly improves production efficiency and drops the hours worked during the month to 19,000. The variable overhead efficiency variance is:

$20 Standard overhead rate/hour × (19,000 Hours worked - 20,000 Standard hours)
= $20,000 Variable overhead efficiency variance

Fixed Overhead Spending Variance

The fixed overhead spending variance is the difference between the actual fixed overhead expense incurred and the budgeted fixed overhead expense. An unfavorable variance means that actual overhead expenditures were greater than planned. The formula is:

Actual fixed overhead - Budgeted fixed overhead = Fixed overhead spending variance

The amount of expense related to fixed overhead should (as the name implies) be relatively fixed, and so the fixed overhead spending variance should not theoretically vary much from the budget. However, if the manufacturing process reaches a step cost trigger point, where a whole new expense must be incurred, then this can cause a significant unfavorable variance. Also, there may be some seasonality in fixed overhead expenditures, which may cause both favorable and unfavorable variances in individual months of a year, but which cancel each other out over the full year.

EXAMPLE

The production manager of Quest Adventure Gear estimates that the fixed overhead should be $700,000 during the upcoming year. However, since a production manager left the company and was not replaced for several months, actual expenses were lower than expected, at $672,000. This created the following favorable fixed overhead spending variance:

($672,000 Actual fixed overhead - $700,000 Budgeted fixed overhead)
= $(28,000) Fixed overhead spending variance

There are a number of possible causes of a fixed overhead spending variance. For example:
- *Account misclassification.* The fixed overhead category includes a number of accounts, some of which may have been incorrectly classified and so do not appear as part of fixed overhead (or vice versa).
- *Outsourcing.* Some activities that had been sourced in-house have now been shifted to a supplier, or vice versa.

- *Supplier pricing.* Suppliers have changed their prices, which have not been reflected in the budget.

Problems with Variance Analysis

There are several problems with the variances described in this chapter, which are:

- *The use of standards.* A central issue is the use of standards (i.e., the budget) as the basis for calculating variances. What is the motivation for creating a standard? Standard creation can be a political process where the amount agreed upon is designed to make a department look good, rather than setting a target that will improve the company. If standards are politically created, variance analysis becomes useless from the perspective of controlling the company.
- *Feedback loop.* The accounting department does not calculate variances between actual and budgeted results until after it has closed the books and created financial statements, so there is a gap of potentially an entire month from when a variance arises and when it is reported to management. A faster feedback loop would be to eliminate variance reporting and instead create a reporting process that provides for feedback within moments of the occurrence of a triggering event.
- *Information drill down.* Many of the issues that cause variances are not stored within the accounting database. For example, the reason for excessive material usage may be a machine setup error, while excessive labor usage may be caused by the use of an excessive amount of employee overtime. In neither case will the accounting staff discover these issues by examining their transactional data. Thus, a variance report only highlights the general areas within which problems occurred, but does not necessarily tell anyone the nature of the underlying problems.

The preceding issues do not always keep accounting managers from calculating complete sets of variances for management consumption, but they bring up the question of whether the work required to calculate variances is a good use of staff time.

Which Variances to Report

A lot of variances have been described in this chapter. Do you really need to report them all to management? Not necessarily. If management agrees with a reduced reporting structure, you can report on just those variances over which management has some ability to reduce costs, and which contain sufficiently large variances to be worth reporting on.

The following table provides commentary on the characteristics of the variances:

Name of Variance	Commentary
Materials	
Purchase price variance	Material costs are controllable to some extent, and comprise a large part of the cost of goods sold; possibly the most important variance
Material yield variance	Can contain large potential cost reductions driven by quality issues, production layouts, and process flow; a good opportunity for cost reductions
Labor	
Labor rate variance	Labor rates are difficult to change; do not track unless you can shift work into lower pay grades
Labor efficiency variance	Can drive contrary behavior in favor of long production runs, when less labor efficiency in a just-in-time environment results in greater overall cost reductions; not recommended
Overhead	
Variable overhead spending variance	Caused by changes in the actual costs in the overhead cost pool, and so should be reviewed
Variable overhead efficiency variance	Caused by a change in the basis of allocation, which has no real impact on underlying costs; not recommended
Fixed overhead spending variance	Since fixed overhead costs should not vary much, a variance here is worth careful review; however, most components of fixed overhead are long-term costs that cannot be easily changed in the short term
Revenue	
Selling price variance	Caused by a change in the product price, which is under management control, and therefore should be brought to their attention
Sales volume variance	Caused by a change in the unit volume sold, which is not under direct management control, though this can be impacted by altering the product price

The preceding table shows that the variances most worthy of management's attention are the purchase price variance, variable overhead spending variance, fixed overhead spending variance, and selling price variance. Reducing the number of reported variances is well worth your time, since reporting the entire suite of variances calls for a great deal of investigative time to track down variance causes and then configure the information into a report suitable for management consumption.

How to Report Variances

A variance is a simple number, such as an unfavorable purchase price variance of $15,000. It tells management very little, since there is not enough information on which to base any corrective action. Consequently, you need to dig down into the underlying data to determine the actual causes of each variance, and then report the causes. Doing so is one of the most important value-added activities of the accounting department, since it leads directly to specific cost reductions. The following table is an example of the level of variance detail to report to management:

Variance Item	Amount*	Variance Cause
Purchase Price		
Order quantity	$500	Bought wrappers at half usual volume, and lost purchase discount
Substitute material	1,500	Used more expensive PVC piping; out of stock on regular item
Variable Overhead		
Rush order	300	Overnight charge to bring in grease for bearings
Utility surcharge	2,400	Charged extra for power usage during peak hours
Fixed Overhead		
Property taxes	3,000	Tax levy increased by 8%
Rent override	8,000	Landlord charge for proportional share of full-year expenses
Selling Price		
Marketing discounts	4,000	Customers took discounts for advertising pass-through
Sales returns	11,000	450 units returned with broken spring assembly

* Note: All amounts are unfavorable variances

The preceding table can be expanded to include the names of the managers responsible for correcting each item noted.

Summary

A great many variance calculations were discussed in this chapter. Just because they have been presented does not mean that it is necessary to create an elaborate reporting structure that contains all of them. Consider instead that management usually does not have time to read such a report, much less act on it. You may deliver a more effective budget report if you spend a great deal of time delving into the underlying reasons for just a few variances, and package the information so that the causes of the variances are readily understandable and can be acted upon at once. Then, in successive periods, rotate through different parts of the financial statements, identifying other areas in which there are actionable opportunities, and bringing them to the attention of management.

Even the best budget reporting does not eliminate the need for "face time" with managers. Schedule time with key managers and use your budget reports as supporting documents as you discuss specific variances, the reasons for them, and recommendations for improvements. This approach is much more likely to result in immediate management attention to key issues.

Chapter 26
Budgeting Controls

Introduction

Control systems are usually intended for business transactions that occur on a regular basis, and which involve the transfer of assets. Budgeting does not initially appear to require controls, since it is only an annual event, and it is not directly associated with accounting transactions. However, confusion can arise because of the multiple versions of a budget that are typically scattered throughout a company. Also, the budget is not directly integrated into a company's operations, and so tends to be forgotten. In this chapter, we describe several controls that address these problems.

> **Related Podcast Episode:** Episode 76 of the Accounting Best Practices Podcast discusses budgeting controls. You can listen to it at: **accountingtools.com/podcasts** or **iTunes**

Budget Creation Controls

A serious problem with any budget is that the normal iterative approach to creating it results in having a number of versions littering the company. The following controls are intended to lock down the final version and ensure that everyone in the company is using it:

- *Approve the budget.* There may be situations where managers claim that they did not approve of some aspects of the budget. To avoid this issue, have the board of directors formally approve a specific version of the budget, and include that version in the board minutes. This tends to quell dissent.

- *Label the final budget.* There will likely be several iterations of a budget, which means that some managers may end up using the wrong version. To avoid this problem, put the words FINAL BUDGET or APPROVED FINAL BUDGET in the footer of every page in the budget. Also state in the footer the date of the budget. Further, print and bind the final version and hand it out to all approved recipients. If you want to be absolutely certain that managers have received this final version, have them sign a receipt when you hand out the final version, and retain the receipts. By taking these steps, it is nearly impossible for a manager to be working from the wrong version of the budget.

- *Match loaded version to approved version.* Once the budget has been approved, load it into the accounting software, so that you can generate financial statements in an actual versus budget format. Given the volume of budget information to be entered, it is quite likely that some of the budget information will be entered into the accounting software incorrectly. Consequently, match the loaded version of the budget to the approved version, and adjust the loaded version for any errors found.

- *Password-protect the loaded budget.* Though unusual, it is possible that an employee could access the accounting system and alter the budget loaded into the accounting system, presumably making their budget versus actual reports look more favorable. You can mitigate this risk by password protecting the accounting software, only giving access permission to certain employees, and by using a change log to track who has made changes to the budget. Also, when you issue the financial statements at the end of each reporting period, consider verifying the budget totals in the statements as part of the standard closing procedure.

- *Password-protect the budget file.* It is quite easy for someone to access the completed budget file and inadvertently make changes to it. To avoid this issue, impose password protection on the file. In addition, archive the file, preferably in an off-site location. Further, consider printing and binding a copy of the budget, and storing it in the corporate archives.

- *Create procedure for changing accounts.* It will sometimes be necessary to delete accounts from or add accounts to the chart of accounts. When you do this, it may be necessary to alter the amounts of any budgets linked to those accounts. For example, when you delete an account, shift the associated budget to some other account; otherwise, the budget totals in the accounting system will no longer match the official budget. Also, if you add an account, it is possible that a portion of the budget charged to another account should be allocated to the new account. To make sure that this is done, create a formal procedure for account changes that includes the revision of associated budget amounts, and require a review every time such changes are made.

Of the preceding controls, the one most likely to mitigate problems is matching the loaded version of the budget to the approved version. If there are many budget line items to be transferred from the approved budget to the accounting software, it is extremely likely that at least a few budget items will be transferred incorrectly. Consequently, matching the loaded version to the approved version is critical.

Budget Integration Controls

An unfortunate reality of budgeting is that, once completed, many budgets are placed in a drawer and ignored until it is time to create a new one in the following year. Consider using the following controls to ensure that the budget is so thoroughly integrated into corporate operations that it cannot be ignored:

- *Include in purchasing system.* If the purchasing department uses a computerized purchase order system, enter the budgeted expense amount into the system for each expense line item. Then, as the purchasing staff enters purchase orders into the system during the budget period, the system accumulates the amount of expense and compares it to the budget; if the accumulated amount exceeds the budget, the system rejects any further purchase orders. For example, if there have already been $48,000 of accumulated purchase orders for office supplies during the budget period, the creation of another purchase order that moves the total past the annual budget of $50,000 will either be rejected outright or cause a warning flag to be generated. This can be an onerous control, especially in the last few months of a budget year, when numerous expense line items are approaching their allowable maximum expenditure levels.

A simpler alternative is to issue a budget versus actual report to managers at regular intervals that warns them of impending overruns in their budgeted amounts. Better yet, generate the report only on an exception basis, so that employees only see those expense line items for which there are few funds remaining.

This control does not work well if you use block budgeting, where funds are allocated to a cluster of expenses, and can be shifted among those expenses at the discretion of the responsible employee.

- *Include in performance appraisals.* If the human resources department manages a periodic employee performance appraisal process, then ensure that they include in these appraisals a comparison of budgeted to actual expenditures for any expenses for which an employee is responsible. These appraisals should be tied to employee promotions and pay rate changes, in order to fully gain their attention. For example, holding expenses below the budgeted amount may earn a department manager a bonus, while exceeding the annual sales quota may trigger the payment of a larger commission to a salesperson.

- *Include in financial statements.* By far the most common budget integration control is to include the budget in the financial statements. The information appears in a separate budget column next to actual results, and may also be presented in a format where the dollar variance and percentage variance between the two figures is stated. This approach presents budget information to management on a continuing basis, but does not force anyone to use the information.

- *Include in responsibility reporting system.* Create a set of reports that are distributed to all employees who are responsible for any parts of the budget, in which are shown budgeted versus actual expenditures or revenues. Any employee receiving these reports should only see the budget line items for which they are specifically responsible. Thus, the engineering manager will receive a report pertaining to the performance of the engineering department, while a salesperson only receives a report for the sales generated by his sales region. This reporting system may result in dozens of separate reports, but is so closely tailored to individual responsibility levels that it is hard to ignore – especially if the company president includes handwritten notes on each of the reports! It should be possible to have the accounting system automatically generate these reports at the end of each accounting period.

The controls outlined here assume that management wants to use the budget as a control device. If they intend to instead use it as an occasional planning tool, it is not necessary to adopt these controls.

Summary

When designing controls for a budgeting process, a key issue to remember is that, depending upon the intentions of management, the budget may be considered an authorization to commit funds. As such, you want to be certain that it has been properly approved, that the correct version is in use, and that there is a proper feedback loop in place to ensure that the organization is aware of it. The system of controls adopted should meet these goals. In the absence of controls, there is a significant risk that a company will commit the incorrect amount of funds to various activities, resulting in inadequate financial performance. Thus, budgetary controls can have a significant impact on the overall performance of a company.

Appendix
Sample Budget

This appendix contains a complete budget model, where each schedule in the budget ties into the other elements in the budget. The model is presented in top-down format, beginning with the revenue budget and ending with the master budget. We will provide commentary on various aspects of the model as we proceed through it.

We begin with the revenue budget, which appears in the following table. This budget is comprised of *product* sales, which means that we will also have to budget for the inventory supporting those sales. The product is sold for $500 per unit and costs $210 to build.

Revenue Budget

	Quarter 1	Quarter 2	Quarter 3	Quarter 4
Treadle spinning wheel				
Asia region	$1,200,000	$1,260,000	$1,280,000	$1,300,000
Europe region	250,000	240,000	260,000	250,000
North America region	650,000	800,000	810,000	820,000
South America region	100,000	125,000	150,000	175,000
Total revenue	$2,200,000	$2,425,000	$2,500,000	$2,545,000
Units sold (at $500 each)	4,400	4,850	5,000	5,090

We then turn to the ending finished goods inventory budget, which generates information needed for the production budget. This budget incorporates a small inventory build in the third quarter to adjust for seasonal sales differences, adds some stock in the first and second quarters to improve the speed of fulfillment, and makes several minor product changes. The result is the ending inventory quantities and dollars shown in the following table. Note that the ending inventory balance is approximately 25% of the total sales in each quarter, which is based on recent history and is therefore expected to be a reasonable estimate of the inventory level during the budget period.

242

Sample Budget

Ending Finished Goods Inventory Budget

	Quarter 1	Quarter 2	Quarter 3	Quarter 4
Unadjusted ending inventory level	2,300	2,600	2,885	2,975
+/- Product changes	0	185	-100	55
+/- Seasonal changes	0	0	200	
+/- Service changes	300	100	0	0
Adjusted ending inventory	2,600	2,885	2,975	3,030
× Standard cost per unit	$210	$210	$210	$210
Total ending inventory cost	$546,000	$606,000	$625,000	$636,000

The following production budget incorporates the expected unit sales and the amount of planned ending finished goods inventory to arrive at the total number of units to be manufactured in each quarter.

Production Budget

	Quarter 1	Quarter 2	Quarter 3	Quarter 4
Budgeted unit sales	4,400	4,850	5,000	5,090
+ Planned ending inventory units	2,600	2,885	2,975	3,030
= Total production required	7,000	7,735	7,975	8,120
- Beginning finished goods inventory	-2,300	-2,600	-2,885	-2,975
= Units to be manufactured	4,700	5,135	5,090	5,145

The following direct labor budget is based on the standard number of employees needed to crew the production line for treadle spinning wheels. The line requires a staff of 20 if no more than 5,000 spinning wheels are manufactured per quarter. The budget reflects an increase to 23 staff for production volumes in the range of 5,000 to 5,500 units per month.

Direct Labor Budget (Crewing Method)

	Quarter 1	Quarter 2	Quarter 3	Quarter 4
Staffing headcount	20	23	23	23
× Quarterly pay per person	$11,000	$11,000	$11,000	$11,000
= Total direct labor cost	$220,000	$253,000	$253,000	$253,000

The following direct materials budget is based on the roll up method, under which we multiply the total amount in the bill of materials by the number of units to be manufactured. The standard materials cost per unit is $163.19. When you add to the materials cost the standard cost of labor, which is $46.81, this sums to the total standard cost per unit of $210.00. The labor cost per unit was calculated in the first quarter, and is $220,000 total direct labor cost divided by 4,700 units produced.

Direct Materials Budget (Roll up Method)

	Quarter 1	Quarter 2	Quarter 3	Quarter 4
Units to be manufactured	4,700	5,135	5,090	5,145
Standard cost/each	$163.19	$163.19	$163.19	$163.19
Total cost	$767,000	$838,000	$831,000	$840,000

The following manufacturing overhead budget does not attempt to break down overhead expenses by department within the overhead area. Instead, it presents information by expense line item. Most of these costs are fixed, so there are only a few changes for scheduled pay raises, a rent increase, and a seasonal increase in utilities.

Manufacturing Overhead Budget

	Quarter 1	Quarter 2	Quarter 3	Quarter 4
Production management salaries	$145,000	$147,000	$151,000	$151,000
Management payroll taxes	10,000	10,000	11,000	11,000
Depreciation	16,000	14,000	14,000	14,000
Facility maintenance	20,000	20,000	20,000	20,000
Rent	60,000	60,000	69,000	69,000
Personal property taxes	8,000	8,000	8,000	8,000
Quality assurance expenses	29,000	29,000	31,000	31,000
Utilities	5,000	5,000	5,000	6,000
Total manufacturing overhead	$293,000	$293,000	$309,000	$310,000

The following cost of goods sold budget is derived from several of the preceding budgets. The gross margin percentage gradually increases over the four quarters, which appears reasonable; it is caused by manufacturing overhead costs increasing at a slower rate than revenues, while the cost of direct labor only increases once, when the crew size is increased in the second quarter.

Cost of Goods Sold Budget

	Quarter 1	Quarter 2	Quarter 3	Quarter 4
Revenue	$2,200,000	$2,425,000	$2,500,000	$2,545,000
Cost of goods sold:				
Direct labor expense	220,000	253,000	253,000	253,000
Direct materials expense	767,000	838,000	831,000	840,000
Manufacturing overhead	293,000	293,000	309,000	310,000
Total cost of goods sold	$1,280,000	$1,384,000	$1,393,000	$1,403,000
Gross margin	$920,000	$1,041,000	$1,107,000	$1,142,000
Gross margin percentage	42%	43%	44%	45%

Sample Budget

The following sales and marketing budget contains no surprises – sales modestly increase, which management believes it can handle with the existing sales staff and some mid-year promotions. The commission is three percent of revenues.

Sales and Marketing Budget

	Quarter 1	Quarter 2	Quarter 3	Quarter 4
Salaries and wages	$180,000	$180,000	$185,000	$190,000
Commissions (3%)	66,000	73,000	75,000	76,000
Payroll taxes	17,000	18,000	18,000	19,000
Promotions	0	25,000	50,000	0
Advertising	20,000	20,000	20,000	20,000
Travel and entertainment	15,000	18,000	9,000	15,000
Office expenses	12,000	12,000	12,000	14,000
Other	5,000	5,000	5,000	5,000
Total expenses	$315,000	$351,000	$374,000	$339,000

The following administration budget has a large salary component, which is for the owner of the business. This means that the social security wage cap is eliminated by mid-year, leaving a much-reduced payroll tax for Medicare for the remainder of the year.

Administration Budget

	Quarter 1	Quarter 2	Quarter 3	Quarter 4
Audit fees	$25,000	$0	$0	$5,000
Bank fees	4,000	4,000	4,000	4,000
Insurance	7,500	7,500	8,000	8,000
Payroll taxes	24,500	24,500	5,500	5,500
Property taxes	0	24,000	0	0
Rent	20,000	20,000	20,000	20,000
Salaries	350,000	350,000	375,000	375,000
Supplies	4,500	4,500	4,500	4,500
Travel and entertainment	9,000	9,000	9,000	15,000
Utilities	7,000	7,000	7,000	8,000
Other expenses	2,000	2,000	2,000	2,000
Total expenses	$453,500	$452,500	$435,000	$447,000

The company has a small amount of research and development activity, part of which is outsourced. It is addressed in the following budget.

Research and Development Budget

	Quarter 1	Quarter 2	Quarter 3	Quarter 4
Contract services	$4,000	$6,000	$6,000	$6,000
Consumable supplies	8,500	8,500	10,000	10,000
Depreciation and amortization	3,500	3,500	4,000	4,000
Office expenses	2,000	2,000	2,000	2,000
Payroll taxes	2,000	2,000	2,000	1,500
Salaries	30,000	30,000	30,000	32,000
Total expenses	$50,000	$52,000	$54,000	$55,500

The capital budget shows the cash expenditures for capital items that are anticipated during the budget period, with most of the expenditures clustered in the areas of production and research and development.

Capital Budget

Expenditure Area	Quarter 1	Quarter 2	Quarter 3	Quarter 4
Production	$30,000	$0	$0	$0
Research and development	0	0	42,000	0
Safety-related	8,000	8,000	5,000	0
Legally mandated	0	0	0	28,000
Total expenditures	$38,000	$8,000	$47,000	$28,000

The following master budget incorporates all of the revenue and expense line items in the cost of goods sold budget, as well as the total expense line from the sales and marketing, administration, and research and development budgets. We then multiply the before-tax profit by a 35 percent income tax rate to derive the income tax. Next, we incorporate the net profit, depreciation, capital purchases, and dividends into a rough estimate of cash flows to determine where there might be cash flow problems during the upcoming year. The company is quite profitable, and the only cash drain is caused by two large dividend payments, which can likely be rescheduled to avoid the negative cash balance at the end of the first quarter.

Master Budget

	Quarter 1	Quarter 2	Quarter 3	Quarter 4
Revenue	$2,200,000	$2,425,000	$2,500,000	$2,545,000
Cost of goods sold:				
Direct labor expense	220,000	253,000	253,000	253,000
Direct materials expense	767,000	838,000	831,000	840,000
Manufacturing overhead	293,000	293,000	309,000	310,000
Total cost of goods sold	1,280,000	1,384,000	1,393,000	1,403,000
Gross margin	$920,000	$1,041,000	$1,107,000	$1,142,000
Sales and marketing	315,000	351,000	374,000	339,000
Administration	453,500	452,500	435,000	447,000
Research and development	50,000	52,000	54,000	55,500
Profits before taxes	$101,500	$185,500	$244,000	$300,500
Income taxes	35,500	65,000	85,500	105,000
Profits after taxes	$66,000	$120,500	$158,500	$195,500
Cash flow:				
Beginning cash	$50,000	-$52,500	$77,500	$7,000
+ Net profit	66,000	120,500	158,500	195,500
+ Depreciation	19,500	17,500	18,000	18,000
- Capital purchases	-38,000	-8,000	-47,000	-28,000
- Dividends	-150,000	0	-200,000	0
Ending cash	-$52,500	$77,500	$7,000	$192,500

We could refine the rough estimate of cash flows to include the cost of the increase in inventory through the four quarters, as outlined in the ending finished goods inventory budget. We could also adjust it for the working capital requirements associated with accounts receivable and accounts payable.

Glossary

A

Activity-based budget. A budget designed to allocate money to specific activities, rather than to departments or other functional areas.

Administration budget. A document that itemizes all administrative expenses for an entity during a budget period.

B

Balance sheet. A report that summarizes all of an entity's assets, liabilities, and equity as of a given point in time.

Benchmark. A financial or operational result of a business unit that is used as a performance standard by another entity.

Bill of materials. The record of the materials used to construct a product. It can include raw materials, sub-assemblies, and supplies, as well as an estimate of the amount of scrap that will be created during the production of the product.

Block budget. A budget in which expenditures are granted without allocation to specific budget line items, allowing managers to shift funds among different expense types as needed.

Borrowing base certificate. A statement of the ending balance of a company's accounts receivable and inventory, multiplied by the allowable percentage of each one against which the business is allowed to borrow. The certificate is signed by a company officer and forwarded to the lender at the end of each reporting period.

Budget. A set of interlinking plans that quantitatively describe an entity's projected future operations. It is used as a yardstick against which to measure actual operating results, for the allocation of funding, and as a plan for future operations.

Budget gaming. Actions taken by managers to alter the result of their areas of responsibility in comparison to the budget in order to increase the amount of the bonuses paid to them.

Budget variance. The difference between the budgeted or baseline amount of expense or revenue, and the actual amount. The budget variance is favorable when the actual revenue is higher than the budget or when the actual expense is less than the budget.

Budgetary assumption. An assumption that sets the boundaries for or derivation of a budget, such as an assumed rate of increase for wages or the ability of a bottleneck machine to run at least at 80 percent of capacity.

C

Capital budget. A document that shows the aggregate expenditures planned during a budget period for various types of fixed assets. It may also compute the amount of depreciation expense during a budget period.

Capital budgeting. A series of steps followed to justify the decision to purchase an asset, usually including an analysis of the costs, related benefits, and impact on capacity levels of the prospective purchase.

Capital expenditure. The expenditure of funds to acquire or upgrade an asset. This is recorded as an asset and then depreciated, rather than charging it immediately to expense.

Chart of accounts. A listing of all accounts used in the general ledger, usually sorted in order by account number. The chart of accounts is used to aggregate information into an entity's financial statements.

Collateral. An asset that a borrower has pledged as security for a loan. The lender has the legal right to seize and sell the asset if the borrower is unable to pay back the loan by an agreed date.

Compensation budget. A document that computes the compensation expense for employees during a budget period, including compensation, payroll taxes, and benefit costs. This budget may be integrated into department-level budgets.

Continuous budgeting. The process of continually adding one more month to the end of a multi-period budget as each month is completed.

Contribution margin. The margin that results when variable production costs are subtracted from revenue.

Cost center. A business unit that is only responsible for the costs that it incurs. The manager of a cost center is not responsible for revenue generation or asset usage. The performance of a cost center is usually evaluated through the comparison of budgeted to actual costs. The costs incurred by a cost center may be aggregated into a cost pool and allocated to other business units.

Cost of capital. The blended cost of an entity's outstanding debt instruments and equity, weighted by the comparative proportions of each one.

Cost of goods sold budget. A document that compiles the budgeted cost of goods sold from the direct labor, direct materials, and manufacturing overhead budgets.

D

Direct labor. The cost of the production labor directly associated with the manufacture of products or the provision of services.

Direct labor budget. A document that computes the cost of direct labor during a budget period, based either on labor routings or the cost to crew a production facility.

Direct materials. The cost of the parts and supplies consumed to create a product. Direct materials are a variable cost.

Direct materials budget. A document that computes the cost of direct materials during a budget period, based on either bills of material or an adjusted historical percentage.

E

Ending finished goods inventory budget. A document that computes the ending finished goods inventory budget, stated in units. It is adjusted for multiple factors, such as seasonal changes, service changes, and internal system changes.

F

Fixed budget. A financial plan that does not change through the budget period, irrespective of any changes from the plan in actual activity levels experienced.

Fixed cost. A cost that does not change in response to activity volume. An example is a rent payment that is fixed under a lease agreement.

Flexible budget. A budget that calculates different expense levels based on changes in the amount of actual revenue.

Forecast. A projection of an entity's future revenues, expenses, and asset acquisitions and dispositions.

I

Incentive compensation. A system for issuing an incremental increase in compensation if a specific target is reached within a certain period of time.

Income statement. A financial report that summarizes an entity's revenue, cost of goods sold, other expenses, tax expense, and net income or loss. The income statement shows an entity's financial results over a specific time period, usually a month, quarter, or year.

Incremental budgeting. The practice of budgeting based on slight changes from the preceding period's budgeted results or actual results.

Indirect labor. The cost of labor used in the production process, but not directly associated with the manufacture of products or the provision of services. Examples of indirect labor are production supervisors and maintenance mechanics.

Investment center. A business unit within an entity that has responsibility for its own revenue, expenses, and assets. Management evaluates the investment center based on its return on those assets invested specifically in the investment center.

K

Key performance indicator. An operational or financial measurement that is used to assess the performance of a business.

L

Labor routing. A document showing the work steps required to complete the manufacture of a product, including the time required for each work step.

Line-item budget. A budget in which expenditures are allocated to specific line items in the budget, and managers are not allowed to shift funds among these line items without permission.

Long term budget. A budget that covers a period of more than one year.

M

Manufacturing overhead budget. A document that itemizes the cost of manufacturing overhead during a budget period.

Master budget. The budgeted financial statements derived from all other supporting schedules in a budget process. The master budget may contain just an income statement, or may include a balance sheet.

Material requirements planning. A computer-driven production methodology that uses bills of material, inventory records, and a production schedule to forecast and order materials, so that those materials needed for scheduled production are available in the correct quantities and on the correct dates.

N

Net present value analysis. A discounted cash flow methodology that uses a required rate of return (usually an entity's cost of capital) to determine the present value of a stream of future cash flows, resulting in a net positive or negative value.

O

Overhead. The cost to support a company's production process. Examples of overhead are rent for the production facility or the cost of product warehousing.

P

Participative budgeting. A budgeting process under which those people impacted by a budget are involved in the budget creation process.

Payback method. A capital budgeting analysis method that calculates the amount of time it will take to recoup the investment in a capital asset, with no regard for the time value of money.

Piece rate pay. A pay method used to pay employees based on the number of units of production completed. To calculate wages under this method, multiply the rate paid per unit of production by the number of units completed in the work week.

Profit center. A business unit or department within a company, for which both revenues and expenses are recorded. This results in a separate financial statement for each such entity, which reveals a net income or loss.

Production budget. A document that derives the planned number of units of production during a budget period, based on forecasted unit sales, planned ending inventory levels, and beginning inventory levels. The budget is stated in units.

Program. The type of service provided by a nonprofit.

R

Research and development budget. A document that itemizes the expenditures related to research and development activities for an entity during a budget period.

Responsibility accounting. A reporting system that compiles revenue, cost, and profit information at the level of those individual managers most directly responsible for them.

Restricted funds. An allocation of funds that is assigned to a specific purpose.

Revenue budget. A summarization of expected sales levels over a budget period, which may alternatively be categorized by product, region, salesperson, or some other category. Most other parts of a corporate budget are based on it.

Rolling budget. A budget that is continually updated to add a new budget period as the most recent budget period is completed.

Rolling forecast. A forecast of key revenue, expense, and cash flow information to which a new period is added as soon as the most recent period has been completed.

S

Sales and marketing budget. A document that itemizes the various expenditures for the sales and marketing functions during a budget period. It may be structured by expense type, territory, or (in rare cases) by customer.

Sales discount. A reduction in the price of a product or service that is offered by the seller, in exchange for early payment by a buyer. An example of a sales discount is for the buyer to take a 1% discount in exchange for paying within 10 days of the invoice date, rather than the normal 30 days.

Short term budget. A budget that covers a period of up to one year.

Semi-variable cost. A cost containing elements of both fixed and variable costs.

Spoilage. The production of goods that cannot be sold at normal prices, due to damage. Normal spoilage is the amount of damage that naturally arises during a production process, while abnormal spoilage exceeds the normal or expected rate of spoilage.

Start-up cost. A cost that is only incurred when a project or product is initially created or launched.

Static budget. A budget that is completed prior to the budget periods being forecasted, and which is fixed for the entire period covered by the budget, with no changes based on actual activity.

Step cost. A cost that does not change steadily, but rather at discrete points. It is fixed within certain boundaries, outside of which it will change.

Sunk cost. A cost that an entity has incurred, and which it can no longer recover by any means. Do not consider a sunk cost when making a decision to continue investing in an ongoing project, since this cost cannot be recovered.

T

Target costing. A process of determining the price point at which a new product can be sold, assuming a certain feature set, which is used in conjunction with a target profit to arrive at a target cost at which a product must be designed.

Throughput. Revenues minus totally variable expenses.

Transfer price. The price at which one part of an entity sells a product or service to another part of the same entity. There are a number of transfer pricing methods, such as using the market price, or a negotiated price, or cost plus margin. Transfer pricing is used to avoid paying income taxes in high-tax regions, and so is a significant focus of government auditing activities.

V

Variable cost. A cost that varies in response to activity volume. An example is the cost of materials used to manufacture a product.

Variance analysis. The difference between actual and planned behavior.

W

Wage base limit. The maximum amount of wages paid in a calendar year to which the social security tax applies. The social security tax is not applied to wages above the wage base limit.

Z

Zero-base budgeting. A budgeting system that requires managers to justify all of their budgeted expenditures, rather than just the incremental changes to the budget used in the preceding year. Thus, the manager is assumed to have an expenditure base line of zero.

Index

254

256

Made in the USA
Columbia, SC
28 January 2018